Strategies and Tools for
Corporate Blogging

Strategies and Tools for Corporate Blogging

John Cass

AMSTERDAM • BOSTON • HEIDELBERG • LONDON
NEW YORK • OXFORD • PARIS • SAN DIEGO
SAN FRANCISCO • SINGAPORE • SYDNEY • TOKYO
Butterworth-Heinemann is an imprint of Elsevier

ELSEVIER

Butterworth-Heinemann is an imprint of Elsevier
30 Corporate Drive, Suite 400, Burlington, MA 01803, USA
Linacre House, Jordan Hill, Oxford OX2 8DP, UK

∞ Recognizing the importance of preserving what has been written, Elsevier prints its books on
acid-free paper whenever possible.

Library of Congress Cataloging-in-Publication Data
Cass, John (Gene John)
  Strategies and tools for corporate blogging / by John Cass.
    p. cm.
  ISBN 978-0-7506-8416-3
  1. Business communication—Blogs. 2. Internet marketing. 3. Business
enterprises—Blogs. 4. Blogs. I. Title.
  HD30.37.C33 2007
  659.20285'4678—dc22

                                                    2007004083

British Library Cataloguing-in-Publication Data
A catalogue record for this book is available from the British Library.

ISBN: 978-0-7506-8416-3

For information on all Butterworth-Heinemann publications
visit our Web site at www.books.elsevier.com

Printed in the United States of America
07 08 09 10 11 12   10 9 8 7 6 5 4 3 2 1

To my father, Gene Cass, for all of your help and support.

TABLE OF CONTENTS

5 Tools for Blogger Relations

6 Writing for Blogger Relations

7 Dialogue and the Art of Conversation for Effective Blogger Relations

8 Brand Strategies for Effective Blogging

9 Blogosphere Communities: Lessons from the Automobile Blogging Community

10 Blogs from the Customer's Perspective

11 The Future of Blogger Relations: Podcasting, Web 2.0, and Social Media

PREFACE

While this book describes some of the benefits of corporate blogging, the book's focus is to give the reader the tools and strategies to develop expertise in how to build a successful corporate blog. This book is not about why blogging is necessary for a company per se; rather, the focus is on enabling the reader to conduct effective corporate blogger relations.

In 2003, when I started blogging I was interested in how businesses can use blogs to reach high rankings in search engines, but quickly discovered blogs do so much more in terms of creating dialogue between companies and their customers. When I was approached by Butterworth-Heinemann Elsevier in late 2005 and asked if I'd like to write a book about the topic of corporate blogging, I was excited to be able to bring together in a book all of the research and ideas I've collected over the last few years. Although many books have been published on this topic, none have really targeted how to conduct blogger relations. This book sets out to help the reader to build a successful blog using blogger relations.

Now here is an overview of each of the chapters:

The first chapter describes the need for blogger relations by describing the evolution of the Internet and the web, and how the development of blogs requires a new approach in marketing if a company is going to be successful in using blogs as a way to reach an audience.

The second chapter provides a template for how to develop both an assessment of a company's resources and the blogging community. The plan and tools will give the reader the framework to decide when and if a company is able to start blogging.

The third chapter provides a plan for developing an effective corporate blogging strategy that will enable a company to blog. Ideas and strategies that are relevant and appropriate for blogging are discussed and described from public relations, search engine optimization, journalism, and online marketing.

The fourth chapter provides direction on how to write guidelines for employees and readers for a blog. This chapter provides examples of the potential harmful consequences of employees publishing online, and suggestions on how to avoid such circumstances.

The fifth chapter examines blogging systems, popular blog monitoring tools, bookmarking tools, CGM measurement companies, and how each system and technology tool can help a company build a blogging practice and strategy. The chapter also describes how to integrate effective blogging strategy into a blog's creative and navigation design.

The sixth chapter describes what writing and research skills are needed for a corporate blog. The chapter reviews some of the different article types from journalism that can be used for blog writing.

The seventh chapter describes the art of blogging conversation, which, unlike advertising and public relations, allow your audience to have instant conversations with blog authors. This chapter also describes how to use dialogue to connect with an audience.

The eighth chapter describes how a company can build trust for their brand using a blog and provides several ideas and case studies that demonstrate how a company might build a blogging program to increase that trust.

The ninth chapter demonstrates the importance of developing an assessment to ensure that a company is able to build a successful blogging strategy by using the example of the automobile blogging community. The chapter uses the blogging community assessment template provided in chapter two to examine the automobile blogging community. The chapter analyzes a list of blogs in the automobile community to provide some suggestions as to how a company might develop a blogging strategy that would work for that community.

The tenth chapter provides a mixture of tips on how to build a blog through a series of quotes from blog reader interviews of several corporate blogs. Reading the real thoughts of blog readers about why they read corporate blogs demonstrates how establishing credibility is very important to the success of a blog.

The final chapter, chapter eleven, describes how podcasters and Web 2.0 websites can be used to build or connect with a community. It also shows how some of the same techniques used in blogging can also be used with new social media to connect with audiences through the web.

I hope you will enjoy reading the book and find the information useful in your own company's blogging efforts. Corporate blogging is still in its infancy, and I continue to watch the development of the technology and the communities as they evolve. If you want to continue the conversation, contact me at jcass@ nwlink.com or post a comment on my blog at http://pr.typepad.com.

John Cass
Arlington, MA

ACKNOWLEDGMENTS

This book would not have been possible without the help of many people. I am very lucky to have a number of people who were kind enough to contribute their time, ideas, and advice. Most importantly, I want to thank my wife, Karin Feeney-Cass, for her support, encouragement, and help in making this book possible. The book was written during the final term of Karin's pregnancy of our son Bram and his birth. Many, many people helped during his premature birth and the two-month stay in the hospital. Without their support, I could not have attempted the completion of the book; my thanks to all who helped. I want to especially thank my mother-in-law and father-in-law, Joan McSweeney and John Feeney, for their support and help with editing the book.

There were many people who helped with the editing of the book, but most thanks must go to my father, Gene Cass. I also want to thank my sister, Tina Clarke, who not only helped with the editing but also provided some good advice on how to structure several chapters. Thanks go to my brother, Dale Cass, for his help with editing, and also providing some advice on how to use some of the more obscure functions of Microsoft Word. Several other people helped edit the book: my thanks go to Jan Pendzich, Joe Lamontagne, Patricia Danehy, and Larry St. Pierre.

An important person to thank for the inspiration for this book is Ian Lurie of Portent Interactive in Seattle, my former employer, who encouraged me to start blogging in 2003 after I had moved to Boston.

A great deal of the book was developed from previous studies and blog posts from the previous three years. Many people have commented on and given me the inspiration for all of the blog posts I have written over the past three years; my thanks to all who have contributed to my blogs.

My thanks to Stephen Turcotte and my colleagues at Backbone Media, Kristine Munroe and Megan Dickinson, for help with the Blogsurvey blog, the Backbone

Media Corporate Blogging Survey 2005, and the Northeastern University and Backbone Media Blogging Success Study. Thank you also to Dr. Walter Carl and his students at Northeastern University for the work on the Blogging Success Study, and the Walter's blog post about synthetic transparency.

Additional thanks go to the following people and companies for their interviews: Tom Abate from the San Francisco Chronicle and MiniMediaGuy blog; Mike Chambers and Eric Anderson from Adobe; Bill Higgins from IBM; George Pulikkathara from Microsoft; Ken Dyck, a customer of Microsoft; Rick Short and Dr. Ron Lasky at the Indium Corporation; Max Kalehoff of Nielsen BuzzMetrics; Michael Cornfield, Ph.D., adjunct professor in Political Management, the George Washington University, and Vice President of Public Affairs, ElectionMall.com; Mary Beth Weber of SigmaValidation; Tim Jackson from Masi Bikes; Christine Halvorson from Halvorson New Media, LLC, and Stonyfield Farm; Robert Moffit of the American Lung Association of Minnesota blog (ALAMN); Jeremy Pepper from POP! PR Jots blog; Jim Cahill and Deborah Franke of Emerson Process Management; and Cathy Taylor from Adweek.

Thanks also to the blog readers who helped me with the content for chapter ten. Special thanks to MASI Guy blog readers James Thomas, Jeff Mosser, and Annie Bakken; Heather Hamilton's One Louder blog readers Viki Lutzhas and Brett Norquist; and Dr. Ron Lasky's blog reader, Don Ballard. Thanks also go to Tim Jackson, Heather Hamilton, and Rick Short for arranging the blog reader interviews.

Thanks go to Lauren Vargas for the inclusion of her blog post, and also to Trevor Cook and Kami Huyse for their comments.

Three people helped with interviews for chapter eleven. I would like to thank them for their great contributions to the book. Neville Hobson of the Hobson and Holtz report at For Immediate Release and NevilleHobson.com; Dan Karleen, one of the founders of Berks.TV, a production of Pipe Up! Media, LLC, an Internet TV channel covering Greater Reading, PA and all of Berks County; and Philip Rosedale or Philip Linden as he is called in Second Life, the CEO and Founder of Linden Lab, the company that built Second Life.

Lastly I want to thank Jane Macdonald, my Acquisitions Editor at Butterworth-Heinemann, an imprint of Elsevier, Inc., for having asked me to write the book, and for having supported me throughout the process.

CHAPTER 1

The Need for Blogger Relations

The evolution of the Internet has been a step-by-step process of technological development, and each technological advance has made it easier to communicate with others. As time has progressed and Internet technologies have become more sophisticated, the use of those technologies for communications has required greater skill and knowledge to communicate effectively with other people via the Internet. After all, making a technology easier to use does not necessarily mean that people understand what the technology does or how they can use it. Each step in mastering each new tool means that people gain technical familiarity and experience that they can apply to the next Internet technological development. This chapter will discuss the evolution of the Internet and the web through the development of email, bulletin board, forums, and blogs. When blogs developed, there were some important differences between previous technological developments and blogs, and those differences resulted in blogs being very successful publishing and communications tools. The differences between forums and blogs illustrate the reasons for the blog's successes in the area of helping blogs to get top rankings in search engines. Blogs are not just tools for getting a top ranking; they also allow companies to connect personally with customers through individual employees.

People have shifted from reading newspapers to using the Internet to obtain their current news. People still watch TV, but sites such as YouTube are indications that online video is shifting viewers from TV to watching videos online. Advertisers are recognizing the shift in eyeballs and are moving resources to create content for the web, not for purposes of traditional advertising but to promote virally campaigns on the web. Newspapers are responding to the shift by beefing up their online editions, launching blogs and podcasts, and more. Online media sites are even starting to involve the audience in the development of content. Tom Abate, a news reporter from Sfgate.com, the *San Francisco Chronicle*'s online site, explained that journalists are "scrambling, experimenting and worrying," and journalists, finding new methods of gathering and writing news, are faced with the changing patterns of media consumption and news development.[1]

The ability to publish and connect with others means that individuals have as much influence on the course of events today as companies once did in the world of mass media with advertising and public relations. Companies have to realize that it is important to listen to the community discussion about their industry online because that discussion can be easily found on the web. The shift in media consumption and the power of customers because of blogs and other social media sites is another reason why companies should start blogging.

Blogs can play a very significant role in how a company connects with their online audience because they are published and controlled by individuals. Even new technologies such as podcasting and video logging are launched through blogs. By necessity, a company relationship with their audience online has to take blogs into account. If companies want to connect with their audience, they have to enter a dialogue with the blogging community. The advantages of blogging are such that companies have to determine how to best use blogging to connect with their audience online. This book is about how a company can use the discipline of blogger relations to blog effectively.

A BRIEF HISTORY OF INTERNET TOOLS

The Internet was built to exchange data and files, and some of those files contained messages; the messages in the files inspired the development of email. Email has been around since the 1970s, when it was initially used by the U.S. government for military uses and by the academic community for collaboration. The first commercial use of the Internet did not occur until the late 1980s, and it was not until the mid-1990s when the World Wide Web grew dramatically that large-scale adoption of email occurred. Consumers used the web to chat with their friends, family, colleagues, and strangers. Email became a means for selling a refrigerator, finding a partner, or hiring a van to move across the country. Because an email can be forwarded and sent via the Internet with little effort, many consumers and companies adopted this new form of communicating. Users quickly realized that private email has the potential for public disclosure, and understanding the dangers, users take steps to avoid private information from being revealed too widely. Email is a less formal method of communication than letter writing that can be used for quick messages or for a longer essay.

Online bulletin boards developed during the 1980s. Bulletin boards were a precursor to the web that allowed people to connect to a single computer and exchange messages and information. Bulletin boards remained popular until the 1990s when web-based forums supplanted them. Forums provide a gathering place for people with shared interests to share and discuss ideas. A forum member might start a conversational thread, but all members of the forum are free to contribute to the discussion. Moderated forums ensure Internet users do not post messages that spam the forum with sales messages, off-topic comments, defamatory language, or obscene remarks. Although the discussion in many forums is often passionate and lively, the members of the forum are able to police themselves. Forums are more successful when more members actively participate in the discussion. Any new members entering a forum will assess a forum's level of activity. If there are a lot of active threads in the forum, potential new members will be more confident that the forum is a good place to connect with other people of similar interests. Forums are places to share ideas about products and vendors. Companies used forums to join in on community discussions, and some forums could have significant impact on a company's business. A math professor found that Intel's chips were causing mathematical errors in calculation applications. The professor tried to contact Intel customer service, but he did not get a response, and after a few tries, he posted the problem on bulletin boards and forums. Intel's share price dropped dramatically as a result of the revelation.[2]

Tim Berners-Lee developed the World Wide Web in 1992 at CERN,[3] a consortium of twenty European countries for the study of particle physics. The web was developed to facilitate collaboration between scientists at the various institutions. Before the web, the Internet had been confined to technology and academic communities. The development of the web transformed the speed of commercial development of the Internet because the straightforward and intuitive design of web browsers greatly simplified the process of locating information, and many more people began using the web to find information and connect with other web users all over the world. As more people became connected to the web, the new users increased the size of online communities already in existence on message groups and forums. As the number of people on the web increased, the opportunity for interaction and discussion about any topic grew exponentially. Subjects that were once thought obscure in a local community blossomed on the web.

Web search engines have been around since the early 1990s. People use search engines to find the topics, people, and communities they seek. Increasingly, consumers use the web to research products and services they wish to consider for purchase. Research indicates that search engines are often the first place Internet users visit to conduct research on the web. Google has become one of the most important search engines for Internet users. Google's method of measuring the ranking of a website in its search engine results is based upon the content of the website and the links to that website. If other websites that are also highly ranked within a Google link to a website, then that website will receive a higher ranking in the Google search results. How search engines use links to rank websites was an important development in how people searched the web. Highly relevant webpages were easier to find as a result of Google's innovative assessment of links. When you consider the volume of activity in forums, there are fewer links to a particular comment thread from other websites. This is because there is less need to link to other websites within a forum, as the discussion is within the forum community rather than between websites.

THE DEVELOPMENT OF BLOGS

During the mid-1990s, people began writing online diaries or journals. Most of those online journals were developed in manual hypertext markup language (HTML), the scripting language used by web designers to build pages. These types of websites became known as a *weblog*, which was eventually shortened to *blog*. Over time, developers built content management tools for managing and publishing content dynamically without having to master HTML. Entrepreneurs refined the content management tools and added more functionality for communicating effectively between people.

Blogs are websites that appear in journal format. Blog authors can write a series of entries, each post appears in sequential order, posts ranging from one to numerous can appear on the home page, and all entries can be archived and accessed through navigation on the home page. Blog authors use a content management system to write a post and publish quickly.

Similar to forums and bulletin boards, blogs allow others to easily interact and converse in a public setting. They allow Internet users to communicate more easily than most websites through tools such as comments, trackbacks, RSS, and social network bookmarking. Interaction is the key to building a successful blog. Technologies such as RSS, trackbacks, and commenting enable more personal interaction between people. Once these new technologies were available within blogs, conversation was facilitated between bloggers and readers.

The most common method of communication between bloggers and their readers is through comments. Blog readers can comment on a blog post by entering a comment within a blog post comment. Blog authors can choose to answer a comment with their own comment in the same post or by writing another post.

Trackbacks are another tool for communication between blogs. Trackbacks allow you to notify other bloggers automatically that you have written a blog article referencing their article. The trackback works by a blog author writing an entry referencing another blog post. The blogger copies a trackback URL from the other author's blog post and uses the URL to notify the original blogger that an entry was written citing the blog post. A ping is sent automatically by the publishing system of the blog that cites the original post. Once the other blog is pinged, a reference and link appears on the other blog, unless moderated by the blogger.

Providing an RSS feed on a blog is a good way to update blog readers of content on a blog. A web feed or RSS feed enables the syndication of one website's content to another website or RSS feed reader. Blog readers can subscribe to a blog's RSS feed. An Internet user can discover if there are any updates to a blog by reviewing their RSS feed reader. Examples of RSS feed readers include Bloglines,[4] NewsGator,[5] and Feedster.[6] Another way to find blog content is through RSS feed search engines. People can search RSS feeds in search engines such as Technorati .com[7] or IceRocket.com[8] by a keyword or a tag. Tags are keywords selected by the author and included as a way to identify a blog post. In addition to RSS, some blogs also provide blog readers with the ability to subscribe by email to the latest published postings by an author.

Social networking sites such as del.icio.us[9] allow blog readers to bookmark a blog article. Social networking is a website that enables its members to contribute content, such as images or text lists, and then search through all of the content submitted by members; thereby, members can find other people with similar interests. del.icio.us provides users with the tools to bookmark and tag any webpage by keyword tags. Registered members can quickly search bookmarked articles using their tags. People searching the del.icio.us website find articles bookmarked and tagged by other users. Social networking websites such as Digg .com[10] give members the ability to promote stories that rise in popularity on the homepage of Digg.com when a user promotes or discusses an article suggested by another Digg member.

The ability to easily set up a blog and interact between blog sites using trackbacks means that blogs have rapidly grown in number and prominence. Blogs can be set up through hosted solutions providers such as Google and Six Apart. Blogger from Google and TypePad from Six Apart are two of the most popular blogging platforms on the market. WordPress is another popular blogging system that has a free server version and a hosted solution.

Communities of blogs typically start with one or two bloggers. Using search engines, bloggers find one another through the keywords used to research blog posts. Over time, the number of bloggers in a community increases as the community matures. It is not surprising that the blogging community in the technology sector has been well established for a number of years, as developers and technologists were the ones who developed blogs to be able to communicate with the world. Blogs were initially personal websites, although many blogs focused on a particular topic. Technological and political topics dominated the writings of many early bloggers.

A corporate blog is a blog published by a company or one of its employees, typically focusing on the company and its industry. In contrast to the growth of personal blogs, the growth of corporate blogging has been slow. One sector where blogs have expanded rapidly is the technology sector. During the early part of 2006, Chris Anderson of Wired Magazine and Ross Mayfield of SocialText instigated the Fortune 500 Wiki Project.[11] The goal was an effort to catalog all Fortune 500 companies with blogs. The majority of the companies in the Fortune 500 engaged in blogging are in the technology or telecommunication industry.

THE DIFFERENCES BETWEEN FORUMS AND BLOGS

Blogs have not developed in isolation. Many prominent bloggers were already leaders in their industry who ran their own websites or were members of industry forums, journalists, or writers of articles in industry traditional media publications. As the number of blogs published by people on a specific topic increased, bloggers have effectively created communities discussing a variety of topics, industries, and personal tastes.

Blogs extend community discussion beyond the confines of forums and bulletin boards. When comparing a customer forum to a corporate blog, a forum is more of a closed community where most discussion occurs inside the forum between members. Occasionally, members refer to outside content and websites, but typically, the discussion is internal to the forum. A forum may be a public website accessible through search engines or, alternatively, a secure forum, available only to registered members. Unlike a blog, typically, forum members do not communicate with other members on other websites; the conversation remains within the forum.

Forums are best moderated, not managed. Rather than the forum operator initiating all of the discussion topics, forum members should be free to discuss any topic they wish. However, if they bring up subjects that are off topic, the forum post can be removed or the forum member reminded to post only relevant topics. A company with a forum can direct an occasional thread; however, members run the best forums.[12] Editorial control of a forum is best left to the membership. There should be some restrictions on what can be posted to reduce off-topic posts and sales pitches. But it is best to give the membership of a forum the ability to pose and answer questions freely. A company can then learn from their customers by observing customer questions and ideas posted in a forum thread.

Forum posts can get easily lost in the large volume of content, which means that they are not always the best way to get information out to customers quickly.[13] In contrast, the sequential design of most blog home pages, the ownership, and the editorial control of blog content makes it easy for writers to focus readers' attention on the last story published. In a forum, on the other hand, the community decides the current discussion topic of the forum.

Blogs have, in many ways, revealed the vibrancy of online conversations in existing online communities. Blog interactions are conversations between websites rather than conversations within a website such as in a forum. For example, discussion in a forum is among forum members rather than between a forum member in one website and another forum member in another website, whereas conversation within a blog can either take place in the comment section of the blog or as a post that sends a trackback to another blog. As part of the process of creating a blog post, bloggers reference other posts and link to those posts in their own entries. This practice of linking between blog authors is a function of transparency between bloggers and part of the etiquette of effective blogging. Linking referenced material within a blog post can both add credibility to an author and ensure there are no accusations of plagiarism.

The cultural phenomenon of linking has an interesting and beneficial effect on blogs. Google and other search engines rank websites based upon content and the keywords contained within the websites. Search engines also rank websites based upon the number of websites that link to a given website or webpage. The more webpages that link to a site that also contains related content, the higher the rankings of the webpage in the search engine results. Blogging includes the process of referencing other blogger's content that can link content to related content on another blog. This effectively gives any referenced blog content a vote of confidence but also a boost in popularity for a website's search engine rankings. In contrast, this ability of bloggers to reference and gain a high ranking on a particular keyword in search engines is not as easily accomplished to the same extent within forums, as forum communication occurs within the forum so there are no links from other websites to help boost a page's ranking for a keyword. Many forums have a lot of relevant content and a number of links. But the possibility of gaining link popularity from links between blogs is far greater within blogging communities compared with forums.

People who use email will receive unwanted spam and unsolicited messages. Blogs receive unwanted messages as well; automated software places sales and inappropriate messages in blog comments and sends trackbacks, with the aim of generating direct traffic and receiving links from the targeted blog. Because of the volume of spam comments and trackbacks on blogs, there has been a movement to restrict the ability of links within comments and trackbacks to add to the popularity of blogs for search engine results. The no-follow tag was developed; here, a link will appear in the comment or trackback, but no benefit will be derived from the link, as the search engines ignore the link when crawling the blog because of the no-follow tag. Many blogging publishing platforms provide blog owners with the ability to turn on the no-follow tag for links and trackbacks in certain sections of a blog. This tag is having some effect in the face of trackback spam, but linking and popularity still plays a big role in the power to boost a website or blog to high rankings within search engine results.

CORPORATE BLOGS CONNECT WITH PEOPLE ONLINE

When a consumer publishes their opinion online, that opinion can be easily found by millions of fellow customers through search engines or word of mouth from friends and colleagues. Other people may consult those opinions when deciding if they should make a purchase; thus, the community of opinion has the power to significantly influence purchasing decisions. That is why it is so important for any company to monitor and be involved in blog customer conversations and, if necessary, to respond. The decisions about products are influenced by what consumers write about products in blogs.[14]

Blogs and forums provide opportunities for product feedback. For a product manager, forums can provide some of the best information on customer ideas and feedback. When a blogger includes the input of customers for product development, a blogger can receive feedback, more links, producing higher sales and turning customers into brand evangelists. Yet, a successful blogger relations campaign has some advantages over a forum. Blogs give companies the ability to interact between other blogs in a totally different way than the closed world of a forum. Blogs give companies many tools of interaction, such as commenting and trackbacks. By setting up a company blog, a company is open to conducting an online dialogue between consumers and bloggers. A company blogger is free to comment and trackback on blogs in the community, and other bloggers are free to comment on the company blog. If a company can run a successful blog, the company can gain links more easily than in a forum. A company also gains the opportunity to have a dialogue with many other blog readers from bloggers who refer to a company blog post. Blogs, in general, provide companies with more ways to connect with a wider audience and community as contrasted with the limitations of a forum, which is confined to a small but active proportion of their target audience.[15]

There is value to engaging your audience in industry forums if that is where the discussion is located. Because of the nature of search engines and the growth of blogging, a company has the ability to make a bigger impact on community discussion by developing content on a blog. That is why it is so important for a company to be involved with both forums and blogs. Although not every audience member is going to click on a company blog, or find the blog, they may find the link on the company website to a forum. Lastly, communicating on a forum answers questions and shows active engagement in the community; you can do all that with blogs and, in addition, have the chance to easily connect with the wider community outside of a forum.

MEDIA CONSUMPTION

Media consumption has changed dramatically since the development of the Web and the Internet. Consumers are favoring the web because of the speed at which news is delivered and the flexibility to control how news is delivered through audio, video, text, and mobile devices. People also have the ability to participate in the news-gathering and news-making process through blogs and other social media websites. The change in media consumption means that new models of sponsorship and advertising will have to be developed to follow people as they switch from traditional media to new social media websites on the web.

A study by the Online Publisher's Association conducted by The Ball State University Center for Media Design, called "A Day in the Life: An Ethnographic Study of Media Consumption," concluded that the web reached 62% of adults. This compares with 73% of adults being reached by radio, 91% of adults through TV, 39% of adults through newspapers, and 31% of adults by magazines. The changes to adult media consumption in terms of the web have been dramatic; the numbers for the web have gone from an estimated 10% in 1995 to more than 60% in 2005.[16]

Consumers are moving away from network TV to cable and local TV and away from newspapers and radio to the web. Young people are accessing news through the web and new devices. Technology is driving the changes in media consumption among the young. The Internet is becoming their primary source for news. Merrill Brown, in an article called "Abandoning the News" for the Carnegie Corporation of New York's magazine the *Carnegie Reporter*, writes that the U.S. news industry is threatened because young people are moving away from traditional sources of news. The report was based on a survey of 18- to 34-year-olds conducted by Frank N. Magid Associates in May 2004.[17]

The Pew Research Center for the People and the Press' research report published in July 2006, "Online Papers Modestly Boost Newspaper Readership: Maturing Internet News Audience Broader Than Deep,"[18] indicates the consumption of news has changed dramatically across media since the mid-1990s (see Figure 1.1).

Regularly watch...	1993 %	1996 %	2000 %	2002 %	2004 %	2006 %
Local TV news	77	65	56	57	59	54
Cable TV news	—	—	—	33	38	34
Nightly network news	60	42	30	32	34	28
Network morning news	—	—	20	22	22	23
Listened/read yesterday...						
Radio	47*	44	43	41	40	36
Newspaper	58*	50	47	41	42	40
Online news three or more days per week	—	2^	23	25	29	31

*From 1994   ^From 1995

Source: The Pew Research Center

FIGURE 1.1   The Changing News Landscape.

The Pew research indicates that the switch from traditional media to the web as a source for news is cutting across all ages of the population (see Figure 1.2).

Advertising is not a dying medium, but it becomes more difficult to reach your customers through advertising because the audience is seeing so much.[19,20] Basically, consumers are seeing more ads and, therefore, because of the high

	Regularly get news online		
	2000 %	2006 %	Change
Total	23	31	+8
18–24	29	30	+1
25–29	31	42	+11
30–34	30	47	+17
35–49	25	37	+12
50–64	19	31	+12
65+	8	11	+3

Source: The Pew Research Center

FIGURE 1.2   Online News Audience Grows Up.

volume of material, have a difficult time remembering the ads. This recall factor applies across all ages of people. The increase in both the amount of media consumption and volume of advertising competition gives an incentive to companies to find more efficient ways to reach customers. Companies should realize that advertising requires more money to achieve the same return on investment than just a few years ago.

People's attention spans for advertising may be low, but their available attention span for content on blogs and online community groups are high. The reason is people have to proactively search for such content, and when they do find content that is highly relevant to them, they pay more attention to it. Companies, therefore, have an opportunity to reach consumers who will increasingly give them more of their attention in the new world of online social media.

Targeting people may actually be easier on the web, because you know fairly definitely that someone accessed a webpage using web statistics tracking software. However, even if media consumption has switched to new locations, it does not necessarily mean that advertising will work on new social media websites. Companies have to develop new approaches to reaching people in the new media. Blogger relations enables companies to connect with people not by selling but by demonstrating the value a company offers through listening to customers, thereby enabling an audience to contribute and participate in the development of a company's products and brand.

CONSUMER-GENERATED MEDIA

All of the electronic content written by people on websites and the Internet may be called *consumer-generated media*, although some also call content generated in a community website *web 2.0 content* or, simply, *writings by people*. The growth of consumer-generated media has been highlighted by the growth of blogging. In 2006, most content developed by people online existed on websites other than blogs. Companies such as Cymfony, Umbria, and Nielsen BuzzMetrics, which provide analysis and monitoring of consumer-generated media, have all discovered that there is more forum content on the web to analyze than blog content. The phrase "consumer-generated media" also refers to the growing power of people to develop news directly instead of the traditional media found in print, radio, and TV, where professional journalists produce content for an audience's consumption.[21]

The content published by consumers on forums, websites, and blogs can now reach a mass audience through the web. The ability of consumers to publish their own content means that it is very easy for them to report on developing news stories, when once only traditional media organizations would have had the resources to publish content that could reach a mass audience. Recent dramatic examples of such citizen journalism include blog postings and photographs from the train bombings in Madrid and London in 2004 and 2005, respectively. Traditional media reporters, in their reports, used personal accounts, photographs, and videos shot at the scene of these events by people because the photographs and reports were eyewitnesses' reports and provided the most up-to-date and best accounts of these stories.

It has now become commonplace for Internet users to look to the web for advice about products and companies. People talk with other consumers to compare and discuss products and vendors. TheKnot.com[22] is a website dedicated to discussion about weddings and marriage. Although one opinion about a product might not influence a user's decision on TheKnot, the combination of many voices in the forum influences a Knot member's decision to purchase.

A video showing a consumer demonstrating how easy it was to open a Kryptonite lock with ballpoint pen had a dramatic impact on the Kryptonite Lock Company. The video was posted on the web, and the discussion about the problems with the Kryptonite lock produced no initial response from the Kryptonite Lock Company on the web. Later, the Kryptonite Lock Company recalled all of the locks at great expense. Blogs played a large role in critiquing Kryptonite for their lack of response and in spreading the story throughout blogging communities.

If a company wishes to alleviate any criticism on the web, they have to be involved in industry online conversations; blogging is one of the best ways to join those conversations. How you join the conversation will depend upon your level of success with your blogging efforts. One story about a company that succeeded in conducting effective blogging is how Macromedia changed their software development process because of the use of blogs.

MACROMEDIA CASE STUDY

Mike Chambers agreed to be interviewed for the Backbone Media Corporate Blogging Survey 2005; he was then senior product manager of developer relations at Macromedia. Subsequently, Macromedia merged with Adobe Corporation. Mike Chambers' blog can be found at http://weblogs.macromedia.com/mesh/. Macromedia was a successful software technology company with many well-known products, including Flash and Cold Fusion.[23]

Macromedia started to blog in 2002 to build a better sense of community and get information to customers quickly. Blogging completely changed the way in which Macromedia conducted its software development process. Slowly, through trial and error, Macromedia determined how to best make the process work. The whole process of using blogs to communicate with customers for the development of new products was a huge success, in terms of better products, more committed customers, more sales, and positive public relations results.

Customers gave input through blogs on feature suggestions. As time passed, Macromedia started to ask what features customers wanted, and those requests began to appear in new versions of products, which were announced on company blogs. The Macromedia programmers would discuss openly on their blogs what needed to be done and reported back to customers if they were able to make any suggested customer changes. Macromedia developed its understanding of how blogging would help their company to get more information from their customers on product development.

If customers are involved in the process of software product development, it changes their perception of the process. Rather than being a case of them versus us, involvement in the process empowers people, and customers start thinking of themselves as part of the Macromedia team. Chambers said, "The customers feel more vested in the whole development process; they have more ownership."

Marketing is not just about promoting a product and making a sale. Forums can help companies build better products through online discussion; similarly, corporate blogs can also provide a mechanism for customer feedback and ideas. The editorial control of corporate blogs and an effective blogging effort can give a company a unique opportunity to demonstrate its brand online by demonstrating that it can provide value and keep promises with its customers.

WHY BLOGGING IS ABOUT MARKETING

Marketing is not just about promotion; the marketing concept is also about discovering the needs and wants of a customer. As the Macromedia case study illustrates, a lot of marketing is about understanding your customer's needs and wants and making sure that you build a product that satisfies those needs and wants efficiently and profitably. Research on blogging[24,25] indicates it is not a good idea for a corporate blogger to focus solely on the blogger discussing their products and services extensively, rather the better blogging strategy is to discuss customer issues and concerns. If a company receives customer feedback and improves its product in response to that feedback, the company will also have improved its brand online. When the customer helps develop the product, customers are more likely to evangelize a product and brand.

If a company does not engage its customers, they will not know that there exists the opportunity to make additional profit and satisfy a number of customers. Use a blog for customer feedback and discussion about products and services and you will help to build your brand online as the Macromedia case study demonstrates. Every customer request received should not mean a change in product design, but it is important to explain why a design change is not possible. Your customers will typically respect your reasons for not making the change.

Marketing is a planning process, and each company has to decide how to get the most return from marketing dollars. Blogs are a good way to connect with customers but might not be the best way for every company. That is why it is important for a company to conduct research into their blogging community to determine if blogging is an opportunity for their company and is right for them.

THE AUTOMOBILE INDUSTRY BLOGGING COMMUNITY

To underscore the need for conducting an effective blogging campaign by a company, it is helpful to review an example of an industry where there is a need for engagement through corporate blogs. The automobile industry is one industry where there is an active blogging community. To understand what drives the development of corporate blogs for automobile manufacturers, a review of the automobile blogging community is necessary. Chapter 9 of this book describes the automobile blogging community in more detail. In the fall of 2006, after reviewing the content of a number of automobile blogs, it quickly became apparent that there are currently three themes of discussion in the automobile blogging industry:

1. A description of a car from the perspective of its drivability, style, power, and value;
2. The current state of the green-car industry, what companies are doing or not doing to help reduce energy consumption and pollution emissions;
3. How badly General Motors and Ford are running their affairs in terms of product development, marketing, and everything else.

Reviewing a blogging community to understand what content is being generated demonstrates the need or lack of opportunity for an effective company blogging effort. The review of the automobile community indicates several opportunities for discussion within the community. When other customers see that a company is communicating with a customer about their concerns and issues in a public blog, the help a company provides to an individual customer is not just solving a customer service issue but helping to strengthen a company's brand in the perception of the readers.

WHY BLOGGER RELATIONS?

If the best way to connect with consumers through traditional media was advertising and public relations, in the new era of consumer-generated media, the best way to connect with consumers and corporate clients who write on blogs is by running a corporate blog. Traditional marketing and public relations tactics are not always the best way to connect with bloggers, especially consumer bloggers. Rather, blogger relations is the best way to connect with bloggers, that is, the process of connecting with peers and audience through blogs to develop relevant content that delivers your message and demonstrates your brand through content and action.[26]

Blogger relations is the opportunity to have a direct conversation with someone through a blog. The open nature of that communication puts constraints and opens up opportunities for both participants. Companies will not succeed with blogging unless their bloggers understand it is more important to build a connection with an audience rather than trying to sell the reader something. A real conversation is what blogging is all about, which is greatly ironic because by not selling you succeed in promoting your brand.

In the traditional setting of media relations, you would never see public relations professionals critiquing a journalist in a conversation where they are pitching a story. With blogging, there are some new rules in how you engage people who are part of online media. It is helpful for companies to distinguish between the conduct of public relations and blogger relations.[27] Blogger relations can include the process of conducting media relations, which I narrowly define as the process of connecting with a member of the media to pitch a story. However, to be truly effective, blogger relations is the process of building relationships, leadership, and a presence in a blogging community by writing posts and conducting a dialogue with fellow bloggers in their community.

The concept of blogger relations[28] is a combination of different skills sets, some of which include public relations. Some of the characteristics of public relations[29] led me to think that public relations will play an important future role as each new technology has opened new opportunities for communication; those characteristics are the following:

- Public relations people have to defend their brand constantly in the media marketplace on a daily basis with journalists; this previous experience of the rigors of the communications market prepares public relations people more than anyone else to our evolving media society.
- Public relations people have to convince journalists and other stakeholders that their story is important to the journalists' and stakeholders' market, selling their story on value to the journalists' audience. The net is the same; website marketers have to provide value or their audience and customers move on to the next site.
- The media world has changed; news is delivered 24 hours a day, 7 days a week, and the Internet is the reason for that change. Traditional public relations powered by Internet tools will be one of few ways to manage the communications pressure to publish quickly and well in the 21st century.

- Public relations strategy focus is on unique characteristics that interest audiences; this approach is the right one for online audiences and how people find information on the web using search engines.

The skills needed for effective blogging in a corporate setting include expertise from many professions: writing, journalism, Internet marketing, public relations, product management and customer service, and many other disciplines. Companies have different goals for blogging, including leadership, customer service, product development, and more. Product development is definitely not public relations, and that is just one reason why effective blogger relations do go beyond public relations. In fact, some of the best returns for blogging come from product development. Macromedia was a great example of a company that used blogs for gaining feedback from their customers and in the process gained public relations and immediate promotional benefits from following a product development dialogue with their customers.

Taking the concept of blogger relations as the way a company can conduct effective blogging, this book will provide strategies and tools for how effective blogging can be implemented within your company and even look beyond blogging to the future of social media websites.

Endnotes

1. Email interview with Tom Abate, news reporter for the Sfgate.com during November 2006

2. PR Communications Blog (2005), *Intel PR Case Study.* Available at http://pr.typepad.com/pr_communications/2005/05/intel_pr_case_s.html

3. Derived from the original French name for the organization—Conseil Europeen pour la Recherche Nucleaire, the organization known since 1954 as the European Organization for Nuclear Research (located on the French/Swiss border in Europe)

4. http://www.bloglines.com

5. http://www.newsgator.com

6. http://www.feedster.com

7. http://www.technorati.com

8. http://www.icerocket.com

9. http://del.icio.us

10. http://www.digg.com

11. Fortune 500 Business Blogging Wiki. Available at http://www.socialtext.net/bizblogs/index.cgi?fortune_500_business_blogging_wiki

12. Blogsurvey Blog, John Cass (2006), *Why Corporate Blogs Provide More Overall Marketing Benefits Than Customer Forums.* Available at http://blogsurvey.backbonemedia.com/archives/2006/02/why_corporate_blogs_provide_mo.html

13. Blogsurvey Blog, John Cass (2006), *Why Corporate Blogs Provide More Overall Marketing Benefits Than Customer Forums.* Available at http://blogsurvey.backbonemedia.com/archives/2006/02/why_corporate_blogs_provide_mo.html

14. Blogsurvey Blog, John Cass (2005), *Forbes Article Claims Microsoft, IBM, SUN and Oracle Bloggers Are Part of an online Lynch Mob.* Available at http://blogsurvey.backbonemedia.com/archives/2005/11/forbes_article_claims_microsof.html

15. Blogsurvey Blog, John Cass (2006), *Why Corporate Blogs Provide More Overall Marketing Benefits than Customer Forums*. Available at http://blogsurvey.backbonemedia.com/archives/2006/02/why_corporate_blogs_provide_mo.html

16. A Day in the Life: An Ethnographic Study of Media Consumption (July 2006). Available at http://www.online-publishers.org/pdf/opa_day_in_the_life_jul06.pdf

17. Carnegie Corporation of New York's magazine, the *Carnegie Reporter*, Vol. 3, No. 2, Abandoning the News. Available at http://www.carnegie.org/reporter/10/news/

18. The Pew Research Center for the People and the Press (July 30, 2006), *Online Papers Modestly Boost Newspaper Readership: Maturing Internet News Audience Broader Than Deep*. Available at http://people-press.org/reports/display.php3?PageID=1064

19. *Financial Times*, Maurice Saatchi (2006), The Strange Death of Modern Advertising. Available at http://www.ft.com/cms/s/910ada08-ffa5-11da-93a0-0000779e2340.html

20. Blogsurvey Blog, John Cass (2006), *Lord Saatchi's 'Death of Advertising' Speech Is 'Utter Rubbish'*. Available at http://blogsurvey.backbonemedia.com/archives/2006/06/lord_saatchis_d.html

21. Blogsurvey Blog, John Cass (2006), *Blogging Glossary of Terms*. Available at http://blogsurvey.backbonemedia.com/archives/2006/02/blogging_glossary_of_terms.html

22. http://www.theknot.com

23. Backbone Media Corporate Blogging Survey, John Cass (2005), *Macromedia Case Study*. Available at http://www.backbonemedia.com/blogsurvey/47-macromedia-case-study.htm

24. Backbone Media Corporate Blogging Survey (2005). Available at http://www.backbonemedia.com/blogsurvey/index.html

25. Northeastern University and Backbone Media Blogging Success Study, John Cass, Dr. Walter Carl (2006). Available at http://www.scoutblogging.com/success_study/

26. Blogsurvey Blog, John Cass (2006), *Blogger Relations Is Not Media Relations for Bloggers*. Available at http://blogsurvey.backbonemedia.com/archives/2006/01/blogger_relations_is_not_media.html

27. Blogsurvey Blog, John Cass (2006), *Click.TV Pitch Program Is Public Relations Not Blogger Relations*. Available at http://blogsurvey.backbonemedia.com/archives/2006/04/clicktv_pitch_p.html

28. PR Communications Blog, John Cass (2005), *Moving PR Forward With Blogger Relations*. Available at http://pr.typepad.com/pr_communications/2005/11/as_described_by.html

29. PR Communications, John Cass (2003), *PR—The Next Internet Revolution*. Available at http://pr.typepad.com/pr_communications/2003/09/pr_the_next_int.html

CHAPTER 2

Determining If Your Organization Should Blog

In the early days of corporate blogging, many employees who started a blog did not always have clear goals and a strategy to follow. Early corporate bloggers had seen the advantages of blogging from people writing personal blogs or from their own experiences with writing a blog. Although most businesses develop a plan when embarking on a new venture, those early company blogging pioneers just went ahead and started a blog, as they wanted to see what results would be produced from corporate blogging, and many would admit they were not exactly sure what results would be produced from blogging but decided to give blogging a try. They quickly learned that blogging allows you to easily interact and connect with an audience online about a topic, whether it is baseball, politics, or software.

There will continue to be companies that start corporate blogging without clear goals and with just a hunch and belief that positive results will come from blogging. Some would argue that the process of blogging enables a company to better connect with their audience, and that alone should be goal enough to start a company blog; however, for those who want to start blogging with a plan, there is one question that needs to be answered before starting: Will a blog help your company reach your organization's communication goals? To answer this question, you will first have to determine if your organization can reach its audience through its blogging efforts. Second, is your organization capable of conducting a blogger relations campaign?

Conducting a blog audit will help you determine if there is an audience for a blog, and this chapter will provide some tools on how to conduct such an audit of your community to help determine if you have the resources available to blog in light of the community audit. Lastly, if you need to justify blogging to your executive team, the chapter provides a blogging report template that can help you get the resources you need to start blogging.

WHY BLOGGING IS NOT ADVERTISING

To determine if your company will reach its audience by setting up a blog, it is important to understand that conducting a blogger relations campaign involves having a conversation with individual bloggers and an audience in your online blogging community. Many marketers understand the process of selling or advertising a product. Advertisers purchase advertising to promote their message with their audience, but corporate blogging is not just about buying an ad. To explain how to build a successful corporate blog, we first have to understand why blogging can be so effective in reaching an audience.

Since the 1960s, the amount of advertising has increased exponentially to inundate people with a higher volume of ads. People's knowledge and awareness of how advertising is attempting to influence them to buy products has also matured. As the number of ads grows, consumer cynicism about advertising increases, and it becomes more difficult to reach customers through advertising. At the same time, visitors to corporate websites may be looking for product information but they do not want a sales pitch. In the 21st century, there is a greater level of skepticism about the motives of companies when sharing information, and customers do not take anything stated by a company at face value. People's media knowledge has created much cynicism about advertising that the assumption is that any corporate message is not to be entirely believed; therefore, you do not get the same chance to tell your story with advertising as you once did. There are more advertisements and more products for people to choose from; therefore, it is more difficult for an organization to cut through the advertising clutter and reach customers even when people might want a product.

A corporate blog in contrast can help a company cut through people's cynicism, allowing them to listen to and explore the value a company can provide. A blog lets an employee reveal their personality and demonstrate their knowledge and passion for an industry, company, or product. Customers view a company's message through the lens of a corporate blog differently from a corporate website, as people's perception about the source of information from a corporate blog is different because they know they are communicating with a person, not a billboard ad or TV commercial. Reading a corporate blog written by an employee who is willing to reveal personal facts, opinions, and anecdotes helps readers to empathize with the blog writer, and what is written on the corporate blog may include much of the same information that is in a company's advertising or corporate website, but because the message is not just another ad, there is a greater willingness to listen to what the blogger has to say.

People throw up barriers to advertising and have skepticism toward any advertising delivered by traditional channels. Corporate blogging can be a way for a company to connect directly, cutting through barriers that existed between a company's marketing messages and the customer. Blogging is a one-on-one conversation between individuals who may chat online about marketing, sharing experiences, discussing ideas, or discussing personal and non-related issues to their industry. Blogging content is read because the content is often not about selling a product or message as is often the case with advertising, but rather what the audience wants to read and discuss.

REACHING YOUR AUDIENCE

There are a lot of blogs on the Internet—tens of millions according to the blog search engine Technorati.[1] Even though there are millions of personal blogs, not every industry has many company blogs. One industry where many companies in the industry have blogs is the technology and software industry.[2] Technology companies were some of the first companies to implement blogs, and many personal blogs were about that industry, as people who wrote and created blogs were initially in those industries, and many of their customers were using blogs, so it made sense that technology and software companies started using them to connect with their customers extensively. Some industries will probably always have a lot of bloggers; they include industries where an audience needs to keep up to date on any changes in the industry quickly. Such industries will benefit strongly from using blogs to update an audience on new developments. Other industries where blogging is important are those that will blog for structural reasons, including those industries with a technically knowledgeable audience. Technology companies often have complex products and services that require a lot of customer support. Corporate blogs can help provide expertise quickly and efficiently. SUN Microsystems, Microsoft, and Intuit are all examples of companies that provide complex products that require a lot of support and training that change rapidly.

One way to determine if there is value in starting a corporate blog for your company is to conduct an audit of the blogs that target your audience. Conducting such an audit can reveal the extent of your industry's blogging community. If the blogging community is large enough, that is a bonus for any company that wishes to start a blog, as running an effective blog is all about interacting with blog readers and other bloggers in your community, and a large community means lots of opportunities to connect. However, if your community is small, you should still consider starting a blog, as there are other factors to consider besides size. Are your customers, journalists who cover your industry, and members of your industry association blogging or reading blogs? Blogging can be a way to reach a small but highly influential group in your industry. If there are only a few blogs that cover your industry, those that do write about an industry will probably be influential. A small existing blogging community may even be something of an advantage, as it enables a company to easily conduct effective blogging by reaching out to a smaller group of bloggers.

Corporate blogs help a company to effectively reach their audience so easily partly because of the influence of search engines. People use search engines to find information, products, and services and enable people on the web to find content on websites easily by using keywords to search for the information users seek. A company gains a competitive advantage if it can achieve a high ranking for its website on a search engine for the keywords its audience uses to find a company. Higher rankings produce more traffic, more brand exposure, and recognition. Part of the process of getting a top ranking on a search engine is producing a lot of relevant content that contains keywords users use to seek industry-related information. Websites that receive a lot of links from other websites that have similar related content on the web receive a boost in rankings in search engines. Blogs are particularly effective in helping companies to get more links to their website through effective blogging.

Linking is one of the factors that give blogging such an advantage in the process of achieving higher rankings on search engines, even if a blogging community is small or the volume of content on the web about an industry is small. A small blogging community in an industry can be just as valuable for a company to help with gaining higher website or blog rankings on search engines.

The size of the blogging community in your industry should be a factor in considering whether your company should start a blog. However, the size of the blogging community relative to the total amount of industry content on the web should also be considered. A small blogging community in an industry where there is a lot of website content will make it difficult for a company to generate sufficient links through blogging to help boost a company's overall search engine rankings. It is always possible to target particular keywords on a blog to just help boost rankings on those keywords. The size of a blogging community and the potential to raise search engine rankings should not be the only factor a company uses in making the decision to blog. Connecting with an audience should definitely be an important goal with blogs, as that is also the strategy that is most likely to help build an effective corporate blogging effort.

Indium Corporation is an example of a company that started the first blog in their industry. Indium Corporation provides solders and electronic assembly materials to the industry. Dr. Ron Lasky, a senior scientist with Indium Corporation has been running his blog since February 2005. According to Rick Short, Indium Corporation's director of marketing, the blog has generated substantial traffic and helped secure more customers for the company. Indium Corporation's customers are engineers who are very wary of sales messages and receiving a sales pitch. The blog by Dr. Ron Lasky, who is one of the industry's senior scientists, is a much more effective way for Indium Corporation to reach customers than a flyer, trade show booth, or salesperson. Customers read Dr. Lasky's blog because it provides insight into customer's questions about the industry, and in the process, Indium establishes a relationship with prospects and customers.[3]

REACHING YOUR AUDIENCE INDIRECTLY

To acquire more customers, sometimes a company has to demonstrate the real value that you provide to your customers beyond just the product. For example, Stonyfield Farm has two corporate blogs, one about organic farming and the other about healthy babies. Stonyfield Farm sells yogurt but does not write about yogurt; rather, Stonyfield's blogs have content that addresses the issues their customers are most concerned about in life as it relates to yogurt—healthy kids and the environment. A conversation about yogurt on the part of Stonyfield would have been a very lonely experiment in blogging, but a conversation about healthy kids and environment as it relates to healthy food and growing kids works because that is what the Stonyfield Farm audience is interested in discussing. The Stonyfield Farm blog was the most successful blog run by Stonyfield Farm. The organic farming blog at Stonyfield Farm is written by one of Stonyfield Farm's farmers. Jonathan Gates, the farmer and Stonyfield's organic farming blogger, writes about whatever is happening in his life, the calving season, or maple sugar season. Although any company can write marketing materials and advice on organic farming and healthy babies, the medium of a blog is perfect for an organic farmer to write about his life. A customer can read in real time on the blog what is happening on the farm. Blog readers can check to see if the farmer is a real person by asking questions to see what response they will receive back from the farmer blogger. The success of the Stonyfield Farm organic farming blog is because it is about one man's unique experiences in running an organic farm. What must seem mundane to the farmer is refreshing, compelling, and entertaining content to most readers. Reading the organic farming blog strongly associates Stonyfield Farm yogurt with organic milk because you can read how the milk is produced on the organic farming blog. The organic farming blog reinforces the healthy nature of the Stonyfield Farm products and the company's commitment to providing organic food. Reading the Stonyfield Farm blogs makes it easier for a customer to associate Stonyfield Farm yogurt with organic farming and healthy kids. When a customer takes a trip to the grocery store and the time comes to make a purchase decision, that association with organic farming and healthy kids will be remembered as a result of the dialogue through blogging.

CONDUCTING A BLOGGING AUDIT

Before starting a blog, it is important that you assess if there is an active blogging readership in your industry's blog community. Is there an active participating blog community or just a few readers? One way to make an assessment of an industry's blogging community is to conduct an online blogging audit of your industry's blogging community. The audit will help determine if there is an active community by reviewing the size of your industry's blogging community and the level of interaction within the audience.

The starting point for any blog audit is a search engine. General search engines and RSS feed search engines can be used to conduct the audit. The keywords used by bloggers in your community can be used as guideposts to find bloggers in your community, and these guideposts can be determined by conducting keyword searches. The presence of such search engines as Yahoo! for finding search results online gives the appearance that the process of auditing a community's blogs might be relatively easy. However, major search engines are designed to find the most relevant content rather than the most current conversations on the web around a particular keyword. This strategy for discovering blogs using major search engines can make finding online customer discussions difficult. RSS feed search engines will help fill the gap between finding the most relevant information on a major search engine and finding the most current blog posts in the blogosphere. RSS feed search engines can be one of the most important tools you can use in finding the relevant blogs in your industry.

RSS feed search engines include Technorati,[4] Feedster,[5] IceRocket,[6] Sphere,[7] and Google's blog search engine.[8] The industry changes rapidly, and there are more to use all the time, and each new engine can provide different tools and results, so it is worth conducting a search for the most popular and useful RSS or blog search engines to use when you start your audit. Posts in RSS feed search engines are typically sorted by the most recent posting, rather than the most relevant post. Bloggers want to read the latest posts published, not the most relevant webpages; RSS feed search engines allow bloggers to keep up with the latest blog posts in their industry.

The RSS feed search engines are limited by their coverage of only RSS feed content and do not provide extensive analysis tools. A new industry, consumer-generated media measurement has appeared to search more content on blogs, forums, and other websites and provide deeper analysis reporting of the indexed content. The new measurement industry seeks to help companies use consumer-generated media research to fulfill product development and marketing communications goals. Measurement companies use observational research methods and powerful automated linguistic algorithms to find opinion and individuals online. Even this new technique has limits, which researchers should bear in mind when working with such metrics companies.

RSS FEED SEARCH ENGINE MARKET OVERVIEW

The reader can get a sense of the differences among a major search engine, an RSS search engine, and the metrics services they provide by reviewing major RSS feed search engines. Major search engines rank their results by the pages with the most relevant content, whereas RSS feed search engines will display their results by the latest post. This means searchers can find the latest but not always the most relevant search results by using an RSS feed search engine.

Technorati.com

Technorati.com is one of the leading blog search engines. Instead of searching websites and webpages, Technorati and other RSS search engines receive updates on new pages and posts by RSS feed. Searchers can find articles by keyword, tag, or website URL. Registered users can also track watch lists of keywords.

Feedster.com

Another important blog search engine, I have personally found Feedster.com to come up with more search finds than Technorati.com. One extremely useful service from Feedster is that the site gives registered users the ability to use Feedster's feed paper to set up your own blog aggregator where you can set up a webpage that displays content from a number of RSS feeds.

IceRocket.com

IceRocket.com is an RSS search engine that has gained significant interest through its responsiveness and updates to technology. The trending tools provide interesting graphs for blog articles and useful data for a blog audit.

Sphere.com

Sphere takes a leaf out of Yahoo! origins and provides a list of featured blogs for important keyword terms. You can also search by time and relevance. The search engine's navigation tool searches by different periods, including 24 hours, 7 days, and 4 months. Sphere also lets you dig deeper to review older posts or just find the latest news on a keyword.

RSS FEED SEARCH ENGINE LIMITATIONS

RSS feed search engines have their limitations. Many of the RSS feed search engines are faced with the problem of spam blogs, otherwise known as slogs. Spammers who set up blogs to sell stuff or build links for their own websites run spam blogs. Some slogs even steal and scrape content from other websites to build the content for the blog.

Google's blogging publishing platform, Blogger, has been a major contributor to spam blogs; Blogger is a free service, and many spammers have taken advantage of the free service to create spam blogs. Those bloggers who search for high-visitor-volume keyword phrases have a difficult time finding relevant blogs that do not include spam. Google has taken steps to reduce slogs, especially now that Google has launched their own blog or RSS search engine.

RSS feed search engines do not yet index the vast amount of consumer-generated media beyond blogs in forums and other secure content websites. Some customers need the content beyond RSS feeds if a company is going to achieve an analysis of the entire online community.

CONSUMER-GENERATED MEDIA IS BIGGER THAN BLOGGING

Blogs only represent a small proportion of consumer-generated media available on the web. Apparently, most content created by people exists in forums. RSS feed search engines do not index most consumer-generated content on the web, as many websites and news groups do not have RSS feeds. To gain insight into an audience's online conversations, it is important for a company to have the tools available that index most online consumer-generated media. Current RSS search engines do not provide sufficient tools to analyze the data indexed by the RSS search engines. It is possible, through manual searching of RSS search engines, to get a picture of an audience's online conversations; it just takes tremendous manual effort to get a reasonably reliable picture of the thoughts and ideas of a majority of customers from consumer-generated media using such tools. RSS search engines can provide enough analysis reporting for a company to build a fairly complete picture of their industry's whole online community.

STEPS TO CONDUCTING A BLOG AUDIT

There are a number of manual steps to complete to build a good audit of a blogging community. There are two goals in conducting an audit of your blogging community. Build a picture of the relative size of the community by assessing each blogger individually and comparing the community as a whole with the total amount of content on the web.

Your first step is to think of a series of keywords your customers would use to describe your company or industry. Let us pick an industry we can use in our example. For the automobile industry, we would choose an initial keyword phrase related to the industry, such as "automobile blog." You would then think of other keywords related to automobile blogging.

There are also several tools from the major search engine that you can use to build your set of keywords, which include the following:

Yahoo! Search Engine Marketing Keyword Selector—The Yahoo! Search Engine Marketing Keyword Selector tool can be found at http://searchmarketing. yahoo.com/rc/srch/. By entering a keyword into the Yahoo! Search Engine Marketing Keyword Selector tool, you will be provided with data on related keyword searches that include your term and an estimated number of times a term was searched for in the last month.

Google Adwords—Google Adwords, Google's advertising website, provides a similar keyword tool to Yahoo! and can be found at https://adwords.google. com. Google's keyword tool lets you generate related keywords for your Google Adwords campaign. But the tool works just as well for generated keywords for a blog audit. In addition to giving some information about search volume for a keyword, the Google Adwords tool can provide additional keyword and phrase suggestions. The keyword tool also has a site-related keyword tool where you can enter the URL for a website and the keyword tool will generate a list of keywords used most often on the website. You can use this tool to spider your own existing website for keywords, and Google Adwords will crawl your website and return a list of your keywords; in addition, you can use the tool to spider other blogs once you develop a list.

You can use the Yahoo! and Google tools to develop a list of keywords and determine the volume of keyword searches on the web in general and the number of times your set of keywords are used within your blogging community. The Yahoo! keyword selector tool gives you the ability to generate the total volume of keyword searches in a single month for a keyword. Use a spreadsheet to keep track of the volume of keyword searches on the web and you will be able to compare this number with the number of times a particular keyword is used within your blogging community. IceRocket provides a useful tool that allows you to determine the number of times each keyword is used by bloggers within a 1- to 3-month period.

IceRocket—The RSS feed search engine IceRocket provides a trend tool that gives the user the ability to track trends on IceRocket by keyword. Enter a keyword into the trend tool and IceRocket will provide the number of posts per day a keyword is cited in the blogs it tracks, the total number of posts, and the average percentage of total posts. You can adjust the trend tool for 1, 2, and 3 months. The higher the number of posts per day, the greater a particular keyword or phrase is used in the blogosphere, as tracked by IceRocket. These numbers can be compared with the volume of keyword searches in general search engines like Yahoo! and Google. The numbers give some insight into the level of blog chatter in a particular community around its set of keywords compared with the volume of searches in general search engines.

If a keyword is generic and can be used in many instances across industries, the data is not very helpful if you are only concerned with one meaning of a keyword, as you do not know how many of the people who conducted a search using the generic keyword meant to use the word in your industry's context or another. Unique keyword phrases that would only be used in a particular community can give a company a fairly good idea of the volume of keyword use in their community.

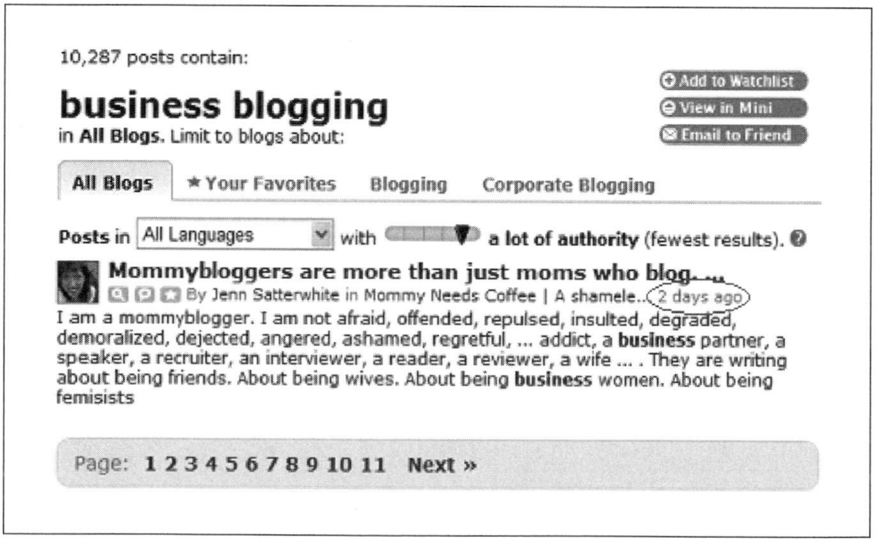

FIGURE 2.1   Results of Technorati.com Keyword Search for "Business Blogging."

ANSWERING THE QUESTION, "HOW OFTEN SHOULD YOU POST?"

IceRocket's trend tool can also be used in conjunction with RSS feed search engines to analyze trends in keyword usage over a set period, with the number of recent posts containing the same keywords in different RSS feed search engines. To determine the number of recent posts on a particular keyword, conduct a search on a keyword in an RSS feed search engine and review the last time the keyword was used in a blog post. Also, look at how many posts contain the keyword. A simple way to discover this information is to scroll to the bottom of a keyword search page and look up the time and date of the last posting for your keyword. Technorati.com gives you the time period of the last post for a keyword search. The period can range from hours to months. The shorter the period of time between the first and last posts indicates the level of community activity around a particular keyword in that RSS search engine. This information enables you to determine what volume of postings are needed if you wish to remain on the top pages of each RSS search engine for a keyword to keep up with other community members.

Figures 2.1 and 2.2 are two examples of Technorati.com keyword searches; the images show the number of posts for each keyword search and the last one or two posts that appear on the first page of the Technorati.com search results

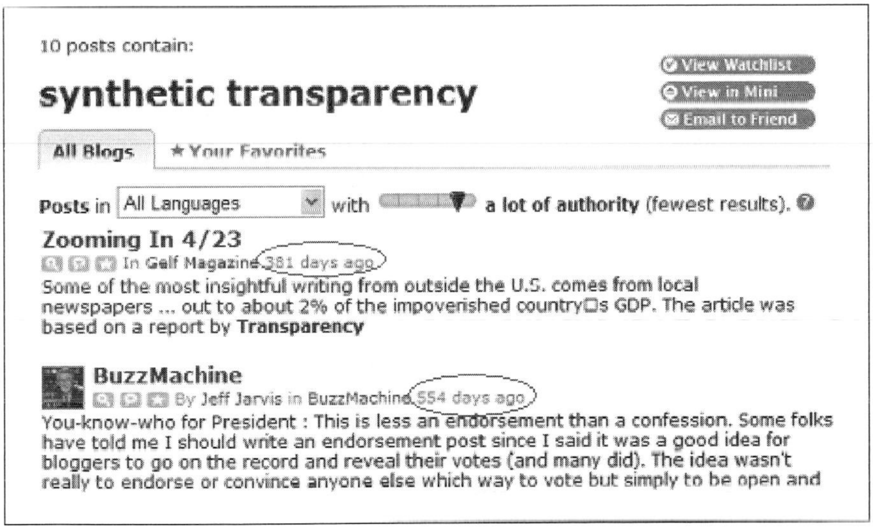

FIGURE 2.2   Results of Technorati.com Keyword Search for "Synthetic Transparency."

for the keyword. The two searches conducted were for the common phrase "business blogging" (see Figure 2.1) and the other search was for the obscure phrase "synthetic transparency" (see Figure 2.2).

On the day of the search, "business blogging" had 10,328 posts, and the last post was written two days earlier; therefore, to maintain a ranking on the first page of the Technorati.com search results, a blogger would have to write at least every two days. For the obscure keyword phrase, "synthetic transparency," there are only ten posts, and the last entry was written 554 days ago, indicating you would only have to write an article once a year on this keyword topic to appear in the search results of the RSS feed search engine.[9]

BLOGGING AUDIT: NEXT STEPS WITH YOUR KEYWORD LIST

Develop an initial list of keywords that you think your community would use in their blog posts. Those keywords will be used to find your blogging community. Once you have developed a short list of keywords, use general search engines like Google and Yahoo! to see what you can find. After finding one or two blogs in your community, read them carefully to make sure the blogs are worth keeping track of. In the process of adding to your list of blogs by conducting keywords used by bloggers in your industry, you can also use the Google Adwords Keyword tool to search each of the blogs and return a list of regularly used keywords on each blog. This process should expand your list of keywords and give pointers for finding more blogs in your industry using the additional keywords.

Many blogs, especially in high-visitor-volume keyword search, are spam blogs, which typically steal content from other blogs and provide no value to your audit. You should be able to quickly determine if a blog is written by a real person and regularly updated. Once you have a list of blogs, check the side navigation of the blog for a blog roll; a blog roll is a list of links to other blogs. The blog roll will have been developed by the blogger and usually lists some of the blogger's favorite blogs in their community. Include those blogs in your list of community blogs to review and monitor. After half a dozen or so blogs, many of the same blogs should start to appear in the blog rolls of other blogs. If you have time, keep track of where blogs link to other blogs. Lots of links to a blog give some clues to the importance of an individual blog in your community and might influence your decisions about which blogs to monitor. When you have exhausted this process, move onto the RSS feed search engines.

RSS feed search engines such as Technorati.com give you the ability to search by keyword directly. However, this process can be very laborious, as you have to search through all of the blogs manually. Technorati.com does provide users with the ability to set the level of authority of a blog—the authority rating is determined by the number of links to a blog from other blogs or websites listed in Technorati.com. The more links, the higher the authority and the greater the chances you will find a good blog worth adding to your list. Besides building a list of blogs for your community, it is also important to assess the relative importance of each blog and the community as a whole. This information will help your company in making a decision about moving forward with a blog. If you decide to blog, the community list will help in understanding the interrelationships and identifying the important bloggers as you start blogging.

Assessing each blog goes beyond a simple numbers game. You will also want to understand each blog's content strategy, blogger background, and the blogger's style of blogging. Following are a series of factors you should record about each blogger:

- Name of the blogger
- Name of the blog
- Website address of the blog
- System used by the blogger
- Interaction elements allowed:
  - Commenting turned on?
  - Trackbacks allowed?
  - Social networking tools enabled?
- Comment tracking tools used by the blogger?
- Blogger background
- Does the blogger answer comments?
- Does the blogger interact with other bloggers in the community?
- Volume of comments received by the blogger
- Technorati.com ranking

Here is an explanation of the list of factors to record for each blogger.

System Used by the Blogger

This is the blogging publishing system used. Blogging systems could include Blogspot or Blogger[10] from Blogger.com, TypePad[11] and Movable Type[12] from Six Apart,[13] and WordPress.[14] There are many other blogging systems available. It is important to become familiar with the many blogging systems available in the marketplace, as the level of functionality of a publishing system can give you some clues as to the level of interaction allowed on the blog and the sophistication of the blogger and the community.

Interaction Elements Allowed

Effective blogging is all about interaction between a blogger and their readers. Commenting and trackbacks are ways for blog readers and other bloggers to respond and give feedback to blog posts. Determine if the blogger has comments enabled or provides bloggers with the ability to send a trackback to a blog. Also, review a website for social media bookmarking tools like del.icio.us[15] and digg .com.[16] The use of social media bookmarking tools indicates a more sophisticated blogger. Reviewing a blogger's bookmarks within social media bookmarking tools can give you some idea of the extent of the research a blogger conducts and also lead to other bloggers.

Comment Tracking Tools Used by a Blogger

There are a few tools used by bloggers to track their blogger conversations. Those include coComment,[17] co.mments,[18] and del.icio.us. coComment enables a blogger to track each comment they post on any blog and allows you to quickly determine the number of conversations a blogger is involved in by signing up for the service and reviewing the bloggers' profile on coComment. The service may also give you some more leads to other bloggers in your community.

Blogger Background

What is the background of the blogger? You can typically research someone's background from their "About" page or by searching through their blog entries to find clues. Is the blogger a traditional media journalist, an industry veteran, a prospect, or an ordinary consumer? Each type of blogger in your industry will bring certain strengths to the community and provide you with an insight into the structure of your industry's blogging community. Is the community made up of professionals and pundits or the type of customers who would be your prospective clients? A background on the blogger, how long they have been blogging, and their reason for blogging will help you to build a good picture of your blogging community.

Does the Blogger Answer Comments?

Enabling commenting on a blog is just the first step in holding a conversation with a blogger. A blogger actually has to answer comments. For companies with lots of customers, the issue of answering customer comments can be more a matter of resources. For instance, on the General Motors FastLane blog, there is a statement on the blog that not every comment will be answered. Whether a blogger answers comments should tell you a lot about how the blogger will react when your blogger posts a comment on their blog.

Does the Blogger Interact with Other Bloggers in the Community?

Effective blogging is really all about having a conversation with others in your community. Reading a blogger's posts will give you some clues to the willingness of a blogger to interact with other bloggers in the community. Does the blogger cite other bloggers in their posts? Do you find their comments on other blogs in the community? Such information will allow you to gauge the willingness of a blogger to interact with you. The level of interaction will also give you some clues as to the level of interaction within your industry's blogging community.

Volume of Comments Received by the Blogger

The volume of comments received by an individual blogger will give an indication of the popularity or notoriety of the blogger in their community. Assessing the volume of comments on several blogs in a community will give you an idea of the level of conversation within the community compared with each blogger in the community. You will be able to identify the leaders in your blog community and some important information about the makeup of the blog readership. As you do not have access to the readership directly, reviewing the comments of other blogs can help to tell you a lot about who is reading the blogs you review.

Technorati.com Ranking

Links give some indication of the standing of a blog on the web and within a blogger's community. If a blog is listed in Technorati.com, the blog will have a listing of the number of other blogs that link to the blog. Use that link ranking to compare different blogs within a community and the community as a whole.

REVIEWING YOUR OWN COMPANY'S ABILITY TO BLOG

Corporate blogging requires a company to have certain resources to be successful and effective at blogging. These include having the right people who can blog, the time to blog, and the ability of a company to be transparent.

Time is the biggest factor in successful blogging, as writing a blog post from scratch can take 10 minutes to several days, depending on the sophistication of the post. Effective blogging requires that a corporate blogger interact with other bloggers in the community. That means your company has to monitor what is said in your community and be ready to respond to breaking events and news through your own posts or by commenting on other blog posts. The first step in starting a blog will be to determine who will blog in your company. Many technology companies such as Microsoft or SUN Microsystems empower any employee to blog in the company but give their employees a set of guidelines on how to blog. Some companies restrict who can blog; for example, Macromedia, before the company merged with Adobe Corporation, restricted the number of bloggers to 50 or 60 bloggers who are mainly in product marketing and development.[19]

Decide who is going to blog within your company, and your choice should depend upon your goals for blogging. In the book, *The Cluetrain Manifesto*, the authors, Levine et al., describe how the Internet is changing the relationship between companies and their customers. The web gives customers more power to control the public discussion about products and vendors, as customers now have easy access to publishing their own content on the web. Because of the collective nature of the web and the use of search engines, customers can build communities that discuss products and companies. One of the tenets of *The Cluetrain Manifesto* is that a company needs to open up to direct communication between customers and employees through the web. Have customers talk with employees directly and empower your employees to build a company that meets the needs of your customers.

As a company, you have to make a big decision whether to allow everyone to blog. Even if you do enable only a few people to blog, one reality is clear with blogging—although many people can write, not everyone can write a blog successfully.[20] Statistics from 2005 for Microsoft and IBM suggest that even with several thousands blogs at each company, the average number of blog posts per month was only between 2.5 and 2.9 blog posts.[21] That is not very many posts for so many bloggers. When assessing your potential bloggers, it is important to determine if your blogger can write, has any personality, and will give sufficient time and discipline to blog.[22] The time required to write a blog, answer comments on a blog, and maybe conduct some commenting on other blogs will depend upon the activity of the community. Reviewing the blog's post period on Technorati.com by keyword or post volume on the IceRocket trend tool will give you some clues as to the amount of activity your blogger will have to commit to have an impact in your community.

Comparing the amount of time it will take to run a successful blog with the time your blogger has available will help determine if it is possible for your company to run a blog. You may find that you need more bloggers to share the burden of blogging. The tasks of blogging are writing, monitoring, and interacting with readers and other bloggers. Monitoring your own blog for comments and the rest of your community is a task that does not have to be completed by one individual. Consider splitting up the tasks of blogging and assigning them to people who will best be able to commit their time.

Just because someone has the time to write a blog does not mean they are always the best people to write your company's blog. As the example of Indium Corporation demonstrates, Rick Short, the marketing director, ran a blog for Indium Corporation, except the topic of the blog was about marketing communications, not the topic that would attract Indium Corporation's engineering-minded customers who are also very gun-shy about marketing messages. Dr. Ron Lasky, one of Indium Corporation's employees, is a senior scientist in the industry, and his blog is read because most of his audience consists of engineers and they take him very seriously, as he is a leader in their industry. Dr. Lasky's blog works because of who he is and his role at Indium Corporation. One of the factors a company should consider in choosing its bloggers is who the audience will want to read when they come to your company's blog.

How your company decides to blog will also affect your company's ability to blog and whether the company should blog. Effective blogging is all about interaction and conversation. Assess both your company's level of transparency with communications tools such as comments and trackbacks and compare that with what your community does. If your company does not want to allow comments or trackbacks, your blog will not be as welcoming to the blogging community as it might be if you did. The blog will probably not be very effective as a tool to interact with customers and your audience. A more traditional website with more content might be the better choice than a blog if you do not want to open up comments or trackbacks. Even if you do allow comments and trackbacks on the blog, deciding who is going to be able to comment and how you react to comments or criticism is very important. Your openness to allowing comments and trackbacks will affect the perception your audience has about your level of transparency. Essentially, by setting up a blog, a company is declaring that it is willing to interact online with its readers and audience. No company is under any obligation to reveal everything through a blog when asked; however, a company should understand that how the company reacts or does not respond to comments and criticism will be judged and commented upon in the blogosphere. A company does not have to post every comment, especially if the comment is obscene, libelous, or against the company's blog reader guidelines, but a company does have to set clear expectations with its readers about what is expected of the readers and what the readership can expect of the bloggers.

THE GM FASTLANE BLOG COMMENT STRATEGY EXAMINED

Two blog readers of the General Motors FastLane blog[23] were interviewed in 2005, and both customers described their experiences with the blog and their impressions of General Motors. General Motors does not answer every single customer comment on their blog. The FastLane blog has received thousands of comments, and General Motors did not have the resources to answer every comment. General Motors, by setting up a blog, had given the impression that the company is open to receiving questions and comments. Several bloggers on the General Motors FastLane blog have explained repeatedly that the company is not able to answer every query on the FastLane blog. However, customers do not read every single post on a blog, so most customers have not read the message and have an expectation that they will receive an email or comment back from General Motors. The two General Motors FastLane blog readers described how disappointed they were that General Motors did not reply to their comments.

The concern for General Motors is that the blog may be giving a negative impression to customers who really are influential in spreading the word among fellow consumers about General Motors products. Carefully consider your comment response strategy with any corporate blogs. The best scenario is to answer any customer queries through your customer service department. If your company is not able to handle the volume of feedback, make a statement to that effect in the comment form.

Setting expectations goes a long way in avoiding customer frustrations; otherwise, your company might give the impression that you are not listening to customer feedback. Now, while this is always bad on an individual connection with a customer, when this happens in full public view on a blog website, the negative customer perceptions can be bad for a company's reputation within their customer community, because thousands, if not millions, of customers see your lack of response and act accordingly.[24]

BLOGGING REPORT TEMPLATE

When the blog audit is finished, its time to assess whether a blogging community is large and active enough to give a company enough justification to start blogging and whether your company is capable of blogging. Depending on who is conducting the audit within your company will determine your next steps. If you are the decision maker, the owner, CEO, president, or a member of the board of directors, you might not need a report of the blog audit to justify a decision to blog. However, if you are the person who is conducting the research and have to present your findings to a decision maker, then you will have to prepare a report.

Elements to include in the report are the following:

Blogging report executive summary—This is an overview of the report's findings, with justification for blogging or not and resources needed to blog.

Background of the company—This should include your audience, the company's marketing goals, and what the company wants to achieve with blogging.

Audit of your industry's blogging community—This is a detailed list of the bloggers in your community, an assessment of the overall community, its size, level of interaction, transparency required, and sophistication, and the bloggers' willingness to blog effectively. Also include the time that will be needed to blog successfully in the community and the assessment of the current issues discussed in your community.

An audit of your company's blogging capabilities—Determine who can blog in your company, the time your bloggers can commit to blogging, the willingness of people to blog in the company, and who would your audience want most to see blogging.

Potential benefits of blogging—Results may come in the form of higher search engine rankings, a higher profile in the community, or being able to communicate much more quickly and effectively with your customers and audience. How does the traffic you might garner from the volume of searches conducted on the web in general compare with the potential benefits from blogging? How will blogging elevate your company's brand in the community? How will the blog enable your company to connect with your audience? If the results help a company to meet their communications goals, then a company should consider blogging, even if the company does not currently have the resources to blog. Good results and a well-written report can provide the justification for providing more resources to the effort of blogging.[25,26]

Blogging justification—The justification for blogging or not blogging should be included in the report. You will need to measure the resources needed to commit to blogging and provide an assessment. Describe the capability of the company to provide those resources and the expected results from blogging.

Endnotes

1. http://www.technorati.com

2. Blogsurvey Blog, John Cass (2006), *Business Blogging Dominated By Technology Companies in the Fortune 500*. Available at http://blogsurvey.backbonemedia.com/archives/2006/05/fortune_500_tec_2.html

3. Taken from interviews with Rich Short, director of marketing for Indium Corporation, and presentations given by Rick Short and Dr. Ron Lasky at the Boston AMA Blogging workshop in June 2005

4. http://www.technorati.com

5. http://www.feedster.com

6. http://www.icerocket.com

7. http://www.sphere.com

8. http://blogsearch.google.com/

9. Blogsurvey Blog, John Cass (2006), *Conversation Search Engine Marketing, Effective Blogging and the Long Tail*. Available at http://blogsurvey.backbonemedia.com/archives/2006/05/conversation _se_1.html

10. http://www.blogger.com/start

11. http://www.typepad.com/

12. http://www.movabletype.org/

13. http://www.sixapart.com/

14. http://wordpress.org/

15. http://del.icio.us/

16. http://digg.com/

17. http://www.cocomment.com/

18. http://co.mments.com/

19. iMEDIAConnection, John Cass (2005), *Case Study: Macromedia and Blogs*. Available at http://www.imediaconnection.com/content/6729.asp

20. PR Communications Blog, John Cass (2005), *IBM Internal Corporate Blogging Strategy Thoughts*. Available at http://pr.typepad.com/pr_communications/2005/06/ibm_internal_co.html

21. Blogsurvey Blog, John Cass (2005), *Average Microsoft Blog Posts*. Available at http://blogsurvey.backbonemedia.com/archives/2005/07/average_microso.html

22. Blogsurvey Blog, John Cass (2005), *Blogging Good Content Requires Quality Not Quantity*. Available at http://blogsurvey.backbonemedia.com/archives/2005/06/blogging_good_c.html

23. http://fastlane.gmblogs.com/

24. Blogsurvey Blog, John Cass (2005), *The GM Blog: Lessons for Customer Blogging Relations*. Available at http://blogsurvey.backbonemedia.com/archives/2005/09/the_gm_blog_les.html

25. Blogsurvey Blog, John Cass (2005), *Why is a blog good for business?* Available at http://pr.typepad.com/pr_communications/2004/03/why_is_a_blog_g.html

26. PR Communications, John Cass (2004), *Corporate Blogs Start Personal Online Conversations*. Available at http://pr.typepad.com/pr_communications/2004/07/corporate_blogs.html

CHAPTER 3

Developing a Blogger Relations Strategy

The ability to publish online easily is a phenomenon that is completely changing how companies communicate with their customers. Mass media gave companies easy access to customers through advertising and effective public relations campaigns. Now that consumers can so easily publish their own content, there are some new opportunities in how a company's message can be delivered to audiences. There are also some new threats if a company does not get involved with this new medium, such as a company not being able to handle a communications crisis in the new medium because they do not have experience with how blogging operates. There are also potential risks from getting involved through blogging directly, especially if the process is not planned and managed well. But if a company commits enough resources and develops a good strategy, the company should be able to turn any threats into successful encounters and avoid risks by being involved in blogging.

Companies now face a new dilemma with content that is published by people on the web. In this new world of easy publishing on the web, customers are free to discuss companies, products, corporate advertising, and public relations campaigns in the traditional media. With the rise of search engines such as Google, customers can find each other's content and discussions extremely easily through search engines. Blogs and forums enable people to connect with one another to discuss the benefits and disadvantages of products together as a community. Customers read other customers content and also respond and discuss with their peers in forums and on blogs. Each published customer article or published comment influences overall opinion about a brand. When an individual writes something thoughtful about the relative merits of a product they contribute to the body of available customer opinion about a product on the web, and other customers can publish their own thoughts on those opinions. Sometimes, the community reaches a consensus about brands, products, and services, but all the content is available through search engines.

Customers are more cynical about company messages in advertising because of the high volume of advertising that inundates them. Customers now have the ability to easily critique a company's products, services, and advertising online. If customers believe a company is selling hype or if a product does not live up to expectation, customers have the ability to publish their opinions on the web, which means that companies cannot hide from complaints or negative opinion about their products and services. A company has to get its message right the first time and back up what it promotes with reality; if not, customers will consider a company's advertising as just more marketing hype and dismiss your company's efforts. Even more seriously for the management of brand's reputation in today's online world is that if your products are discussed negatively, that negative discussion may be on the web forever to be found through search engines by customers and competitors. When a company does not respond to customers' complaints, the audience will probably assume that such negative opinion must be correct. In contrast, it is remarkably easy to demonstrate that your company is listening by responding to customer concerns. Online audience engagement is not just about responding to complaints, however; it is also about effective communication. In this new world of blogs, it is about understanding that part of the message to customers through blogging is about building trust, which can be accomplished by fulfilling expectations consistently by backing up any claims with products and services that meet expectations.

Successful marketing through blogs and forums is all about engaging your customers with relevant information they want to read, which may be industry-related information, updates on products, or answering customer questions about how to use a product. Some of the benefits of blogging for a company are higher search engine rankings, engaging customers, and creating higher brand awareness, and these are accomplished by stating opinions and giving leadership on current topics of discussion in an industry, whereas an audience can interact with a company more easily through a corporate blog, thus giving their opinions and feedback about products and what the future should hold for the industry. Blogging can enable a company to keep up with the speed and flow of the customers' conversation about a company's products and competitors' products online.

To receive the most benefits from corporate blogging, a company has to become an effective blogger. Outreach is important in blogging, but pitching bloggers may not be the best way to reach them. To conduct an effective blogging campaign requires a combination of skills that already exist from within the disciplines of public relations, search engine optimization, journalism, and online marketing. Bloggers also need an entirely new set of skills within the new discipline of blogger relations. This is the new discipline that enables a company to engage its audience online by combining old offline skills with the new online communications skills. As blogger relations borrow much from other professions in terms of strategy, this chapter will review what public relations, search engine optimization, journalism, and online marketing can provide to the new discipline of blogger relations, and pulling it all together will help you create a plan for developing a corporate blogging strategy for effective blogging.

HOW TO EFFECTIVELY CONDUCT CORPORATE BLOGGING

Blog marketing gives you the opportunity to comment on other people's blogs in your community, whose readers might be your customers and prospects. Blogger outreach to other blogs means you have the opportunity to converse on a wide number of blogs in your community, whose audience is exactly the audience you want to reach. When you do comment and interact with another blogger, the effort should not be about attempting to grab attention or interrupting the blogger.

There is a technique in public relations that enables companies to gain media attention. That process of drawing attention to your company is called media relations, and it involves the process of reaching out to journalists to pitch stories. Media relations can also involve building relationships with journalists in your industry.

Blogger relations is the process of developing content on the blog, and conducting outreach to other blogs results in a company building a connection with other bloggers and the audience in their community. That connection will be built through credible posts that enhance the authority of a blogger and reveal enough about the blogger so that the community has a sense of the person through his or her writing and begins to trust the blogger. A successful blogger relations campaign involves outreach to other blogs with the purpose of developing a connection with bloggers and blog readers.

It is possible to use media relations' tactics with bloggers by asking bloggers directly to write a story about a product. To ask for attention in the online community, if executed well, may produce results. However, your outreach is really best conducted minimally and simply where the content is relevant to the blogger and their audience, perhaps through a short email with a brief introduction to another blogger, describing what you want the blogger to do.

The most important strategy in blogger relations is where a blogger receives attention by not pitching for attention. Blogging is definitely about reaching out to your audience; however, it is best not to interrupt with a sales pitch a blogger whose blog is focused on their interests and issues. In fact, asking a blogger to interview you for their blog, review your product, or link to your blog may be construed as interrupting the blogger. However, chatting with a blogger about their latest blog post, even critiquing the post, or asking the blogger if they will commit to an interview on your blog is not. To succeed in the discipline of blogger relations, focus on what the other blogger wants to discuss and you will be conducting blogger relations effectively.

After many discussions with corporate bloggers at software companies,[1–3] I have discovered that the people who are often the most effective bloggers in a company are the product builders or technical support people who can help a customer to get the best out of that product. The reason for this is that those disciplines focus on what their customers want to talk about most, such as making the product work, discussing the future of the product, and how to use the product. That is an important lesson when your company approaches blogging: Make sure you put your message within the context of what people want to hear.

Blogging as a cultural phenomenon is all about informal conversations, building relationships, and creating goodwill that establishes credibility. Any expert gains credibility when they discuss all sides to an argument. If an expert is pitching a product, or interrupting another blogger to gain attention, then the expert's credibility is lessened. Many marketers have documented the decline in the effectiveness of advertising during the last 40 years. Seth Godin even coined a phrase for the phenomena, "interruption marketing,"[4] which describes advertising as an interruption to a customer's life. Interruption should be the activity to avoid for any blogger; therefore, ask if you are interrupting someone's life, thoughts, and conversation when you approach the blogger. If you are interrupting another blogger, you run the risk of losing credibility, and credibility is the currency corporate bloggers hope to achieve in developing relationships and awareness in their industry.

Guerilla marketing and word-of-mouth marketing are the processes of people talking about your company between their friends and associates without being paid or prompted. Word of mouth is best when it happens spontaneously. It is difficult to artificially generate spontaneous attention for a company. Blogger relations holds out the possibility of doing just that, generating word of mouth about your company and product by not using promotional tactics. Within the medium of blogging, a company can describe their product, industry, and thoughts in a way that is conversational and informal. Using blogger relations as an approach, a company will gain credibility and allow a company to break through a customer's cynicism about marketing and advertising.

Unless there is seriousness to your writing and you are making a genuine attempt to conduct a dialogue with your community, customers and the press will quickly identify hot air and no substance and conclude your company's blog is a shrill or sales mouthpiece. You risk your blog being ignored or even criticized by taking such actions. In contrast, if you do have something worthwhile and relevant to publish, you will demonstrate your expertise in your industry by the posts you make.

Blogging is one of the best ways to reach your audience, because a blog gives the writer the space to write. You will be able to publish enough content regularly that the content becomes dialogue between the blogger and the audience. Blogging also allows a blogger to find their own style because it gives the blogger the freedom to reveal what he or she is really like to the world, and such writing can be compelling if the writer's experiences are of interest to their audience.

PITCHING A BLOGGER

The standard for deciding if you can interrupt a blogger is the relevancy of the story you want the blogger to publish; this has also always been true when contacting journalists. Conducting blogger relations in the same way tactics for media relations are implemented can be very effective. However, it is important to consider that someone who wishes to establish themselves as an authority probably should not also practice interruption tactics in a blogging setting, as using such tactics will lessen the blogger's credibility. Of course, it just depends upon the circumstances of the blogger and company; there will always be situations when experts will develop new products or an idea and ask their community for feedback. Where the relevancy of such questions is high, not only will the expert get results but their credibility will also be enhanced. However, to practice systematic pitching, or interruption marketing, one runs the danger of ruining a blogging expert's reputation in their blogging community.

Blogger relations can be defined in two ways. One, you interrupt other bloggers to pitch them a story, and two, a blogger joins in on an existing conversation and introduces a company message as it relates to the conversation. Both definitions of blogger relations can and will have results but also may produce unintended consequences. The pitching technique is an interruption to the immediate attention of any intended bloggers who are the focus of a pitch. A blogger who uses this technique risks losing credibility if the recipient believes the pitch was not relevant to them. Bloggers who read another blog's articles and determine that there is a post where they can contribute something of value to the original article or to an ongoing discussion in the blog's comment section will be focusing on content and relationships and implementing the conversational approach to blogger relations.

One way to ensure that your conversations in the blogosphere are relevant to your company, and not just to the participants, is to pick conversations that are related to issues you would discuss on your own blog. To find those conversations, you would target the keywords your audience uses to search for topics related to your industry. By conducting those searches, you will have content associated with the issues and keywords you are targeting as a company, whether that discussion is on your own blog or in the comment section of another blog. It is important to be involved in the discussion wherever it takes place. An audience will read your company blogger's contribution to the discussion whether the audience discovers the blog discussion through other blog links or by finding the page through a search on a search engine. Making sure your conversation is relevant to the blogger and your own company helps you to reach your audience. It also gives a blogger more opportunity to enhance their reputation in the wider community by writing a relevant comment.

If you must use both the pitching and conversational approaches to blogger relations, try splitting up the responsibilities for each approach between a company's blogger and their public relations professionals. Dividing the approaches between people will allow your expert blogger to maintain their credibility. There is something to be said for the blogger to blog and a media relations person to pitch stories to journalists. When you are attempting to gain credibility as an expert it is difficult to maintain your credibility if one moment you are writing eloquently on your subject and the next moment you are trying to sell the audience something. Public relations people save their company or client a lot of time when they are the first point of content for the media and public. Communications professionals provide some distance between the journalist and a company. There will always be companies with bloggers who use both pitching and conversational approaches to blogging. However, for the long term, a company should consider what roles they want their bloggers to assume. It is important to understand that, sometimes, when you interrupt others to grab attention, you will not succeed in gaining anyone's attention, but when you focus on developing great content and conversation, invariably, your company always wins. If not through a sale, at the very least, by having another page of content indexed in Google with the relevant keywords your audience uses to search for your company. Any company should ask itself this question, "Do your company experts have the time to spend on attempting to grab attention by interrupting people, when they already have little time to blog as it is?" Rather, if you must pitch, leave that up to the public relations folks.

It is my belief from observation and conversation with corporate bloggers that you are better off not interrupting bloggers. Strangely enough, the interruption process is the part of blogger relations that borrows the most from some of the techniques in media relations; although the technique can work, and companies have shown the technique to work extremely well.[5,6] The media relations technique of pitching when used in the context of blogger relations is not the most effective technique for all bloggers to use. Public relations professionals, or for that matter, bloggers in general, are not effective bloggers when they conduct outreach in the same way public relations professionals practice cold pitches to journalists. Pitching in this way can be effective. However, if your goal is effective blogging through spreading your message by word of mouth, pitching a story will not achieve your goal because pitching is not word-of-mouth marketing; it is really media relations because you conducted outreach to get attention for your story, idea, or product. The technique can be very effective if used correctly; if you want to be an effective blogger for the long term, the strategy to follow is one of conversation with bloggers as it occurs.

PUBLIC RELATIONS

The profession of public relations has more to give the new practice of blogger relations in terms of techniques and expertise than any other profession. The public relations profession helps companies to communicate their message effectively so that goodwill is generated toward a company. Public relations departments manage internal communications and media relations, can be involved with crafting a company's brand messages and crisis communications, and are increasingly responsible for managing the relationships with online communications in the world of consumer-generated media.

Skills provided by the public relations profession that will help with blogging include the following:

- The ability to develop a relationship with other business people,
- The ability to conduct a dialogue with other business professionals,
- The expertise to look beyond the moment, and predict the future consequences resulting from any company actions,
- Public relations people have to convince journalists and other stakeholders that their story is important. Public relations people sell their story on the value it will provide to the journalist's audience,
- The media world has changed, news is delivered 24 hours a day, 7 days a week, and the Internet is the reason for that change. Public relations professionals who are experienced in the pace of the news cycle have the training, techniques, and discipline to keep up.[7]

Most critically, when communications crises arise that require delicate management, public relations professionals have the skills to manage the crisis.

Initial mistakes and errors by a company can easily be compounded by further errors when managing a crisis. It is the job of public relations professionals to provide advice on what steps and language to use to reduce bad will created by any initial mistakes. It can be a very difficult course of action for a company to be open about its mistakes. There may be legal implications for a company if mistakes are admitted. Those legal consequences have to be balanced against the damage to a company's reputation when the company does not admit fault, error, or take steps to remedy a crisis.

Despite the skills public relations professionals have with communications, the writing of a corporate blog is often best conducted by people other than the communications professionals in a company. Blog readers are often looking for expertise not held by a communications professional or want to read about the topic or industry of interest from an expert in their field. A number of technology companies including Microsoft, SUN Microsystems, and Adobe have adopted blogging into their corporate communications practices. Invariably, the most successful technology blogs in terms of reaching their audiences at these companies are run by product builders and customer-facing staff.

In the Backbone Media Corporate Blogging Survey 2005, Mike Chambers from Macromedia, the product manager for Flash, explained how Macromedia's product managers and developers used blogs to communicate effectively and quickly with their customers.[8] The writers of corporate blogs at Macromedia may not always be formally trained in public relations, but their audiences wanted the ability to communicate directly with the people who design and build the Macromedia products. It is in the nature of blogging that the elements of interaction that include commenting and trackbacks, require that bloggers act quickly to respond to customer and blog reader comments and questions. In the online world, people expect you to respond to their comments or lose interest. In a traditional media relations setting, a public relations professional might be the best individual to manage the process of setting up an interview between a journalist and a product manager. In contrast, in the world of corporate blogs, the best device for managing discussion between the customer and product manager is the product manager's blog.

Think carefully who should be blogging in your company. Blogging opens up more possibilities for senior product builders in a company to communicate directly with customers, as a new degree of efficiency in communications is possible with blogging because individual employees can communicate directly with a number of customers at the same time,[9] where once a product builder would not have had the time or inclination to answer all customer questions. Answering questions on a blog not only resolves an issue for the customer who asked the question but also demonstrates to an audience through the process of conducting a dialogue the value a company can provide.

Blogging propels non-communications staff into the role of the spokesperson for a company in a very public way. Now that blogging places once internal staff in such public roles, non-communications staff has much to learn from their public relations brethren. Public relations people have never been the only spokespeople within a company, it has been the role of product marketing people to communicate with many stakeholders inside and out of their company to develop and manage products. However, any non-public relations professional who finds themselves in the role of a corporate blogger can learn the techniques of effectively communicating and generating goodwill for a company from a public relations professional.

WHAT CAN BLOGGERS LEARN FROM PUBLIC RELATIONS?

Blogger relations strategy borrows a lot from public relations strategy; in fact, the really good public relations people who conduct media relations do not try to sell the product. First, public relations people should try to understand the needs of the audiences, what interests them, and what is on the top of their mind in current industry discussions. Public relations people review their products and brands looking for the unique characteristics that have great relevancy for an audience. If public relations gets it right and has a good sense of the market, every time a public relations person approaches a journalist with a story, what the public relations person has to say is relevant and useful to the journalist and the audience. Blogger relations can be enacted in just the same way, although typically most bloggers will not have overall strategy in mind on every single blog post, or comment, rather they will think about strategy in broad terms, generally developing content that describes the unique characteristics of a company. On a day-to-day basis, with the demand for content, bloggers will discuss non-product and, sometimes non-strategic related issues on a blog. Surprisingly, that wider discussion is important, as it demonstrates that the blogger is not just a marketing shill but also a person with opinions and personality. In fact, many blog readers say learning about a blogger's experiences and life puts what the blogger has to say in perspective and connects them with bloggers. If a blog reader feels connected and trusts the blogger, that connection and trust extend to how a blog reader views the blogger's company. Be that as it may, here are some strategies and techniques that blogger relations can borrow from public relations for effective blogging.

Building a unique blogging content strategy—Public relations professionals focus on the unique characteristics of a company to understand the most important value a company provides to its customers. A company has to understand the unique strengths that are most relevant to its audience. Successful blogging involves writing a lot of content, but what does a company actually

write? It is important to create a strategy to develop the most relevant content for an audience. Relevancy is the key in public relations, and it is also the key in corporate blog marketing. Developing a story that is relevant to an audience will increase your chances of having your story published. In the blogging world, you do not have to worry about being published, but you do have to worry about attracting an audience. To attract an audience, you have to make sure your blog contains relevant content for your audience.

Understanding the importance of dialogue—Effective blogging is about building relationships with other bloggers and blog readers. Sometimes, that means knowing how to respond to questions and blog comments, and, sometimes, it means being willing to go out into your blogging community and discuss issues on other blogs. Public relations is one marketing profession that already has the expertise and skills on how to approach someone with an idea or story and have that message heard and be taken seriously enough to have an article published based on the initial conversation. Review the techniques that public relations professionals use in building dialogue with an audience.

Public relations professionals build relationships with traditional media professionals. They have to understand how to develop a story that is relevant to a journalist's audience and know whom to approach and how to approach them. Blogger relations is similar, in that a blogger has to take the time and care to review the work of a blogger whom they would like to interact with before posting a comment or sending an email. If a blog's content is relevant to a company's audience and a company has something relevant and valuable to add to the conversation, then it is safe to contribute to the conversation.

There are very big differences between how a blogger might be approached and how a journalist may be approached. Bloggers are interested in discussing ideas about their topic or industry. Bloggers welcome debate and even sometimes disagreement. Although public relations professionals may present different opinions to a journalist, typically, a public relations person will not directly disagree with a journalist's opinion and work. In the world of blogging, it is possible for a reader to make a comment on a blog that disagrees with a blogger. Many bloggers welcome the discourse if that discussion is civil and seen as being initiated with the aim to discuss ideas or find out information. Constructive criticism and debate play a big role in blogging, for it is through different opinions that bloggers develop a reputation of authority and credibility in their community. Even so, public relations approaches for handling criticism and discussion can help with effective blogger relations.

Understanding the importance of developing relationships—Knowing whom to contact for a story is a very important problem in media relations. Public relations professionals spend a lot of time developing media contacts and maintaining them. With the advent of the web and blogs, to determine which bloggers to contact, there are new skills to learn. The same principles applied

by public relations in building relationships with the journalists who serve an audience apply in building relationships with the bloggers who connect with your company's audience. The methods for finding bloggers are not yet as obvious as they are in media relations; in media relations, you can easily get a list of publications or a database of journalists. In a blogging community, there may be many more bloggers than journalists who cover the same industry. Finding those bloggers requires a process of identifying them through search engines such as Google or Technorati. Then, you have to read and conduct a narrative analysis of the blogs you have discovered to determine the relevancy of each blog to your audience. Measuring the importance of a blogger can be difficult; however, a blogger with a lot of links in a community is probably some indication of their influence within a community. What is really essential is understanding the relevancy of a particular blogger's content to your audience and your own company's goals. In addition, you also have to understand how a blogger wishes to be engaged, if at all, as how they wish to be approached will affect your outreach to a blogger. In public relations, the process of maintaining your media contacts database is constant; the same applies to the process of maintaining a database of your blogging community.

Public relations strategy helps you to focus on your unique strengths— Blogger relations can change the role of communications and public relations staff. People interested in a company do not necessarily need to talk with communications staff to act as the go-between with a blog. Rather, public relations professionals can shift some of their focus from tactics to providing strategic advice on how to build a successful blogging practice and respond to communications incidents where their expertise is needed.[10]

The future of public relations in the world of blogger relations—Blogger relations involves skills from many different existing professions, public relations, search engine optimization, web design, and journalism. To be successful in the new world of blogging, public relations professionals will have to educate themselves on all of the skills needed to help a company's or client's efforts. The public relations discipline is one of the professions poised to grow significantly from the growth of blogging. Public relations professionals have many of the skills and strategies needed to be successful in today's new media world, but public relations professionals have much to learn from other professions if they are truly going to be successful in blogging.

Lastly, blogging is not just about public relations. Blogging also involves customer service and product development. In fact, some of the best returns for companies from blogging come from product development. Companies can use blogs for gaining feedback from their customers and in the process gain public relations and immediate promotional benefits from following a product development dialogue with their customers. Therefore, it is important for public relations professionals to educate themselves on how these other disciplines

affect blogger relations. That expertise includes search engine optimization skills, online marketing, and the journalistic approach.

SEARCH ENGINE OPTIMIZATION

Search engine optimization is the process of optimizing content on a website so that webpages rise to the top editorial rankings in important search engines such as Google, Yahoo!, and MSN. Search engine optimization optimizes the content and structure of a webpage to gain higher rankings on a search engine. The content on a page, links to a site, and the ability to get indexed in a search engine are the three important factors in achieving a higher ranking in a search engine. Companies value top positions in search engines because so many people use the web to find information to help in making choices about products and companies. Achieving a top ranking on a search engine will influence the amount of traffic that comes to your website.

The most important search engines all have editorial listings and sponsored ads. Advertisers pay for the sponsored ads. According to research, a smaller percentage of customers click through on the ads compared with the editorial listings. A search engine selects the most relevant site on the web for a particular keyword and then displays a link to the site in the editorial listings of a search engine. Google was one of the first search engines to increase the ranking of a website based upon the number of links a webpage receives from other websites that contain similar content and keywords.

Lots of advertisers spend a higher proportion of marketing dollars on pay-per-click (PPC) advertising compared with the amount of resources they commit to building effective organic search engine optimization for their web presence. However, the returns from organic search engine optimization are much greater than from pay-per-click advertising. The reason fewer dollars are spent on editorial search engine optimization compared with the pay-per-click campaigns is that it is a lot easier to develop a simple ad on a search engine compared with developing an entire website with a lot of good content. One activity really only takes a lot of money, whereas the other takes a lot of time on the part of employees.

Although the advertising dollars spent on blogs has certainly grown, the amount of money spent on building an effective blogger relations practice is still small. The number of companies that are blogging is small   only 10% of the Fortune 500 companies had a blog in the fall of 2006. Blogging appears to be following in the footsteps of the organic search engine optimization industry and developing slowly. Some of the reasons for the slow development is the amount of time it takes to run a successful blogging practice and concerns over bad publicity generated by running blog. Not only do you need the time to write,

but you also need the time and expertise to interact with your customers and audience.

HOW BLOGGING HELPS WITH SEARCH ENGINE OPTIMIZATION

Now that the reality of the new blogging economy has hit the mainstream, search engine optimization content strategies once used for traditional websites are just as relevant for building your blogging strategy.[11] Blogs are important to search because of the way blogs are designed and implemented, and blogs can help a company to achieve great results for all three of the following factors:

1. Blogs are powered by content management systems that allow non-technical people to update content quickly. Also, culturally, it is very acceptable to post content more frequently than a normal website. Content is an important factor in ranking webpages in a search engine.

2. It has been difficult to get a website to link to another website by simply asking a webmaster to link a site, and blogs have solved that problem. Bloggers link to other valuable content on a regular basis; if your content is valuable, you will receive a lot of links without having to ask for the link. Links are how the main search engines judge the relevancy of a webpage.

3. Getting into a search engine is the first step toward achieving a high ranking; it is not just about getting the home page into a search engine, you also need to build a website that has all of its content indexed, and blogs design can help you achieve this. Blogs are designed well for accessibility and indexing by search engines.

Blogging provides a way for companies to easily build relevant content and gain links, so that a company can boost its rankings in the search engines by using an effective blogging strategy. If your content is relevant, your customer community will vote for its relevancy by linking to the content. To build a website that achieves high search engine rankings, you have to ensure your content is relevant and valuable for your audience and that the content features the keywords you are targeting. The key in blogging is to identify the content strategies that will encourage interaction and linking to a company's blog, and the same goes for any writing you conduct on other blogs in the blogosphere, including commenting and trackbacks.

Customers have the ability to create and publish their own blogs. Over time, a blogging community develops, and what is discussed on one blog may be quoted or followed by another. As these customer blogging communities develop, the opportunities and threats for that community to praise or criticize a company increase in effectiveness because the mechanism for gaining high rankings in a search engine includes the quantity of content around a particular topic. The community can quite easily propel discussion about a company or product to top rankings on the most important search engines. Where once in the world of television advertising customers did not have the power to significantly influence dialogue on national TV, a mass of people with their own websites actually may have more power to influence what is seen on the web through the search engine.

The question for any company in developing a corporate blog is, therefore, what content strategies should you develop to get the most recognition from each audience?[12] Developing content that interests your audience and is relevant will get a company the most attention and links from their audience. To conduct a successful blogging campaign that affects a company's search results requires that all content in a blog contain the keywords your audience uses to search on the web. Once someone finds the blog through a search engine, the content on the blog must be relevant to an audience. If a company's product is complex or requires explanation, customers will want to ask questions online about how a product works. That is how many corporate blogs have developed relevant content for many blog readers, by helping customers to understand how to use a product.

A company first develops a content strategy that will be of interest to the community as a whole, as this will produce the most results for a blogging campaign. The Backbone Media Corporate Blogging Survey 2005 includes blogging strategy examples from Microsoft, Macromedia, and others that demonstrate a company can gain the most from blogging when their content strategy is focused on customer's ideas and feedback,[13] as customer feedback produces the greatest opportunity for creating customer evangelists, more links, sales, and higher search engine rankings.

HOW BLOGS ARE POWERFUL TOOLS FOR COMMUNITY OUTREACH

Blogs, by their nature, are community online tools, very similar to forums in that they allow easy interaction and communication between online users. Although forums are typically closed communities where discussion takes place within the community, blogs are more open; conversation takes place both on the blog and between websites. Members run the best forums, in that the editorial control of a forum is best left to the members of the forum. Blogs, on the other hand, allow a company to control the editorial content of the website. Yet, similar to email and forums, a company can use an informal conversational style of writing.

Although forums can provide some of the best information on customer ideas and feedback, a successfully run blogger relations campaign has some advantages over a forum. When a blogger focuses on the ideas of a customer for products, a blogger can receive ideas, more links, and higher sales and turn customers into evangelists. Blogs give companies the ability to interact, link, and receive links to other blogs, unlike the relatively closed world of a forum, where conversation happens within the forum, not between websites. Blogs give companies many tools of interaction, such as commenting and trackbacks. By setting up a company blog, a company declares that the company is open to conduct an online dialogue between bloggers and an audience. A company blogger is free to comment and trackback on blogs in the community, and other bloggers are free to comment on the company blog. If your company can run a successful blogging operation, you will gain links and the opportunity to have a dialogue with many other blog readers from the blogs that refer to your blog posts. Blog writing encourages linking, as authority and credibility come in part from stating evidence and other blogger posts. As a result, blogging has a culture of linking to other blogs. Linking is important for search engine rankings and online marketing, in general, in terms of higher search engine traffic and direct traffic.

Corporate blogs allow more interaction between other blogs and websites than forums. That flexibility to interact in the wider online customer community means that blogs can give companies additional benefits in the areas of higher search engine rankings and exposure to new audiences beyond forums. Forums and blogs play a vital role in the online design tools for interaction with customers, and although the total amount of content in blogs may be less, it is the open nature of blogging that allows interaction between individual bloggers that gives blogs their special role in the world of product development, marketing, search engine optimization, and public relations.

WHAT CAN BLOGGERS LEARN FROM INTERNET MARKETERS?

Corporate bloggers can learn a lot from the search engine marketing industry on how to achieve top rankings on search engines. Bloggers can also learn a lot from other aspects of Internet marketing. Internet marketers have sent customers a lot of email and posted many banner ads, and in the process, some Internet marketing professionals realized that selling to someone who does not want to hear your message is a waste of time and will only annoy the customer you interrupt. Permission marketing, a concept developed by Seth Godin, is the idea that a marketing company should only follow-up with people who wish to receive information about a company [14] The same principle applies in blogger relations—it is better if you only chat with other bloggers who want to talk about the same topics.

Internet marketing professionals use web statistics tools to measure the effectiveness of their efforts. There are online tools for measuring the volume of traffic on a blog, such as RSS feed search engines. There are also tools for measuring the rankings of a blog or website on the search engines. Web Position Gold from FirstPlace software[15] provides a tool for measuring the ranking of a webpage on all of the major search engines for a large number of keywords. You can use the software to track your position and progress over time. Bloggers should use such search engine measurement techniques to determine if their blogging efforts are producing traffic or higher rankings on search engines. Keep a monthly track of the results, in terms of your traffic and the keywords people are using to find your blog.

Probably, the biggest lessons bloggers can take and apply from Internet marketing is around the philosophy of how you interact to users on the blog. Internet time, similar to the news cycle, runs 24 hours, 7 days a week, and it is important to show that your website is active by updating content and by responding to comments and questions quickly. Also, Internet marketers are very aware that the easy navigation of a website or blog is very important to the success of a website; this includes features such as giving people the option of searching a blog for content using a search box on the blog and providing many different ways to navigate your content. Search is also an important design consideration for your blog; it is important to make sure you include the keywords in your blog that your audiences use to find you so that the blog can be easily found on search engines.

Conversation online is something Internet marketers are very familiar with; they understand that you have to develop automated systems that update people when a comment is posted, as long practice has taught Internet marketers that people forget to return to the same website. Be helpful and do not assume that people will come back to your blog if you post a follow-up comment to a blog reader's comment; make sure you let them know you posted a comment, preferably with an automated email. Use strategies of good navigation and automated communication throughout the design of your blog and how you interact with blog readers, and you will make life easier for your audience.

Internet marketing people have really learned the benefits of building strong communities and letting the community grow a website through their contributions. Community contributions are what make Ebay,[16] Craigslist,[17] and YouTube[18] all successful. Consider using social marketing strategies for the development of your blog. Invite other people to make contributions from the community, and feature interviews with other bloggers regularly.

Becoming the catalyst for a community project can gain many benefits for the community and you indirectly. Consider how you can develop community projects with the rest of your blogging community. You do not have to do all the work yourself. If you help to initiate a project that builds a stronger community, even if the project might not be directly related to your company or products, the benefits of establishing yourself as a credible resource to your blogging community are priceless.

WHAT JOURNALISM CAN TEACH BLOGGERS

Now that people can develop their own content on the web, rather than work through traditional media publications to get out a company message, companies have the ability to connect directly with audiences who read and write blogs by developing their own blog and joining their industry's online conversation.

Journalists play a useful role by reporting to the society. They seek out the stories that will most interest their readers and attempt to provide objective reporting based on facts by checking the authenticity of their stories. The journalistic approach provides the credibility media publications need to attract readers. With the growth of citizen media, once the journalist is removed from the media distribution channel, what then happens to the content of the story? If corporate bloggers are writing about the top stories in an industry, does objective reporting go out the window in such situations?

In the new age of citizen journalism, blogs, and social media websites, journalism appears to have less relevancy than before because it is associated with professional mainstream media. Rather, the journalistic approach has greater relevancy because of blogging, and many bloggers do resemble journalists in their approach to writing. In fact, some are journalists: Jeff Jarvis from BuzzMachine[19] and Stephen Baker from Business Week[20] are examples. Another journalist, Tom Abate, is a reporter for the San Francisco Chronicle and also a blogger; he writes the MiniMediaGuy Blog. He believes that journalism might be the new rhetoric and suggests, "Journalism may be the fact-based, persuasive style of writing that acknowledges the many facets of a story, situation or person, but nevertheless leads to some point."[21]

Reporting the facts does not appear to be what a lot of blogging is about. Many blogs are more about opinion than facts; at least, for example it seems opinion is more important than fact in many political blogs. However, in the corporate blogging world, many blog readers are attracted to employee bloggers for their content, content that is relevant and gives information about the products readers use or their industry. Cold facts do not necessarily keep those blog readers coming back for more; sometimes, opinion and filler pieces do, anything that reveals the tastes and personality of the corporate blogger, which will build a connection. But products and brands are not built on opinions and taste alone; even the most highly fashionable accessory has to work. So the humdrum of corporate facts builds and establishes credibility for corporate bloggers. Here is where, as Tom Abate suggests, "the style, value, ethics, and approaches of journalism may be ideally suited to helping people express themselves in this media age," for customers want authenticity, credibility, and dialogue to be able to put trust in a blogger and the brand he or she represents. To achieve all that, bloggers have to be themselves and also keep to the same standards journalists follow. Tom Abate describes how journalism really "applies only to communications that are intended to persuade or inform. Conveniently, the norms of journalism transcend written media. Journalism aspires to be fair, factual, and concise in any media, or combination of media types."[22]

The issue of standards, especially transparency in writing, has affected the development of blogging culture. There is much debate about what standards bloggers should use in their writing. Journalism can provide some standards for blogging to use with helping to establish credibility. Corporate bloggers can also use some of the experiences and lessons from journalism to develop standards in writing that fit the norms of their blogging community.[23]

Reviewing the origin of journalistic standards, we find that Walter Williams, the first dean of the Missouri School of Journalism, developed the journalist's creed in 1908. The creed holds journalists to certain standards. The creed goes someway to defining journalism. Here is the creed:

> I believe in the profession of journalism.
>
> I believe that the public journal is a public trust; that all connected with it are, to the full measure of their responsibility, trustees for the public; that acceptance of a lesser service than the public service is betrayal of this trust.
>
> I believe that clear thinking and clear statement, accuracy and fairness are fundamental to good journalism.
>
> I believe that a journalist should write only what he holds in his heart to be true.
>
> I believe that suppression of the news, for any consideration other than the welfare of society, is indefensible.
>
> I believe that no one should write as a journalist what he would not say as a gentleman; that bribery by one's own pocketbook is as much to be avoided as bribery by the pocketbook of another; that individual responsibility may not be escaped by pleading another's instructions or another's dividends.

I believe that advertising, news and editorial columns should alike serve the best interests of readers; that a single standard of helpful truth and cleanness should prevail for all; that the supreme test of good journalism is the measure of its public service.

I believe that the journalism which succeeds best—and best deserves success—fears God and honors Man; is stoutly independent, unmoved by pride of opinion or greed of power, constructive, tolerant but never careless, self-controlled, patient, always respectful of its readers but always unafraid, is quickly indignant at injustice; is unswayed by the appeal of privilege or the clamor of the mob; seeks to give every man a chance and, as far as law and honest wage and recognition of human brotherhood can make it so, an equal chance; is profoundly patriotic while sincerely promoting international good will and cementing world-comradeship; is a journalism of humanity, of and for today's world.[24]

The creed is not the only standard or code for journalists. The Code of Ethics for the Society of Professional Journalists has four overriding standards for journalists to follow[25]:

- Seek the truth.
- Provide a fair and comprehensive account.
- Strive for thoroughness and honesty.
- Integrity is the cornerstone of credibility.

Reviewing each of the standards, we can discuss their relevancy for effective blogging.

Seek the truth—On the issue of keeping the public's trust by seeking the truth, a corporate blogger's goals are often different from a journalist, they have to consider the goals of their company. It is a rare journalist who will suppress the news. The demands of a company may limit what a corporate blogger will reveal to their audience. Corporate bloggers have responsibilities, and if revealing information may harm a company, the blogger will not reveal confidential information.

An audience will desert a blogger quickly if the blogger does not write the truth on a consistent basis and is discovered. It is not right for a corporate blogger to obscure the truth. It is correct for a blogger to set expectations about what they can and cannot reveal on a blog. Integrity does not have to be compromised, but neither is a blogger under any obligation to reveal corporate secrets that may affect a company's competitiveness.

Provide a fair and comprehensive account—Reviewing the Code of Ethics for the Society of Professional Journalists, its first requirement may give the corporate blogger pause for thought. The requirement states: "Test the accuracy of information from all sources and exercise care to avoid inadvertent error. Deliberate distortion is never permissible."

Testing the accuracy of information from all sources is not always possible. How many times will a blogger check a source quoted in the *New York Times* or *Washington Post* article? Probably not that often, because the expectation is that the reporting was accurate and verified in such premiere newspapers. Bloggers will take the information reported in those newspapers as fact and base their articles on that information. However, if you were a professional journalist writing a piece that includes the same sources as another newspaper story, you would check the accuracy of those sources or find your own. Maybe the same should hold true for bloggers, instead of just citing a traditional media article, think twice about publishing an article that references a media publication without checking the original or finding another source. It is not always possible to check every fact reported in other publications and blogs. Many blogs have to rely on others to report the news for them to create their stories, especially if those blog articles are opinions about what has happened in the news. However, the concept of providing a comprehensive account is a useful lesson in thinking about the issue of checking accuracy of information. Repeating unsubstantiated facts leads in some cases more to rumormongering than reporting.

The issue of accuracy of information is very important to a corporate blogger. If you are attempting to gain a reputation for leadership in your industry, it is important to give an accurate picture of the realities of your company and industry. Otherwise, your credibility will be questioned, and over time, people will not consider your writing to be worth reading because they doubt the integrity of the information published on the blog. If you are writing about your own company where you have no direct knowledge of the subject, you should double-check with colleagues to make sure your facts are correct.

A company does not have to be entirely transparent in writing a blog post, but if you were reading an article that sought to convince you that the article was written by an expert in the industry and that article failed to mention important facts any expert should know or who would research, you would question the credibility of the article and its author. An irreverent example of the importance of revealing all the facts to establish credibility comes from the film *Miracle on 34th Street*, where Edmund Gwenn plays Kris Kringle, or Santa Claus. Kris gets hired at Macy's flagship store in New York. However, when Macy's does not have a toy a child wants for Christmas, he recommends another store to the child's parent, and because of his recommendation to go to a competitor, he nearly gets the sack. All turns out well because the customer who received the fair advice from Kris tells the store supervisor she will be buying from Macy's from now on because of Kris' honesty. Kris generates such goodwill among many customers that Macy's decides to adopt the practice throughout all of their stores. Effective bloggers are like Kris Kringle in the film *Miracle on 34th Street:* you gain more credibility when you dare to give your blog readers all the facts.

Strive for thoroughness and honesty—Bloggers must reveal their connection with partners, employers, and customers. Corporate bloggers can certainly be paid by someone who the blogger writes about, as long as the blogger discloses the relationship.

Integrity is the cornerstone of credibility—If all that journalists have is their integrity, the same holds true for corporate bloggers. Bloggers do not have the same responsibility to reveal everything, but they have to make sure expectations are set with their readers about what they can and cannot reveal. Otherwise, if blog posts are considered inaccurate, blog readers will go elsewhere.[26,27] As a journalist gains a good reputation for accuracy in reporting, a blogger gains authority and credibility if he or she writes clearly and with accuracy and fairness.

Bloggers are often critical of others if they think there is cause. Giving an opinion before researching all the facts is possible with both journalists and bloggers. An audience will desert a blogger quickly if a blogger writes untruths on a consistent basis and is discovered.

Editorial process—One way blogging is different from journalism is that there is typically no editorial process in the production of content for a blog. The lack of editorial oversight and the ability of the audience to interact almost instantaneously with a blogger in a public forum through commenting make blog writing different from the way journalism was practiced just a few years ago.

THE BLOGGER RELATIONS STRATEGY PLAN

Putting all the resources together from the different disciplines of journalism, Internet marketing, and public relations, you can create a plan that will help you in developing a strategy for your blog.

Evaluate the keywords used by your audience in order to determine which keywords to use in your content and in the structure of your blog and which keywords to monitor the web for stories that directly affect your company and industry.

After conducting an audit of your blogging community, you will have a good understanding of what topics are discussed by many of the bloggers in your industry. Put that knowledge to good use when you brainstorm for ideas on how to develop content for your blog and who should be the writer. Think about how your products and company will help your customers, and put the value you provide to your customers in the context of their current issues.

Put public relations planning techniques to good use when you are thinking about conducting blogger relations. Develop your list of bloggers to read on a regular basis, and understand that it is important to act quickly when you see a story pop up where you can comment or write a post. Monitor your list of industry blogs and keep a list of watch keywords to find other websites, blogs, and stories that would be of interest to your audience or that would give you the opportunity to comment.

Lastly, although it is important to be yourself when blogging, blogging is not just about the facts, and it turns out that if you really want credibility and to be believed, you have to keep some standards about the facts you use; that is where reviewing the journalistic approach will help you to steer the right course for gaining credibility and trust with your audience.

Endnotes

1. Backbone Media Corporate Blogging Survey, John Cass, Stephen Turcotte, Kristine Munroe (2005). Available at http://www.backbonemedia.com/blogsurvey/

2. Global PR Blog Week 1.0, John Cass (2004), *Microsoft Corporate Blogs & Other Stories*. Available at http://www.globalprblogweek.com/archives/microsoft_corporate_.php

3. Global PR Blog Week 1.0, John Cass (2004), *Corporate Blogging Survey*. Available at http://www.globalprblogweek.com/archives/corporate_blogging_s.php

4. Permission Marketing, Seth Godin, edition (May 1, 1999), Simon & Schuster, New York

5. Blogsurvey Blog, John Cass (2006), *Blogger Relations Is Not Media Relations For Bloggers*. Available at http://blogsurvey.backbonemedia.com/archives/2006/01/blogger_relations_is_not_media.html

6. Blogsurvey Blog, John Cass (2006), *Click.TV Pitch Program Is Public Relations Not Blogger Relations*. Available at http://blogsurvey.backbonemedia.com/archives/2006/04/clicktv_pitch_p.html

7. PR Communications Blog, John Cass (2003), *PR—The Next Internet Revolution*. Available at http://pr.typepad.com/pr_communications/2003/09/pr_the_next_int.html

8. Backbone Media Corporate Blogging Survey, John Cass, Stephen Turcotte, Kristine Munroe (2005). Available at http://www.backbonemedia.com/blogsurvey/

9. Blogsurvey Blog, John Cass (2006), *The New PR Is Part of Blogger Relations*. Available at http://blogsurvey.backbonemedia.com/archives/2006/06/the_new_pr_is_p.html

10. PR Communications Blog, John Cass (2006), *PR Truth*. Available at http://pr.typepad.com/pr_communications/2006/05/pr_truth.html

11. Blogsurvey Blog, John Cass (2005), *'Blogging Relations': The Concept that Combines PR & SEO*. Available at http://blogsurvey.backbonemedia.com/archives/2005/07/blogging_relati.html

12. Blogsurvey Blog, John Cass (2005), *Benefits of Business Blogging*. Available at http://blogsurvey.backbonemedia.com/archives/2005/10/benefits_of_business_blogging.html

13. Backbone Media Corporate Blogging Survey, John Cass, Stephen Turcotte, Kristine Munroe (2005). Available at http://www.backbonemedia.com/blogsurvey/index.html

14. Permission Marketing, Seth Godin, 1st edition (May 1, 1999), Simon & Schuster, New York

15. http://www.1stplacesoft.com

16. http://www.ebay.com

17. http://www.craigslist.org

18. http://www.youtube.com

19. http://www.buzzmachine.com

20. http://www.businessweek.com/the_thread/blogspotting/techteam.html

21. Tom Abate (2006), Email interview with John Cass.

22. MiniMediaGuy Blog, Tom Abate (2006), *Rhetoric 2.0?* Available at http://minimediaguy
.org/2006/03/13/rhetoric-20/

23. PR Communications Blog, John Cass (2006), *The Journalist's Creed.* Available at http://
pr.typepad.com/pr_communications/2006/02/the_journalists.html

24. Missouri School of Journalism (1908), *Journalist's Creed* Available at http://www.journalism
.missouri.edu/about/creed.html

25. Society of Professional Journalists, *Code of Ethics.* Available at http://www.spj.org/ethicscode
.asp

26. PR Communications Blog, John Cass (2006), *Checking Sources in Corporate Blogging.* Available
at http://pr.typepad.com/pr_communications/2006/07/checking_source.html

27. PR Communications Blog, John Cass (2005), *Moving PR Forward with Blogger Relations.*
Available at http://pr.typepad.com/pr_communications/2005/11/as_described_by.html

Blogging Guidelines for Companies

Blogging is a technological change that requires a cultural awareness, for those people who publish, in how to conduct themselves on the web. The new environment of customers and employees self-publishing their writing on the web poses new challenges, some of which may have harmful consequences for companies. Where once only politicians, journalists, and celebrities had ready access to the world through the media, now ordinary citizens have the ability to publish on the web through blogs, and blog readers might publish content on a corporate blog that the company would really rather they did not.

The ability to publish content on the web means that employees can publish on the web either in a corporate blog or on other websites. The possibility exists that once private conversations at the company water cooler can be quickly and easily published on the web for the world to read. Some employees might write something that produces harmful consequences for a company. There are incidents that demonstrate the dangers of not explaining the consequences of posting remarks on blogs to employees that had harmful consequences for an employer.

This chapter will describe some of the possible harmful consequences of employees publishing comments on the web through a number of case study examples. To avoid similar problems in your own company, it is important to write guidelines for your workforce. We provide a list of factors to include in your company's blogging policy and guidelines. However, it is important to realize that you cannot completely rely upon published guidelines to protect you, as there are limits to the law. Rather, it is also important to work with your employees to educate them on the potential consequences of publishing on the web.

The same holds true for your audience; publishing guidelines does not mean that you will meet their expectations, especially if the audience has not read them. What is really important is the realization that you have to set realistic expectations with your audience. Some companies unintentionally set the wrong expectations with blog readers; we discuss a mechanism for measuring whether you are setting expectations correctly and provide employers with tips on how to handle anonymous commentators. Lastly, we end with an overview of how to write guidelines for your blog.

JEREMY HERMANNS AND THE ALASKA AIRLINES DECOMPRESSION INCIDENT

Even companies who do not build and maintain a corporate blog can experience harm from blogging. Employees can write content that might harm the reputation of a company by writing on other blogs as Jeremy Hermanns' blog post on the Alaska Airlines decompression story demonstrates.

Jeremy Hermanns[1-5] and his fiancée survived a horrendous experience when their Alaska Airlines flight decompressed. Jeremy is a blogger, and he wrote about the experience on his blog[6] and also included digital photographs he took with his Treo camera during the incident. The Alaska Airlines incident was a terrifying incident for all of the passengers and air-flight staff involved; fortunately, everyone survived the incident.

Jeremy's blog post about the event received several hundred comments, including several critical comments. Those critical comments were vitriolic toward Jeremy and his assessment of his experience on the flight. Jeremy was intrigued by the critical comments, which were so unlike most of the other comments he had received from many blog readers who had expressed warmth. Researching the identity of the people who made critical comments, he discovered that a number of the comments were allegedly from people with an Alaska Airlines IP address.[7]

Jeremy Pepper, owner of the blog *Pop! PR Jots* and respected public relations blogger wrote a blog post about Jeremy Hermanns' experiences with the decompression on the Alaska Airlines flight, the post Jeremy Hermanns wrote on his blog, and the critical comments he received. Jeremy Pepper analyzed the public relations issues arising from the commentary on Jeremy Hermanns' blog from the people who were allegedly identified as Alaska Airlines employees by Jeremy Hermanns. If, indeed, Alaska Airlines employees made critical comments on Jeremy Hermanns blog, in his post Jeremy Pepper thought the comments damaged Alaska Airline's reputation.[8]

The Alaska Airlines decompression incident and the critical comments left on Jeremy Hermanns' blog demonstrates that in today's online world, a company needs to have a clear communication crisis plan in place with a consistent message for all employees. When an employee states something on a public website that features or affects a community's discussion about a company, that employee is representing the company. However, if an employee does not have a clear picture of how to represent a company online or a company's policy specifically states that employees cannot discuss company activities without prior approval, then the potential for criticism and embarrassment is there.

In the world of consumer-generated media, the alleged example of somebody from an Alaska Airlines computer making negative comments on Jeremy Hermanns blog demonstrates that even if a company has a communications policy in place, it is probably more important to educate your employees on how to act in a crisis with developing news that affects your company. In his post, Jeremy Pepper suggested companies set clear policies for their employees on how to act in public on crisis communications incidents.

Developing and publishing a consumer-generated media policy for a company is not enough, although it may avoid some damage and inappropriate comments. A company should seriously think about educating their workforce on how employees express their opinions publicly on the web. Public and anonymous comments can get national and international attention, causing much negative press, in the same way that the negative comments by an alleged Alaska Airlines employee did on Jeremy Hermanns blog. Running workshops and discussing the consequences of individual employees publishing comments about a company online will probably have more effect than dusty employee handbooks.

JEFF JARVIS OF BUZZMACHINE AND THE GCI INTERN INCIDENT IN DELL

Jeff Jarvis is a well-known blogger who was also a former TV critic for *TV Guide* and *People*, creator of *Entertainment Weekly*, Sunday editor and associate publisher of the *NY Daily News*, and a columnist on the *San Francisco Examiner*.[9] Jeff Jarvis has written about his experiences with Dell computers and the company's poor response to his complaints on his BuzzMachine blog. His blog posts about his experiences with Dell acted as a catalyst and focus of attention for the customer service troubles Dell has been experiencing in recent years.[10] Jeff Jarvis tried an experiment with Dell; he posted articles on his blog to see if Dell was listening to their customers on the web and would respond to him about his problems with his Dell machine. The company did not respond in time, and so Jarvis decided buy an Apple computer.

When Dell launched a blog called the *Direct 2 Dell* blog, Jeff Jarvis criticized Dell's implementation of the blog launch on a blog post, suggesting that Dell still has to "join the conversation" with their new blog.[11] Jeff Jarvis admonished Dell for examples of poor customer service reported by many Dell customers on his blog. What was interesting about the post was that in the comment section of the blog, he received a critical comment. The critical comment was from one of the employees of the agency that was hired to monitor blogs for Dell. The employee named Chris left the following comment.[12]

> Hey Jarvis, I honestly think you have no life. Honestly? Do you have a life, or do you just spend it trying to make Dell miserable? I've been working with Dell the past three weeks researching trashy blogs that worms like you leave all over that frigen blogosphere and I cant honestly say that Dell is trying to take a step towards fixing their customer service. They hire guys like me to go on the web and look through the blogs of guys like you in hopes that we can find out your problem and fix it. But honestly I don't think you have a problem Dell can fix. Your problem is you have no life.

Jeff Jarvis took Chris at his word and investigated Chris' IP address; he discovered that the comment left on his blog did, indeed, come from the agency that monitors the web for Dell. The company is called GCI Group, a division of Grey Worldwide, a large advertising agency. He wrote about the incident on his blog.[13] One of the agency's staff got back to him with an email, which Jeff published on his blog.

> Paul Walker of the GCI Digital Media Practice, employer of "Chris": Jeff Hunt forwarded your email to me and asked that I look into the comment posted on your blog from a GCI Group IP address. I looked into the matter, and I can confirm the comment was left by a summer intern who got caught up in the emotion around your postings. This afternoon he obviously decided to let you know what was on his mind. In afterthought, he likely would choose his words more carefully. It is important that you understand the intern's comment in no way reflects the points of view of Dell or GCI. Dell's aims with its one2one weblog are positive and they have every intention of making it a forum for open conversations with Dell customers.

Along with publishing the email, Jeff Jarvis criticized Dell again, saying,

> The person who answers the phone — or now responds to a blog
> post—is acting on behalf of Dell and to the customer is Dell, since that
> person is our connection to Dell. See the AOL cancellation video. Every
> one of your "customer service" employees and every one of your "public
> relations" employees in every encounter represents your company. That
> has always been the case. Only now, we can record their actions and
> report them to the world. There are many Chrises in many companies.
> The fact that they feel they can treat customers this way is a good
> indication, though, of the culture and management of the companies that
> employ them.[14]

The intern's comment could have caused more bad publicity for Dell and its
agency GCI. However, Paul Walker's email reply helped to defuse some of the
tension around the issue, as there were no further blog posts from Jeff Jarvis on
the subject.

The Dell intern incident demonstrates the dangers of not explaining the
consequences of posting offensive remarks on blogs to employees. Employees
from the lowest to the highest level have to understand the consequences of their
actions. To try to protect itself from the potential consequences of employees
posting harmful remarks, a company can take steps to educate employees and
develop guidelines for how to publish on the web. It is also good practice to inform
all non-blogging employees about the consequences of making disparaging
remarks to a customer on the web. Write a policy on what employees should
do when writing comments on blogs about their company or representing their
employer. Use some of the available case studies to illustrate to employees what
to avoid.

THE MARK JEN STORY

Mark Jen was a new developer at Google who had only been with the company for a
few weeks; he wrote about his experiences there on his personal blog, comparing
the benefits package provided by Google with his old employer, Microsoft.
Google fired Mark Jen because of the articles that mentioned the company,
specifically citing the disclosure of internal confidential information as being a
factor in the dismissal. Mark Jen had written about some future Google projects
and discussed financial projections. Mark Jen had removed the offending posts
at the request of Google and later stated he would have pulled down his site if
his employer had requested it, but Google let Mark Jen go anyway. The Mark Jen
story shows the importance of setting a good blogging policy and educating your

employees on how to write blogs that conform to those guidelines.[15,16] Writing blogging guidelines will help employees steer a safe course when writing on the web, and ensuring your employees are fully aware of the guidelines and the consequences for not following them will hopefully avoid much harmful consequences for companies and employees.

WRITING BLOGGING GUIDELINES AND EDUCATING EMPLOYEES

Blogging guidelines can provide a roadmap for both employers and employees to help avoid any missteps on a blog that might cause problems for everyone involved. Most employees will understand that what is written on a blog will be seen by the world, just as it would be inappropriate to disclose confidential information or be disrespectful to a customer in a telephone call or email, the same is true for blogging. Most employees understand that remaining respectful in all communications is the right approach and will follow any company guidelines.[17]

Guidelines, however, do not guarantee that employees and blog readers will follow them. Guidelines for blogging may provide some protection to avoid bad publicity and diminished credibility, as the new world of people publishing on the web requires an understanding of how to react to customer comments and blog posts. A company also has to understand how to research and write blog posts. It is important to take the time to think about every post before you publish, as that preparation may save you from embarrassment and public criticism. When an employee writes on a blog, it is important that employees consider their obligations to an employer and colleagues, even if the blog posting is on the employee's corporate blog or a personal blog.

Listed below are some issues that will help a company in the process of developing their corporate blogging policy. Use these issues as a starting point to develop your own corporate blogging guidelines:

Does the blog represent the employee's or company's opinion?—Even if a blog is clearly branded as being associated with a company, that company should make a decision as to whether the views expressed on a company blog are the personal opinions of the employee or represent company policy. If blogs were ever closely associated with a company brand, then readers will assume that whatever is published by an employee is the opinion of the company, and the only way to distinguish personal blogger opinions from company viewpoints is to make such a statement on every post; otherwise, people will not find the statement. Many bloggers include such legal disclaimers in their side navigation, or in the about section of their blog, and sometimes in the comment section of their blog posts.

Respecting copyright, fair use, and financial disclosure laws—If quoting material from other sources, make sure you quote only short excerpts from copyright material and link to quoted web materials. Be aware of your own company's or another company's confidential or other proprietary information, and do not disclose such information. Do not cite or reference clients, partners, or suppliers without their prior agreement and approval. If you are ever unsure about the information on your blog, check on the accuracy of your information with a manager, other department, or even an external blogger before your post is published.

Respect your audience—Do not use ethnic slurs, personal insults, obscenity, and others, and show proper consideration for your audience's privacy and for topics that may be considered objectionable or inflammatory. In addition, linking to inappropriate, pornographic, or illegal material on corporate computers might harm existing corporate relationships, to such extreme circumstances, that an employee might subject an employer to tort liability, where the publication of such material causes injury to another person. A court might consider that the employer has neglected proper oversight of an employee's workplace and allowed such activity to happen.[18]

Copyright, fair use, and respecting your audience all fall within the realm of creating "potential liability for criminal activity" by an employee for an employer. Employees might cause libel by misrepresenting other parties. Defamation of other individuals or organizations can have serious implications for a company if sued, not just in the costs of handling the court case, but also the effects such a court action might have on the reputation of a company.

Correcting mistakes—Be the first to correct your own mistakes, and do not alter previous posts without indicating that you have done so. An example of a blogger altering an original post happened when a reporter for the *Boston Globe*, Jenn Abelson, wrote an article about a blogger receiving payment from advertisers in return for the blogger advocating the advertiser's product on a blog. The blogger received payment from an advertiser, without revealing the payment. The blogger, Jeff Culter, wrote a story about DotFlowers.com 1-800-flowers on his website, where he endorsed the florist but did not reveal the payment he received for writing the post; in addition, he initially stated he had purchased flowers from the florist. After the interview with the *Boston Globe*, Jeff then corrected the initial post to state that he had not made a purchase but did not inform his readers that he had made a correction to his post.[19-21]

When mistakes occur on a blog, those mistakes can cause disagreements and misunderstandings. Double-checking sources for information and confirming the accuracy of the facts are ways to avoid embarrassing mistakes. Be the first to correct your own mistakes, and do not alter previous posts significantly without indicating that you have done so. Minor changes in spelling and grammar are perfectly acceptable to most bloggers, but changing the meaning and context of a blog post is something entirely different.

Identify your role and position in your company—Especially if you or your company has an interest in what you are writing about on the blog. Describe your company's interest or your own in the subject by citing the connection to people, organizations, or events in a post.

Disclosing private information—There may be negative consequences from disclosing private information on a blog, and employees should be careful in disclosing their own private information. When someone reveals private information on the web, that information can remain on the web for a very long time and be found through search engines. Many workers disclose their personal information on the blog to build a better relationship with their audience, but it is important to be aware of the dangers of revealing too much private information. Possible dangers include identity theft and stalking by strangers. It is also important to ask someone else's permission before disclosing another person's private details.

Consider the level of interaction—You will have to consider if your company will allow comments and trackbacks on your blog, and if those comments are critical, will your company still publish? You do not have to accept obscene statements but if someone writes a thoughtful critical statement, it is a good idea to allow the comment or trackback to be published and then to respond to any critical statements quickly. If you do not publish such critiques on the company blog, you will be accused of not allowing criticism on your blog, and someone in your audience may assume the criticism is correct even if it is not. You will be far better off if you address any critics with your own response, and more than likely the issue will be defused by a strong defense.

Do not delete any comments unless the comments are spam or off the topic from the original post. If you receive a large volume of comment spam, comments on a corporate blog can be moderated to cut down on spam comments. If you do moderate posts, it is important to quickly post comments within one business day of operation. If you are on vacation, assign another employee to post your audience's comments. If that person is unsure about posting a moderated comment and does not post a comment, have him or her get back to the commentator with an explanation that you will be back in a few days.

Employees disagree with the company—Are your employees allowed to disagree with their company on industry issues or internal company policies? Provided an employee's tone is respectful and not a personal attack, there are some advantages to having a company that is open to constructive criticism on company blogs. Microsoft dared to let Robert Scoble criticize the company and its practices; he has changed the perception of Microsoft in the minds of many customers during the years he wrote a blog there.[22] However, there are times when employees can overstep certain boundaries, such as the Mark Jen story, and there will be harmful consequences for the company and its employees.

Discussing the competition—Will your corporate bloggers comment on the company's competitors? There are many circumstances where an employee might mention and discuss competitors on a blog within the context of a discussion about industry issues. Keep your employees up to date on your industry's restrictions on collusion with competition when discussing competitors. You do not want to fall foul of the antitrust or anti-competition laws Also, it just makes good common sense that any blog discussion about competitors is respectful.[23]

THE COMPANY HANDBOOK AND EDUCATING THE WORKFORCE

Does your company have a company handbook with guidelines about communications outside of the workplace? As your staff will be familiar with the existing policy, there may be no great stretch to apply them to your blogging policy and guidelines. If there are current external communications practices in place, this document can be your starting point for the development of your guidelines. When IBM created its blogging guidelines, the company based them upon its existing communications policies, and not only did the blogging guidelines receive general agreement from IBM's attorneys, which made the blogging policy development process faster, the employees were also already familiar with the policy.

As an employee, when you say something in public about your company, you are representing the company's position, but do you know what your company's position really is and how it should be presented? Companies need to set clear policies for their employees on how to act in a communications crisis. Companies might have communications policies in place; however, in the world of consumer-generated media, it is important to educate your employees on how to react to developing news if they are thinking of writing something about their company on the web. Merely setting a policy is not enough, although it may avoid some damage and comments. A company has to act seriously by educating employees about their policy on communicating in today's new world of consumer-generated media. Seminars and workshops will work better than emails or unopened employee handbooks.

UNDERSTANDING THE LIMITS OF THE LAW

The purpose of blogging guidelines is to set expectations with all of the parties involved. Setting expectations with employees and customers about a company blog will help avoid misunderstandings and criticism. All employers have limits to what they want revealed on a public website. A company does not have to reveal confidential or competitive information. By setting expectations and being transparent about those limits, a company can protect itself from harmful posts and comments A company can hope to protect itself by publishing disclaimers about the content on the blog. Some of those disclaimers can help and some may not, and it purely depends upon the interpretation of the law by a court during a case.

Most states in the United States allow employers to hire employees on an at-will basis rather than for cause basis; thus, employees can be terminated from their employment for any reason without cause. Sometimes, employee handbooks can alter this at-will relationship by a company handbook, stating that the employee will be treated fairly and not terminated unless the employee's performance has been unsatisfactory. It is possible to set expectations of what can be discussed in the blogosphere by employees by establishing those expectations in an employment contract and requiring an employee to sign their employment contract when the employee is hired.[24] There are exceptions to the at-will clause in an employment contract where the employer would harm the public's interests if the termination were allowed to succeed. The circumstances where the termination of employment of an employee by an employer is against certain public policy standards include whistle-blowing, exercise of statutory right, refusal to commit an illegal act, and performance of a statutory duty.

Any legal disclaimers on a blog that state a company is "not responsible for information posted," "the content," and "a user reads them at their own risk" might not actually work in a court of law. However, the U.S. § 230 of the Communications Decency Act of 1996 does protect hosts and users of websites from being considered responsible for any content that might be published on their website. The hosts and users are protected against any torts that cause injury to another person, which would be brought against them for other Internet users publishing any content on a website.[25]

Companies will use legal disclaimers to protect themselves from any legal action brought against a company because of the content published by other website users or where a company wishes to moderate or alter the content published by Internet users. We see an example of these types of disclaimers in the blogging legal disclaimer on the Cisco Systems blog, where the Cisco disclaimer also requires Internet users who publish content to agree that the Internet user is responsible for the content published on the blog.[26]

Another limit to the law is where even defamatory statements on a blog might not be enough for a court action to succeed by the defamed parties because the credibility of blogging is such that any statements have to have some basis in fact and blogging does not provide enough credibility. The *Cahill v. Doe* case demonstrates this.

Patrick Cahill and Julia Cahill v. John Doe

In the case of *Patrick Cahill and Julia Cahill v. John Doe* numbers 1, 2, 3, and 4, 879 A.2d 94, an elected town official and his wife, Patrick and Julia Cahill, brought a defamation suit against four John Doe defendants because of the statements those four defendants made on a blog. The defendants allegedly defamed the reputation of Patrick and Julia Cahill on the blog. The plaintiffs, Patrick and Julia Cahill, were able to discover the IP addresses of the defendants but not their identities. The Cahills asked the courts to require the Internet service provider to provide the identities of the four defendants. One of the defendants filed a motion to prevent disclosure of their identity and the matter went to court. The court decided to deny the defendant's motion to stop the revelation of their identity. John Doe appealed this decision; however, the appeals court reversed the decision and sent it back to the original court. The appeals court stated in this case that the plaintiffs must prove that statements made in a blog are factually based and therefore recognized as defamatory statements by the community rather than mere opinion by an anonymous commentator. However, one decision does not necessarily mean that other court cases will result in the same decision. It is best to advise employees who write online that what they say may have harmful consequences for a company.

Legal disclaimers and guidelines may help a company if something bad happens; but really, a company should focus on prevention. Educating a workforce is the best way to avoid having to take legal action and risking bad publicity when things do go wrong.

TRANSPARENCY IN A BLOGGING POLICY CAN SET EXPECTATIONS

Transparency is about setting expectations with your audience. It is easy to understand how transparency works in the context of blogging when it is thought of in the same way branding works for company products and services. Writing a blog is all about developing a brand. A brand is a promise to a customer about what he or she can expect to receive in terms of a product, the product itself, time delivered, and how it is delivered. Being transparent on a blog is no different if a company sets expectations with readers what they can expect from the blog. There will be fewer unhappy readers as long as the bloggers fulfill their promises.

Not every blogging community is the same, and standards change. A company should research the standards of openness and transparency currently used in their blogging community. Do the majority of the blogs in your community allow comments and trackbacks? Is comment moderation widely used or not? The standards in your community will help to determine if a company will be able to work within those community standards when they publish their blog. Setting audience expectations about what readers can publish on a blog and what company bloggers will write reinforces a company's brand because the company is willing to be transparent about its blogging activities. Hoping for the best and not allowing commenting may not get you into trouble today, but who wants to take that risk when there is no need to do that?

BUILDING A USABLE BLOGGING POLICY

Writing disclaimers and blogging guidelines might protect you from legal liability, but not meeting your audience's expectations about running your blog will definitely tarnish your reputation in the eyes of your public. A company cannot risk being perceived to lack interaction with customers because of its comment policy or a lack thereof. In addition, many companies take serious steps to set expectations with their audience but through a lack of understanding of the usability of a website miss the opportunity to meet customer expectations.

Dr. Walter Carl, a professor of advanced organizational communication at Northeastern University, defined the term *synthetic transparency* on his blog by stating, "Synthetic transparency involves using blogs to give the impression of openness, honesty, and transparency but without really doing so." The term can provide a test for companies who are developing corporate blogs, as it provides a yardstick to measure their own blog's level of transparency.[27]

Josh Hallet,[28] a blog designer and consultant, had previously discussed the issue of transparency[29] on his blog and thought that, "Making a big deal out of the fact that you are 'transparent' only makes me suspicious that you are hiding something."

Although Dag Hammarskjöld, Swedish diplomat, secretary general of the United Nations from 1953 to 1961, and recipient of the Nobel Prize in Peace in 1961, said,

> You are the lens in the beam. You can only receive, give, and possess the light as the lens does. If you seek yourself, you rob the lens of its transparency. You will know life and be acknowledged by it according to your degree of transparency, your capacity, that is, to vanish as an end, and remain purely as a means.

Both Hammarskjöld and Hallet hold the position that the more you try to appear transparent, the less likely it is that you will be perceived as being transparent. Corporate bloggers can give the appearance of transparency by giving their audience the ability to interact with them easily by setting up comments and allowing trackbacks; yet, if a corporate blogger does not really engage their audience when they pose a question through a comment or trackback, the company is not really transparent. This means that even when you have commenting and trackbacks working on your blog to encourage interaction with an audience, these measures only give the appearance of transparency; actual transparency exists when online tools such as commenting and trackbacks are used and bloggers respond to queries posted by their audience.

Fredrik Wackå, a blogging consultant in Sweden, states that, "A blog that's just the old press releases is no blog and it will never have the positive effect a blog can have. I think we all agree to that."[30] He is right. A blog that just rehashes the same old press releases without any interaction with its audience is not a blog. Corporate blogs are different from corporate websites, and there are different expectations as to the level of transparency on a corporate website compared with a corporate blog. People will expect the content on a corporate website to reflect the marketing messages of a company in a very positive way, as advertising does. Visitors would not expect to find criticism or negative feedback on a corporate website. Although on a blog, there is the expectation that there is the possibility of finding some thoughtful critiques of ideas (and even products) from the audience. Blogging is, after all, about the ability of an audience to join in a conversation with the blogger and their community, and sometimes conversations involve disagreements between participants.

Fredrik Wackå went onto say, "But I also think that many would agree that we can't talk about everything in a blog. There is information that would hurt us if it became publicly known (deals being negotiated, for example). Does that mean that blogging by definition is synthetic transparency? In that case, could it be any other way? Or how can we achieve authentic transparency and still have a job?"[31]

Essentially, it is up to a company and blogger to set the guidelines of what they will be willing to discuss on a blog. You should set your own standards for the level of transparency on a blog and reveal those guidelines both formally from a link on the blog and within a post or on a comment. You should not assume that blog readers would be able to find your published guidelines in a link in the side navigation. The best approach in setting expectations is to publish blogging guidelines when it comes to commenting in a post or send to people who comment on your blog an email containing your guidelines.

As one of the largest companies in the United States to blog, the General Motors FastLane blog has generated a lot of press. The FastLane blog has posted that all comments are read, but not every comment can be answered. Two readers described their experiences by commenting on the General Motors blog, and the expectation was that any comments would receive a response because the readers did not see the blog posts that set the expectation that not all comments would be answered.

General Motors has limited its level of transparency by giving the appearance of being willing and able to answer comments, yet they have a formal policy, which they have posted several times, of not replying to every comment. New customers to the blog will not read every post; therefore, if General Motors wants to ensure that a new reader sees their blogging policy, it is important to post the guidelines in many places. Otherwise, misunderstandings will arise, which will cause frustration in readers about the level of interaction on the blog. The General Motors blog is being unintentionally synthetically transparent, and they can remedy the situation by placing statements about their policy just underneath every post and before the comments section on a post.[32]

One blog that is very open about restricting their level of transparency is the American Lung Association of Minnesota blog. During 2005, Robert Moffit of the American Lung Association explained how his association decided not to allow comments on their blog. There is an active blogger pro-smoking community in Minnesota, and the association was concerned that if they allowed comments, pro-smoking bloggers' comments on their blog might disagree with the association's position. He was concerned that the board of directors of the association would require the removal of any critical comments or decide to shut the blog down. Rather than face those possibilities, he went ahead with a blog that does not allow commenting. In effect, the organization set the expectation with the reader that they cannot interact in a public way on the blog. The association has received some criticism through direct emails for not allowing comments on the blog. However, at this stage in the development of the association's blog, such a design makes sense for that organization.[33]

Is the American Lung Association of Minnesota being intentionally synthetically transparent or since they are upfront about their level of transparency by not allowing comments, is the association just defining what level of transparency the organization is willing to accept? I would suggest it is the latter; by establishing the design of the blog without comments, the association makes a clear statement about their level of transparency, and there can be no misunderstandings here. The American Lung Association of Minnesota is not being synthetically transparent.

Giving the appearance of transparency is easy to achieve but hard to maintain, as the General Motors FastLane blog example demonstrates. A corporate blogger really has to measure their level of synthetic transparency on their blog in general and on every post. Measuring requires a yardstick, and the definition of *synthetic transparency* provides a tool for corporate bloggers to determine a blog's level of transparency.

Managing transparency as new issues arise within blog posts is difficult; just as a blogger checks for spelling mistakes and grammatical errors, a corporate blogger should check for the transparency of each post and if it meets their stated blog policy guidelines. Charlene Li provides some advice on setting a blogging policy for a corporate blog.[34] Although blog design is really the easy part of measuring the transparency of a blog, a blogger can design their blog in such a way to clearly set expectations with their readers.

By setting a benchmark, the phrase *synthetic transparency* will help companies to set expectations about what blog readers can expect from corporate blogs, and corporate bloggers can use the term to determine if the design of their blog is unintentionally synthetically transparent and if a post meets their own blog's guidelines.

DEALING WITH ANONYMOUS POSTS AND COMMENTS

Blogs may allow people to post content anonymously[35]; those that do allow anonymous comments play a valuable role in giving people the opportunity to express their views openly without fear of reprisal. However, there is also the danger that views expressed or "facts" stated might not actually be true. Yet, if your company is the object of criticism and does not follow up with a comment to a critical statement on the web, you run the danger of your audience assuming the criticism must be true. If someone does make an anonymous comment, the reader cannot always put the anonymous poster's words in context. What if the poster is a competitor, a disgruntled employee, or even an ex-spouse? Without that identity, any information should always be looked at with a jaundiced eye.

When someone criticizes a company incorrectly or posts or sends in a rumor anonymously, a strategy to combat such anonymous criticism would be to question the credibility of the poster. It is difficult for the reader to really understand if a criticism is accurate or fair when they do not know the identity of the person who commented. You would combat the criticism by commenting on the blog and citing your company's side of the story every time an anonymous comment is made. By telling your side of the story in a critical attack by an anonymous party, your company gains credibility by being prepared to be open. You might ask why the commenter is not open. Consistency and discipline would gain you credibility in this case because your critic is anonymous. You, or the audience, might question the legitimacy of the anonymous commenter, by asking if he or she is hiding anything. If you do, you might then enter into a debate with anonymous commentators. Having a conversation with an anonymous commentator poses its own problems. Ways to combat and stop that difficult situation from arising would be to start off by saying your company will not have a debate with someone whose identity is unknown, in that way, by setting reasonable expectations, the audience will be more supportive of your company. Although you might not debate them, you should definitely defend your own position.

HOW TO WRITE GUIDELINES

When starting to write a blogging policy and guidelines, it is important to have everyone who will be concerned with your blog involved in the process of developing your company's policy and guidelines, especially the people who are going to be writing the blog. Create a blogging guidelines team. Review and consider each set of issues for development of the policy for your blog with the team. If your legal department is nervous about your company blogging, it is always important to remember that lawyers have to serve the business. A company has to take some risks if they want to be successful in building the business.

Discuss how your company wishes to interact with blog readers. You may discover that, initially, people in your company will be reluctant to allow a greater level of openness. That is all right, as developing a blogging policy is a process—one that takes time and careful thinking as to what will work for each company. Initially, your company may decide not to do certain things, such as allowing trackbacks or comments. Typically, when people are thinking about these issues, they go through an education process. First the value of blogging is described, second it is explained that interaction with a blog's readership is required to build a blog that produces any value; otherwise, the blog will not be worth implementing, then people generally decide to allow commenting and a higher degree of transparency. However, do not expect everyone to be on board right away. You might even launch with one set of guidelines, and then change them over time to suit the company as understanding grows and progress is made with the blog.

It is important to set expectations with blog readers and employees about communication within the blog. People might be disappointed and even criticize you for the level of openness and transparency you implement, but if you set expectations about what you will or will not do and also explain the reasons why, there will be fewer surprises, and most people will understand reasonable limitations.

In creating your finished document, write guidelines that are simple to read and easy to understand. Do not use legalese; otherwise, people will not read the document. Also, build a document that illustrates how each policy will work in practice. Have your legal or human resources team write not just a blogging policy but also a series of stories or case studies that help illustrate blogging guidelines for a company. Educate your workforce on how to apply the guidelines, and when you post the guidelines on your website, make sure you do not unintentionally set the wrong expectations with your audience through the poor placement of your guidelines document on your blog.

Endnotes

1. Blogsurvey Blog, John Cass (2005), *Alaska Airlines Flight Decompression PR Issue*. Available at http://blogsurvey.backbonemedia.com/archives/2005/12/alaska_airlines_flight_decompr.html

2. Seven Generational Ruminations Blog (2006), *Hyped Up Panic on Jeremy Hermanns Dot Org about Alaska Flight #536—Rapid De-Pressurization, and Panic at 30K Feet.* Available at http://www.7gen.com/node/979

3. USAToday.com (2005), *Blogger's Aircraft Emergency Account Draws Praise, Scorn.* Available at http://www.usatoday.com/news/nation/2005-12-29-aircraft-blogger_x.htm

4. SeattleTimes.com (2005), *"Absolutely Terrifying" Flight after Ground-Crew Mistake.* Available at http://seattletimes.nwsource.com/html/localnews/2002707386_plane28m.html

5. ABC News (2005), *Terror at 26,000 Feet.* Available at http://abcnews.go.com/GMA/Travel/story?id=1448260&CMP=OTC-RSSFeeds0312

6. Jeremy Hermanns dot org Blog (2005), *Alaska Flight #536—Rapid De-Pressurization, and Panic at 30K Feet.* Available at http://jeremyhermanns.org/me/alaska-flight-536-rapid-de-pressurization-and-panic-at-30k-feet/

7. Jeremy Hermanns dot org Blog (2005), *Alaska Airlines Comments on My Story.* Available at http://jeremyhermanns.org/me/alaska-airlines-comments-on-my-story/

8. Pop! PR Jots, Jeremy Pepper (2005), *The PR Issue Behind Alaska Airlines Decompression.* Available at http://pop-pr.blogspot.com/2005/12/pr-issue-behind-alaska-airlines.html

9. http://www.buzzmachine.com/index.php/about-me/

10. BuzzMachine Blog, Jeff Jarvis (2005), *Guardian Column: Dell Hell.* Available at http://www.buzzmachine.com/index.php/guardian-column-dell-hell/

11. BuzzMachine Blog (2006), *Well, Well, Dell.* Available at http://www.buzzmachine.com/index.php/2006/07/10/well-well-dell-2/

12. BuzzMachine Blog, Jeff Jarvis (2006), *Well, Well, Dell: Chris Comment.* Available at http://www.buzzmachine.com/index.php/2006/07/10/well-well-dell-2/#comment-88833

13. BuzzMachine Blog, Jeff Jarvis (2006), *Some Friendly Advice from Dell.* Available at http://www.buzzmachine.com/index.php/2006/07/11/some-friendly-advice-from-dell/

14. BuzzMachine Blog, Jeff Jarvis, (2006), *Some Friendly Advice from Dell.* Available at http://www.buzzmachine.com/index.php/2006/07/11/some-friendly-advice-from-dell/

15. c/net News.com, (2005), *Google blogger has left the building.* Available at http://news.com.com/Google+blogger+has+left+the+building/2100-1038_3-5567863.html

16. NinetyNineZeros Blog, John Cass, (2005), *the official story, straight, Straight from the Source.* Available at http://99zeros.blogspot.com/2005/02/official-story-straight from source.html #comments

17. PR Communications Blog, John Cass (2004), *AMA Boston Panel on Corporate Blogging.* Available at http://pr.typepad.com/pr_communications/2004/11/ama_boston_pane.html

18. Columbia Journal of Law & the Arts, 27:1, Gutman (2003), *Say What? Blogging, and Employment Law in Conflict.*

19. PR Communications Blog, John Cass (2005), *The Boston Globe Was Correct.* Available at http://pr.typepad.com/pr_communications/2005/07/the_boston_glob.html

20. PR Communications Blog, John Cass (2005), *Blogger Endorses Product Without Revealing Payment.* Available at http://pr.typepad.com/pr_communications/2005/06/blogger_endorse.html

21. Off On a Tangent Blog, Steve Garfield (2005), *Boston Globe Gets the Story ~~Wrong~~ Right.* Available at http://offonatangent.blogspot.com/2005/06/boston-globe-gets-story-wrong-right.html

22. Scoblizer Blog, Robert Scoble (2005), *A Little More on Mark Jen's Story.* Available at http://scoble.weblogs.com/2005/02/09.html

23. U.S. Department of Justice, *Sherman Antitrust Act: Antitrust Division Manual.* Available at http://www.usdoj.gov/atr/foia/divisionmanual/ch2.htm#a1

24. Columbia Journal of Law & the Arts, 27:1, Gutman (2003), *Say What? Blogging, and Employment Law in Conflict.*

25. Wisconsin Lawyer, Jennifer Peterson (March 2006), *The Shifting Legal Landscape of Blogging.*

26. http://blogs.cisco.com/AON/archives/2005/10/

27. Advanced Organizational Communication Blog, Dr. Carl Walter (2005), *Corporate Blogging as Synthetic Transparency?* Available at http://cmnu531.blogspot.com/2005/11/corporate-blogging-as-synthetic.html

28. Hyku Blog, Josh Hallett (2005), *At Last: Synthetic Transparency.* Available at http://hyku.com/blog/archives/000884.html

29. Hyku Blog, Josh Hallett (2005), *Transparency, How Far Do We Go?* Available at http://hyku.com/blog/archives/000467.html

30. CorporateBlogging Blog (2005), *Blog Transparency—Synthetic or Authentic?* Available at http://www.corporateblogging.info/2005/11/blog-transparency-synthetic-or.asp

31. CorporateBlogging Blog (2005), *Blog Transparency—Synthetic or Authentic?* Available at http://www.corporateblogging.info/2005/11/blog-transparency-synthetic-or.asp

32. Blogsurvey Blog, John Cass (2005), *The GM Blog: Lessons for Customer Blogging Relations.* Available at http://blogsurvey.backbonemedia.com/archives/2005/09/the_gm_blog_les.html

33. Blogsurvey Blog, John Cass (2005), *Non-Profit Blog Marketing.* Available at http://blogsurvey.backbonemedia.com/archives/2005/10/nonprofit_blog_marketing.html

34. Charlene Li's Blog, Charlene Li (2004), *Blogging Policy Examples.* Available at http://forrester.typepad.com/charleneli/2004/11/blogging_policy.html

35. Scout Blog, John Cass (2006), *Corporate Guidelines for Using Blogs, and Forums.* Available at http://www.scoutblogging.com/guidelines.html

CHAPTER 5

Tools for Blogger Relations

Building an effective blogging effort requires some technology and tools to power your blog conversations. You will want to pick the blog platform that will enable you to be the most effective blogger. This chapter reviews some of the functions of the major blog publishing systems as they relate to effective blogging strategies.

Monitoring the web is not just about using search engines; the best ways to remain in contact with blogs is by using an RSS feed reader and comment monitoring tools. Once you have found a good blog post, there are some bookmarking tools you can use to find them again. If you need more in-depth analysis and audience conversations within and beyond blogs, there are measurement companies that provide some tools that can help you to crawl the entire web and pinpoint the people and conversations that will have a big impact on your company, and this chapter explores how consumer-generated media (CGM) companies can help you search the web in greater detail.

Effective blog design is not really just about developing a good creative look, although this is certainly important, it is also about making sure you have some of the right elements to ensure blog readers can find you, navigate your blog, and converse with you easily. The chapter finishes with some tips on how to incorporate good blog strategy into your blog design.

BLOG PUBLISHING PLATFORMS

This section on blog publishing platforms focuses on Six Apart's Movable Type system to highlight the blog publishing features that provide the functionality and tools for a company to become effective bloggers. Coverage of other blog publishing systems gives a brief overview of some of the other tools' features that are available. Refer to each product's website for a more in-depth review.

There are currently many different blogging platforms on the market. This list of blog publishing systems is definitely not meant to be exhaustive or indicate that these are the best publishing systems available, although the products of WordPress, Drupal, and Six Apart are some of the popular blogging systems available. Use this section as guide for considering how to use blog publishing systems for effective blogging.[1]

Six Apart

A husband and wife team, Ben and Mena Trott, created Six Apart during the fallout of the last Internet bubble in 2001; the couple developed their blogging publishing system while looking for work.

Based in San Francisco, Six Apart has grown to be one of the most successful corporate blog publishing platform companies in the market. The company's products include Movable Type, the company's server solution, and TypePad, a hosted solution. Other products include LiveJournal, a hosted solution purchased by Six Apart, and Vox, another hosted solution and Six Apart's answer to MySpace.[2]

Six Apart provides powerful content management systems that are the backbone of its blog publishing platforms at a low cost to the customer. The platforms also have the flexibility to be customized by developers and customers.[3]

Movable Type

Movable Type is Six Apart's professional-level blog publishing platform. The blogging platform for many corporate bloggers, Movable Type provides companies with a tremendous amount of flexibility. Customers can download the software to their own server or host and then customize the software. Movable Type provides the stability and infrastructure to support a single blog or hundreds of blogs.

Movable Type provides a number of features for interaction both on the blog and between blogs, including commenting and trackbacks. Plus, there is a lot of room to add additional features with the ability to develop plug-ins for the blog publishing system and have access to a large library of plug-ins from their developer network. The flexibility to easily add plug-ins and the developer network are two of the strongest reasons why companies should actively consider the Movable Type platform. As Movable Type's developer network grows, the number of plug-ins available increase.[4] While most personal blogs can probably be accommodated with many basic blogging platforms, Movable Type's robustness makes it a strong favorite with consultants and companies for their blogging platform.

The software does require technical knowledge and sophistication to run and is suitable for companies with web departments or technical agencies; however, there may be better solutions for a company looking for a customizable solution without too much complexity.

Some of the features in Movable Type that help a company to build a blog that enables effective blogging include the following:

Multiple blogs—Movable Type allows you to create multiple blogs and manage those blogs from a single interface. This is especially important for employers who are thinking of allowing many employees to blog externally. If your company is going to follow the strategy of deploying multiple blogs similar to that of Microsoft, SUN Microsystems, and many of the larger technology companies that are conducting corporate blogging, Movable Type's blogging platform will give your company the flexibility to develop many blogs on one server. You may not have thousands of blogs like Microsoft or IBM, but whether you have 5, 10, or 70, you will want a blogging platform that allows you to create many blogs and give you different levels of security for each of your blog authors.

Easy-to-use content management system—The Movable Type interface for publishing is easy to use for non-technical experts. Movable Type is a powerful content management system that allows a blogger to write content and publish with one or two clicks of a button. No help from the IT department is needed once your blogger is trained in the use of the software. In addition to text publishing, an array of fonts and sizes, hyperlinks, files, and images can be embedded or hyperlinked within each article.

Customize your blog's look—The Movable Type templates are fully customizable, so you can design your blog to include your existing company images.

Community interaction—Blogs are designs of websites that allow a lot of interaction between the blogger and his or her audience. A comment dialog box allows a blog reader to make a comment on a blog post. Because of the increasing volume of comment spam, many bloggers moderate comments before publishing them. Comments are just as important to a blogger as blog posts. Blogging is about dialogue, and the opportunity to interact with your audience is important to developing an active dialogue.

Commenting is a two-way street once you have received a comment from a blog reader and you make a comment in return; unless the reader returns to the post to review the comments, the reader might not know you made another comment. Consider using the plug-in within Movable Type that will allow your readers to subscribe to individual article comments by email or any comments generated on the blog. This email subscription feature can also work for a category of articles. Rather than having to remember to come back to the article to determine if someone has made another comment, a reader will be able to receive an automatic email update as the conversation occurs in the comment section of an article on your blog.

Also consider installing the Movable Type plug-in for an email subscription form to your blog. Your readers may have RSS feed readers, but some will not, and subscribing to a blog through email is a way to preserve a connection with people rather than just using an RSS feed.

Avoiding comment and trackback spam—Movable Type version 3.2 or higher[5] gives you some powerful features to manage community interaction. Comment and trackback management are important features, as bloggers are facing increasing problems with comment and trackback spam, where malicious spammers send irrelevant comment and trackback spam, whose sole purpose is to annoy, produce links, and gain traffic. With Movable Type, comments and trackbacks are automatically monitored for junk items from known offenders, plus a rating system can be used to rate each comment to determine each comment's probability of being spam. Once spam is discovered through the rating system, comments will be moved automatically to the blog publishing system's junk folder.

Comments and trackback moderation can be turned on to allow moderation before being published on your blog, and no comments or trackbacks are published before being reviewed by your blogging team.

Catchpa, or "completely automated public Turing test to tell computers and humans apart," is a popular plug-in that has proven to be an effective deterrent against spam comments. Blog readers who comment are required to transcribe text from an image that is readable only by a human in order to post to a comment page on a blog. Catchpa reduces the source of much comment spam from software robots, and thus effectively reducing comment spam by 90%.

Comment spam can be a real problem for some corporate bloggers, who are usually receiving 30 to 100 spam comments in a day. This volume of comment spam increases the time it takes to manage a blog and does not actually produce any results. Catchpa and other plug-ins give Movable Type users the ability to fight back against spam in comments and trackbacks. However, there are good and bad Catchpa plug-ins, and the developer should test the Catchpa installation to be sure that the images can be read.

Archiving your content—Archiving is an important feature in any blog publishing system. Blog posts appear initially on a blog's home page, and as more posts are made, the blog post moves down off the home page. If the article was not automatically archived it would disappear from the navigation of the home page of the blog unless referenced through another link. Blogs have the ability to produce a lot of content easily. Each page has its own permanent page, and those pages are archived to ensure a permanent record. The archiving features in Movable Type allow companies to archive posts by a period of time, such as a month, giving your readers the opportunity to search your archives back in time.

Archives are extremely important to blog readers, especially when a blog reader visits a new blog for the first time. The age and size of an archive will go some way in convincing that it is worthwhile maintaining a connection with the blog. Also, consider developing a "best-of" list for your articles that you consider are the best articles or that have generated the most traffic.

Categories—Bloggers use categories to characterize each blog post. Using keywords and phrases for categories, a blogger can build a body of work around a particular theme. Bloggers find categories are a great navigational tool that makes it easier to find past articles around a subject, while blog readers use categories to navigate through a blog's content for interesting posts. Movable Type allows you to develop an unlimited number of categories for your blog, and you can also pick multiple categories for the same article.

Navigating your blog with search—Add search function into your blog, as many of your blog readers will want to use a search box to find articles in and navigate around a website. Movable Type provides some options for search functionality.[6]

TypePad

Launched in July 2003 by Six Apart founders Ben and Mena Trott, TypePad was designed from day one to be a subscription hosted blogging solution. TypePad has many of the same features of Movable Type.

TypePad may be a hosted solution, but it is also possible to use your own domain name with the service. Depending on the license you pick, a company can have an unlimited number of blogs. This is good for a company that wants many of its employees or customers to blog.

WordPress

A community of developers who wanted to build an easy-to-use, free, downloadable, open source server blogging system developed WordPress. The software continues to be maintained and updated by a community of developers. WordPress is one of the most popular open source blog publishing platforms available. Early versions of WordPress date back to 2001. The product is simple to install and has a large number of plug-ins. Many major bloggers and corporate blogging companies choose WordPress as an option.

Automattic, the for-profit company that produces WordPress.com, the free, hosted and simpler version of WordPress, plans to make money by selling upgrades to WordPress.com, charging hosting fees, selling services, and providing a great anti-spam service called Askitmet.

WordPress incorporates many of the services provided in Movable Type and TypePad, so here are some of the highlights of the services provided by WordPress that are worth mentioning:

Documentation makes you ready to go—The biggest strengths of WordPress .org are its good navigation design, links to a lot of resources, and great advice on how to install and modify your WordPress installation.

Multiple authors—There is a multiple user version of WordPress called WordPress MU, but it is not as well supported as the single user version of WordPress, a distinct disadvantage for companies because if you have a production server, you do not want to have any problems with software and not have any backup help to support software.[7]

Pingbacks—Pingbacks are similar to trackbacks, except that instead of a blogger having to manually cut and paste a trackback URL into the ping field of the blog management system, the blog software automatically notifies the other blog's publishing software through a pingback that the link exists when a blogger includes a URL to another blog article. If the other blog has pingback functionality, it picks up the link and displays it on the blog post.

WordPress has many of the same standard features of other good blog publishing systems such as Movable Type, commenting, comment moderation, search, and others.

Drupal

Dries Buytaert was the lead developer on the Drupal blog system in Europe during 2000 and 2001. The Drupal content management system is an open source solution supported by a wide community of companies and developers. Not just a blog publishing system, Drupal has a powerful content management system that is a free solution for highly dynamic community websites. The Howard Dean campaign during the 2004 U.S. presidential election used the Drupal system to build blogs and community websites.

If you are looking for a solution where many users can sign up to publish content on the same website, Drupal is an excellent choice.

ExpressionEngine

ExpressionEngine was developed by pMachine, Inc., a company founded by Rick Ellis. The application that was to become ExpressionEngine was first developed in 2001. ExpressionEngine is a powerful content management system for websites or blogs. You can purchase a license of ExpressionEngine and download the solution or host ExpressionEngine through pMachine, Inc.[8]

Member management—With ExpressionEngine, you have the ability to sign up unlimited members, and members can sign up for accounts themselves. This feature gives companies the ability to easily develop online social communities.

Communications—ExpressionEngine provides some email list management features up to the level of customizing email templates. Not every blog reader will have an RSS feed reader, and this email list feature provides another way to keep in touch with your readership.

Closing Remarks on Blog Publishing Systems

There are many blog publishing platforms beyond the four systems mentioned in this chapter. I have reviewed some of the most popular on the market. When evaluating different blog publishing systems, it is important to conduct a search of the current systems available and determine if each system is keeping up with the current interaction tools needed for effective blogging. Build a list of criteria for what you will need from a blog publishing platform and make sure the system you choose meets all of your company's needs.

BLOG MONITORING TOOLS

This section on monitoring tools looks beyond RSS feed search engines and describes three critical tools for monitoring your community, helping in conducting blogger outreach, and finding a post again.

RSS Feed Readers

A feed reader is basically a reader of RSS, Atom, XML, and other associated web feeds. Web feeds allow blog readers or other web content readers to keep in touch with their favorite content remotely, without having to give a publisher their email address. Instead of a publisher sending email out to a list of subscribed members, blog readers subscribe to a feed and review content when and where they wish to look at it. Blog readers use RSS feed readers to read web feeds and keep in touch with their favorite blogs and websites through a feed.

A number of RSS feed readers exist, including NewsGator,[9] FeedDemon,[10] Bloglines,[11] and Feedster.[12] For more feed readers, refer to the Directory of RSS Aggregators at http://www.aggcompare.com/.

Effective corporate blogging requires that your bloggers and/or communications team monitor the web for the latest updates in your industry. A feed reader is a great way to monitor the current conversations in your blogging community and also an excellent way to find more blogs to read.

Many blogs provide RSS feeds; simply take a blog's RSS feed and put the feed into your feed reader. Quite a few RSS feed readers give you point-and-click functionality to easily subscribe to feeds.

To encourage more readers to subscribe to your blog's feed, make sure your web feed information is prominently displayed on your blog. Many feed readers have blog feed subscription buttons that can be placed on your blog to make it easier for your readers to subscribe to your feed. Pick a few of the more popular feed reader subscription buttons to make it easier for your readers to subscribe. To determine what is popular today, review a few popular blogs and make a list of the popular feeds—those are the feeds that should appear on your blog.

One especially useful feature of some feed readers is the ability to share your subscriptions with other feed reader users or on your blog's website. You can access these subscriptions through the feed reader management systems once you have subscribed or review them through a blogger's website. Many bloggers post their RSS feed subscriptions on their website instead of a weblog roll because it is easier to update their RSS feed reader than the weblog roll. One popular RSS feeder, Bloglines.com, gives users the ability to share lists of RSS feeds. I have found this to be particularly useful when giving a client a list of the blogs in their community discovered through a blogging audit. In addition, Bloglines.com users can choose to make their RSS feed subscriptions public through a link. The Bloglines subscription system allows you to determine which users have subscribed to your feed, and it is also possible to click on each person's subscription and then review all of their Bloglines' RSS feed subscriptions. The ability to read other blogger's subscriptions can give you access to more blogs, which you can add to your blogging community audit, but it can also give you an idea of the popularity of a particular blog's RSS feed if there are a lot of subscriptions from many readers.

Comment Monitoring Tools

Blog comment monitoring was a real problem even as recent as 2005. There was really no way to track conversations happening on other blogs. If you only made one or two comments a week, it would be a relatively easy matter to surf a blog and determine if anyone had responded to your comment. But if you make a lot of comments and you were notified by the blog with an email of a new comment in reply to yours, it becomes increasingly difficult to track all the different conversations you conducted across the blogosphere. Del.icio.us provided an early solution to the blog comment problem, but it was not very satisfactory. People would bookmark their comments in blogs with a tag that indicated they had just commented, such as "tracking + comments." The only problem with this use of Del.icio.us is that you have to return to each individual site where you commented to determine if anyone had responded. In 2006, a number of comment monitoring services were launched, and here are a few of them.

coComment

coComment built a search engine for crawling comments on blogs. Initially, the service only tracked comments visited by coComment users. coComment users had to bookmark each comment by using a widget within their book marking tools in their browser. coComment is not very different from Del.icio .us, except coComment has a dedicated website for comments. Each comment was displayed in last date order, which made it easy to see which comment was most recent. If you commented on a blog where other users made comments, you could determine that a comment had been made without having to return to the original blog. However, it would require everyone to adopt the service for the system to have any hope of being useful.

Fortunately, coComment upgraded their service so that you have the ability to track comments on blogs by users who are not coComment users. This means you can track all of the conversations from the coComment interface rather than using an RSS feed reader. When another comment is made on a blog and you log into the interface, it is possible to quickly determine if someone has made another comment, as any new comments appear in boldface in the coComment interface. The interface makes it easier to find the conversations where something happened. You can even use coComment to read the comments from within the user interface. You only have to go to the original blog if you want to make a comment, a big time saver if you make a lot of comments and want to review your comments to determine if you should make another entry. Only some blogging platforms will allow this feature; fortunately, the big platforms, such as WordPress, TypePad, Movable Type, and Blogger, and others are covered.

coComment has some social media search tools. The service lets you find the bloggers who are registered coComment members who write the most comments. You can search for the most comments posted on a particular tag term. You can even subscribe to another user's comment; this feature makes coComment a great tool for understanding what is happening inside your community.

coComment and other services may just have solved one of the recurring problems of blogging, tracking your online conversations in comments remotely.

Co.mments.com

Co.mments.com is very similar to coComment in that you can track your comments using a bookmark within your browser. When you log into your Co.mments.com page, you can see each conversation you are involved in and determine quickly if there are any more comments. One outstanding feature of Co.mments.com is email notification when one of your conversations has an updated comment; however, Co.mments has none of the social media search tools you receive with the coComment service.

Commentful

Commentful also has a comment-tracking interface. If you are a Firefox browser user, Commentful lets you install a blinker extension for Firefox. If there are updates to comments, an icon in your Firefox browser blinks. Commentful works with many blogging platforms and also supports Digg, Flickr, and some forum technology. There are no social media search tools, however.

BLOG SOCIAL BOOK MARKING TOOLS

Blogging is a conversation, and those blogging conversations take place on and between blogs and bloggers. The most popular way to find those conversations is through search engines. Social book marking sites now also enable Internet users to easily find similar content and conversations through tags, keywords, and searches.

This ability to aggregate content in social book marking sites is important. Such sites give corporate bloggers the ability to not only find content easily, but also to connect and find other members of a particular community. Social book marking websites can help you identify those members of the community who sometimes contribute the most to the blogging community.

Del.icio.us

Del.icio.us is a social book marking service for Internet users. Del.icio.us allows you to bookmark any webpage within the site and track the page over time. Users register online at Del.icio.us, and once they sign up, members can bookmark any page on the web within Del.icio.us and at the same time assign metadata that describe the book marked page. Metadata includes a description and notes about the page, the URL, and associated tags. A tag is a keyword that describes an article or webpage. For example, if you were book marking a page about plumbing in Del.icio.us, you would use the tag "plumbing."

In addition to the ability of book marking a page and searching those book marked pages anywhere from a web connection by logging into Del.icio.us, other Internet users can search all of the documents tagged by everyone who uses Del icio.us. The Del.icio.us system is effectively a directory of pages, each tagged with keywords by people who have read and categorized the webpage. The human editing provides a valuable resource for any web searcher who is looking for articles on many topics. Del.icio.us also lists the number of other Del.icio.us members who have bookmarked any webpage, thereby providing some insight into the relevancy of particular webpages—the pages with more bookmarks are considered more valuable by a larger number of people. Anyone can search Del .icio.us to discover the articles Del.icio.us members consider the most important webpages on a particular keyword or topic.

Digg

Digg is a user-supported website where stories are submitted by users to the site, and each story receives votes to either propel or bury stories within the site. Digg and sites like Digg, including newsvine.com, furl.net, fark.com, reddit .com, and many other social media websites, allow you to bookmark articles and, if the community promotes them enough, propel them to the front page of each site. One benefit of using these sites is promotional; if you write an article that is enjoyed or seen as valuable by the community and they promote the article, expect a lot of traffic. Another benefit is using these sites to find more people in the community you are targeting.

CONSUMER-GENERATED MEDIA (CGM) MEASUREMENT COMPANIES PROVIDE COVERAGE AND ANALYSIS

To get a sense of current trends in all customer conversations on the web, companies need to monitor their community wherever users generate content on the web, be that blogs or forums. Beyond the popular RSS feed search engines listed in Chapter 2—Technorati.com, Feedster.com, Sphere.com, and IceRocket .com, there are other tools and services available for auditing and monitoring blogs. These services can be called CGM measurement. The companies that provide CGM measurement services help marketers to search the parts of the web that search engines and RSS feed search engines are not indexing. RSS feed search engines do not yet index the vast amount of published content beyond websites without RSS feeds and those found in forums and other secure content websites. The list of companies providing services that provide deeper analysis tools than RSS search engines includes Nielsen BuzzMetrics, Umbria, and Cymfony.

Max Kalehoff of Nielsen BuzzMetrics described his assessment of the challenges of using existing search tools to find customer conversations. He said,

> Most blog search tools are free consumer services that provide an anecdotal view of the content created in blogs. But if a company is performing sophisticated market research and wishes to tap into the much larger pool of unstructured data that exist in the growing universe of CGM—i.e., message boards, product sites, and emerging consumer-generated multimedia—then free search tools and marginal research methodologies quickly become inadequate. Free blog search engines are important tools that foster the blogosphere by helping people navigate, discover, subscribe and have access to basic profiles. I agree with the saying that they are public utilities that promote conversation. But they are a far cry from the breadth and depth available through full-scale CGM research services.

CGM measurement companies compile databases of all freely available content on the web around a particular industry. If needed, measurement companies also develop relationships with secure content owners by asking permission to index and filter data from forums and other secure websites where CGM is produced.

The measurement companies use sophisticated data-mining techniques to mine their indexed data and provide a clear picture of what is happening for their client's customer community. Data-mining techniques enable the measurement companies to produce custom research that can provide a range of metrics, from measurement of the level of brand awareness among a large population to the identification of key motivators for being favorable toward a brand.

The ability to rank information, websites, and individuals on the web is the key to the worth of CGM measurement research. A measurement company can do the following:

- Determine topics of conversation and rank them by relevancy to a community;
- Determine the level of connection between one brand and another through the analysis of conversations;
- Measure the level of discussion around product or topic;
- Trend customer awareness of products over time.

TABLE 5.1   Critical Key Metrics from Raw CGM

Volume	How many comments about your brand?
Reach	Depth of exposure, impressions viewed by others
Dispersion	Distribution and vitality of issue or conversation
Sentiment	To what extent are messages favorable or non-favorable?
Emotion	How did consumers feel? Betrayed? Confident?
Issue	What specific issues are being discussed in brand buzz?
Source	Where is conversation occurring? Boards, Blogs?
Author	Is author credible? What kind of consumer?

All of these data can be used to identify key purchase-decision drivers among customers online.

Max Kalehoff explained how his company prepares and delivers analyzed data to customers: "Nielsen BuzzMetrics" starts by collecting large volumes of CGM—literally billions of discussions— into its database. The service uses a data-mining system similar to major engines, such as Google, but fine-tuned for the specific purpose of measuring and analyzing CGM. As the raw unstructured data enter the system, the software identifies the source, the author (or user handle), and the date and time the content was created. The software then standardizes the data into one relational database, which becomes the starting point for applying linguistic technologies and performing rigorous analysis. This raw CGM is transformed into a variety of critical key metrics, as shown in Table 5.1.

Ultimately, these metrics are applied to help marketers answer some of the most pressing brand questions, such as.

- How do consumers/customers feel about my brand … right now?
- How many are talking (volume), and who is being impacted (reach)?
- What issues are being discussed? Which issues are coming around the corner?
- Who is talking and where, and are they influential?
- Can I influence, control, or manage word of mouth?
- Did my marketing engage, resonate, or "echo" with consumers?"

How CGM Measurement Companies Analyze Data

Online CGM represents an opportunity for companies to understand their customer's online conversations; however, that opportunity only exists if companies can filter their data. With such massive amounts of data from thousands, if not millions, of online conversations, it is impossible for a company to use people to conduct this sort of analysis, here then is where natural language processing or latent semantic analysis can be used to automatically review online conversations and then filter the compiled conversations for useful analysis.

Latent semantic analysis is a technique whereby researchers using automated tools can understand human languages. Here is the definition for natural language processing from Wikipedia of how the process works: "Natural language generation systems convert information from computer databases into normal-sounding human language, and natural language understanding systems convert samples of human language into more formal representations that are easier for computer programs to manipulate."[13]

Max Kalehoff from Nielsen BuzzMetrics gave some insight into how his industry uses these techniques:

> We work with advanced linguistic technologies which enable rapid and automated analysis of consumer sentiment, as well as brand linkage to various keywords. If one hundred million messages all mentioned your brand, can you separate the positive messages? And amongst those positive messages, can you identify the top drivers of those discussions? Or can you identify which keywords or concepts are most closely associated with your brand?

CGM Observational Research Techniques

Traditional market research techniques use representational sampling techniques to determine predictive models of future customer behavior. CGM measurement market research collects data passively, which means that the consumer insights derived are unaided and lacking of many traditional research biases. CGM measurement companies such as Nielsen BuzzMetrics suggest that their research will give a company more insight into ideas of what their customers, prospects, and competitors' customers think and say to one another and what they will actually do when making a purchase decision.

The bottom line is that the data reveals findings not from an average cross-section of consumers but from those who are so engaged or passionate about a subject that they are willing to go online and talk about it unprompted. These consumers are often among the most difficult to identify and study in traditional survey research methods. Moreover, people who buzz online also tend to organize themselves in communities that reflect their own interests, life stage, or psychographics.

A Critique of CGM Observational Research Techniques

Michael Cornfield, PhD, adjunct professor at the Graduate School of Political Management, The George Washington University, and Vice President of Public Affairs, ElectionMall.com, explained how he uses consumer-generated data in his research. Michael Cornfield describes himself as providing a "narrative analysis" similar to a "literary critic" when using CGM research. Whereas companies like BuzzMetrics provide data that pinpoint the key individuals in online communities, he takes that data to actually conduct narrative analysis of each identified influential person or website in an online community. His analysis filters the individuals and websites further to discover the most influential people and blogs in their community. Michael states that,

> He studies web content samples and data (consumer- and also producer-and media-generated content) to identify who is playing key roles in the community conversation about a company, controversy, or other subject. Who's the big booster, critic, arbiter, advocate, etc.? What are they like? I also identify the main story lines and the turning points in the action on those lines: what incidents cause traffic to spike, critics to go mum, etc. The posting of a document and the spreading of a meme can form the basis for such incidents; of course, offline events also result in the conversation turning for/against/toward/away from a subject.

Michael Cornfield is a social scientist, and he thinks any researcher should be aware of some of the problems with blog metrics and CGM metrics services; his overview of the issues includes the following:

- This is not sample research, as the participants are self-selecting.
- It is better to use quantitative data for the initial analysis of the volume of data that exists on the web and, thereby, discover which individuals and websites are the centers for discussion on the web.
- Use quantitative research with a qualitative analysis of individual's blogs and web content to find those people who provide the most valuable contribution to a community.
- There might be problems with qualitative analysis, as those chosen individuals may not be representative of the group and so may not be predictors of future community direction.
- You can mitigate for a lack of representation by tracking individuals over time to determine if predictive models come to pass.

Although he has some reservations about using this type of research, he does believe the research can be tremendously valuable for companies and states that,

> Before the Internet came along, community conversations were far less legible than they are today. Although we can't analyze those conversations with probabilistic precision, as with survey research, we can learn a great deal from a combination of statistical and narrative analysis. PR and marketing strategists gain from this pioneering research—and, in a way, so do consumers and citizens, because they are being heard more in their natural (as in unprompted by a researcher) state.

Mary Beth Weber of Sigma Validation,[14] a market research validation company, described her thoughts about the nature of CGM and its validity when comparing opinions about products across an entire population, especially in the context of blogs. She said, "If someone is going to blog about a company or product, they will have had either an exceptionally good experience or an exceptionally bad experience. So if you are listening to customer bloggers you may think you have more problems than good, as typically people are more motivated to express their bad experiences." This is one of the biases of CGM, that you may not get the entire picture of everyone in the community about a product.[15]

Using CGM Data

CGM data analysis is being used by companies to provide insight into the buzz around products and brands in different industries, from the pharmaceutical to the television industry. The measurement data is helping companies make advertising and product choice that involves hundreds of millions of dollars of marketing promotions and product development dollars. Such CGM data is already important to business.

Blogger relations is the process of writing relevant content and connecting with an industry's bloggers by linking and commenting to other blogs. Successful blogger relations can bring dialogue, links, higher rankings, product ideas, and new customers. Knowing which blogger to target can be achieved with major search engines and RSS search engines, but the process of identifying the key players takes time. Measurement services can help corporate bloggers reduce the time it takes to discover the important websites in their industry and help with the process of monitoring more of their community's online presence.[16]

EFFECTIVE BLOG DESIGN FOR BLOGGING

Effective blog design includes the design of a blog, its navigation elements, and its communication tools. Blogs have a lot of standard elements, articles, comments, categories, and archives; all of which need to be presented well within the blog template design. Those elements put a lot of constraint on what is possible with a blog design. The focus for your company should be on making sure your blog is easy to navigate to find the content and easy for visitors to connect with the blogger.

Blog creative look—Some companies do not put a lot of effort into the look and feel of their blogs. This might be because they did not have the resources to create a highly designed look for their blog, but there is some thinking in the blogging community that a highly designed blog might cause some blog readers to question its credibility. The blogs developed in the early blogging days of Macromedia were a great example of blogs that used simple and plain templates for their blog designs. The choice of design really must depend upon your audience and the impression your company wishes to present. A plain, simple, and creative look makes sense for a highly technical audience that is very interested in any technical details your company wishes to provide. For other companies, a more complex and compelling blog design will be important, especially if the audience expects good design from that company. Consider your audience when it comes to building a design that is right for your company blog.

How blog readers find articles within a blog is very important to the success of your blog—make the navigation very intuitive and easy to use for blog readers.

Categories—Consider what are the most important topics you write about, and include them in your categories. Blog readers can click on an individual category and review all related materials. Each category also creates a separate page. If you develop a lot of categories, having a long list gets confusing after awhile. Consider installing a category cloud widget for your category navigation; the cloud alphabetically arranges the words together, but the categories that have the most articles will have a larger font. Your readers will be able to pinpoint the main themes of your blog with a quick glance. The cloud navigation may also give you a reminder to write more articles on themes you want to concentrate upon. Many people think about search engine optimization when selecting their categories, picking categories that include the keywords their audience use to search for them on the web.

Blog roll—There is a strategy in Internet marketing that if you make your website really useful, more people will come to the website and also link to it. Providing a blog roll of your industry will encourage more people to bookmark your website. In addition, blogging is about reciprocity; linking to other people in your community will help you to establish relationships with bloggers in your community, who may also return the link

Recent comments—Blogs allow people visiting the site to comment on articles. People are interested in what other readers have to say about your work. Making sure your recent comments navigation links are prominently displayed will demonstrate to readers you have an active community and also entice readers deeper into your blog. One page you might consider developing is a page that links to all the comments made on the blog. This feature is typically not available for most blogs and will probably require some extra custom programming; such a page will allow blog readers to dig deeper into your conversations with readers.

Blog search box—Some people click on links to navigate a blog, whereas others use the search box; thus, make sure you have a search service on your blog; otherwise, many blog readers will not search any deeper into your site than the home page.

Search engines—Make sure your website is fully optimized for the keywords your audiences use and your brand keywords. Include the keywords in your categories, tags, title articles, and the body of your content. Also include those keywords in your metatags, description, keyword lists, and the title of your blog. Targeting your keywords will help blog readers to find you through search engines if you manage to get highly ranked on your keywords.

Blogging is all about dialogue, and facilitating that dialogue through comments, trackbacks, and personal information will help you to continue conversations once initiated.

Comments—If commenting is turned on and/or comments are moderated, make sure that it is functioning properly, and as much as possible, answer any comments you receive, as this is one of the most important things a blogger can do to encourage conversation and dialogue on their blog.

Email subscription—RSS feeds are standard on blogs. However, not every reader uses them, yet they provide an email subscription box for people who prefer to receive an email updating them of your latest posts.

Using trackbacks—The best way for a blogger to alert another blogger that he has mentioned his work in a blog post is to use a trackback. Trackbacks send a notification to a blog that another blogger has written a post citing a blog article. To send a trackback, a blogger has to copy and paste a trackback URL from a blogger's article into the ping field of a blog content management system. Once the blog post and trackback ping are published, the blog content management system notifies a ping server that the page has been updated. The ping server then notifies the original blog's system that a trackback has been sent from another blog. A link appears automatically underneath the post of the original blog, which links to the article of the blogger who sent the trackback ping.

There is an increasing amount of trackback spam from malicious blog spammers, and so many blog publishing systems allow bloggers to monitor trackbacks before publishing a trackback.

Search engines give higher rankings to those websites that have more links from relevant websites. Trackback spammers send trackbacks to attain more links to get higher rankings on search engines and receive direct traffic. The correct etiquette in using a trackback is to reference any blog post where you wish to send a trackback. Writing a comment about the content of a blog article on another blog will increase the likelihood that a blogger will publish any trackbacks sent to them.

Successful trackbacks, like successful blog marketing, can only be achieved if a blogger understands that he is having a dialogue with other bloggers. Merely targeting other blogs for links will probably only get your trackback deleted and may also give you a reputation for spamming among your industry's community of bloggers. Do not send a trackback to a blog post unless you want to comment indirectly through a trackback or you wish to reference some information provided by a blogger's article. Only send a trackback if your post is relevant to the other blogger's article. Lastly, do not randomly send trackbacks to a blogger's article when your own article does not even reference the post or has nothing to do with the content on the blog.

Endnotes

1. Author's note: I have used both TypePad and Movable Type blogs. My current personal blog, PR Communications, is powered by TypePad.

2. http://www.myspace.com

3. http://www.sixapart.com/about/index

4. http://www.sixapart.com/pronet/plugins/

5. Blogsavvy Blog (2005), *Giving Blogs with Movable Type*. Available at http://blogsavvy.net/giving-blogs-with-movable-type

6. http://www.sixapart.com/movabletype/features

7. http://mu.wordpress.org

8. http://www.pmachine.com

9. http://www.newsgator.com/home.aspx

10. http://www.newsgator.com/NGOLProduct.aspx?ProdID=FeedDemon

11. http://www.bloglines.com

12. http://www.feedster.com

13. http://en.wikipedia.org/wiki/Natural_language_processing

14. http://www.sigmavalidation.com

15. Blogsurvey Blog (2005), *Validating Customer Generated Comments on Blogs and the Web*. Available at http://blogsurvey.backbonemedia.com/archives/2005/11/validating_customer_generated.html

16. Intelligence Briefing, John Cass, Vol. 3 No. 3 April/May (2006), *Discovering your customer's opinion about your company with consumer-generated media measurement*. Edited by Edward A. Crowley, published by Photizo Group.

CHAPTER 6

Writing for Blogger Relations

In Chapter 3, we discussed what skills bloggers could draw on from public relations, journalism, and search engine marketing. In this chapter, we continue on that theme and explore some of the writing and research skills a blogger can learn from journalism and determine the writing skills that are needed by corporate bloggers to write a blog.

The reality of the new media world is that every Internet user has the ability to develop content on the web very easily. The world of blogging allows interaction between writers and readers, which changes the relationship between the two, as the possibility of a dialogue means that smart bloggers write articles that foster dialogue with their audience. Correspondence is nothing new in journalism; what is new is the speed of the dialogue between writer and reader—a blogger can write a post, publish it, and a few moments later, a reader will have read the article and made a comment. This is very new in the world of reporting and publishing, and this changes the dynamic of how a blogger writes on his or her own blog and in the outreach conducted to other blogs in a community.

Although different tactics are needed to connect with readers and bloggers through writing on a blog, many public relations professionals would argue strategically that blogging is still just a communications channel between a company and an audience. The techniques to reach the audience might have changed but, fundamentally, the goal is still the same; use media to send a company's message to its customers and stakeholders.

The elements of successful blogging are writing, research, and interacting with an industry's blogging community. This combination of skills and practices makes blogging different from communications strategies for traditional media. Essentially, the difference is how you write to interact in a blog; however, to write well, you have to ensure your material is unique or compelling content. Writing good content requires research, as tremendous credibility is attained when you write with authority. Basing your writing on good source materials and double-checking facts before publishing helps to establish that authority. Research skills are critical to effective blogger relations, as part of the dynamic in blogging is keeping up with the important sources of information so that what a blogger writes is current. The process of research includes monitoring news sources, conducting searches, and building relationships with community members.

WRITING EFFECTIVELY

Most blogs are powered by content management systems that enable a blogger to write an unlimited number of articles of varying lengths. So in a sense, blogs do not really put any constraints on the length of an article or the number of posts that can be published on a blog. To write effectively for a corporate blog requires that a blogger understand that any constraints of the medium are really a function of the audience or how a blogger connects with the audience through his or her blog, for example, if the audience prefers short news articles to long essays, or if the audience wants to read technical information without personal details.

A corporate blogger has to be attuned to what content will interest and sustain an audience. In the profession of journalism, there are a number of different forms of written pieces, and many of these types of writing formats can be used by bloggers. The news reporting style of the article is very important for attracting an audience and bringing them back repeatedly, and the focus of reporting is the up-to-date news, whereas feature articles address non-breaking news stories, and features are less prominent in newspapers but are a mainstay in magazines.

Features, news reporting, and filler articles were all developed within journalism to fit the needs of different audiences and the media business. Within the context of blogging, the different article formats journalists write for newspapers and magazines take on a different relevancy. Some formats are more relevant to the blogging medium, some less so, as each format is not always as useful for writing a blog post as it is for journalism. Bloggers use article formats that appeal to their audience and their own writing style.

Blog articles are found, read, and navigated through differently from print newspapers and magazines because blogs are online. The factors that influence the usefulness of a particular format of writing for a blog include the following:

- The look and presentation within a blog.
- How blog readers find articles.
- Reasons for an audience to return.

This chapter will review the different types of writing formats developed within journalism, along with an explanation of each format's relevancy and usefulness to a corporate blogger.

REVIEWING THE FORMATS OF ARTICLES

Features

The topic of a feature article is typically not a current news item. The format for features can be quite broad, including interviews, essays, how-tos, and reviews. A feature reviews what interests the audience rather than focusing on an immediate news item. Journalists use feature articles to widely explore the human-interest issues behind a news story.

Corporate bloggers use the format of the feature extensively, as the format can give bloggers the time to explore the background to important issues in their industry or community. Blogs are perfect for the journal entries, but not every blogger has the time to write a personal narrative of his or her daily work life. Many corporate bloggers write feature blog entries about their overall experience by examining particular incidents within their work life. The personal narrative connects the reader to the blogger, and the description of work life establishes the blogger's experience and expertise. Many important blog articles that attract a lot of attention and help establish the credibility of a blogger in their community use the format of a feature article.

How-tos

Another format of feature article writing that bloggers use are how-tos. These articles take the reader through each step of how to do something and in the process really demonstrate the expertise of a blogger within his or her industry. In the Backbone Media Corporate Blogging Survey 2005, many bloggers stated that gaining thought-leadership or establishing their credibility through suggesting new ideas in the community is important. How-tos are particularly useful for building a webpage that might be highly ranked on search engines, as searchers will often search for definitions and articles that explain how to do something.

Interviews

Interviews are widely used by bloggers to build relationships with other bloggers in their community. Especially for new business bloggers, interviewing other established bloggers in the community can be a great way to make a contact and learn more about the industry. Bloggers will also use a series of interviews with industry members to enhance larger feature pieces, gaining quotes and additional ideas to add depth to the article.

Product Reviews

Product reviews and analysis are particularly relevant for new technological developments and are regularly found on blogs about the technology industry. Detailed feature blog posts that include a review of how a blogger used a new technology are very common in the business technology blogging communities. Articles that review current trends in technology sometimes have snippets of quotes from many other blogs, which help to describe the current community ideas about a new technology's progress and development. Use online research in your community to determine if other bloggers have reviewed products; add those to your articles, especially if by quoting different blogs you can show a spread of opinions about a product.

Essays

Essays are a format of feature articles that journalists use to convince or inform their audience. Not all essays are formal in tone; many can be light but typically persuasive in nature. Bloggers will use this format extensively to try to convince their audience of the idea or position the essay discusses. Bloggers can break up their essays into different sections and run the sections in a number of blog posts for several days or weeks.

New Journalism

New journalism is a style of writing that developed during the 1960s. Journalists combine the objective approach of news reporting with the subjective approach of fictional writing. New journalism is about facts, but those facts are combined with the writer's or subject's personal thoughts and feelings.[1] The format of new journalism articles is used by many bloggers in that opinion, thoughts, and feelings about events, products, and situations are in many cases most of what bloggers describe on their blogs. From a pilot on the Southwest Airlines blog[2] describing his experiences landing a plane to the organic farmer on Stonyfield Farm blog[3] posting images of the morning milking, employees and writers for corporate blogs describe their reality. In doing so, bloggers demonstrate the relevancy of their world to the reader by describing their subjective perspectives on their experiences.

The blog format is a series of posts in diary format and is very much derived from journals in that people write in their blogs their personal perspectives on events and situations. Corporate blogging is a type of writing that can be an effective way to get the facts to an audience quickly and is a clear objective of many bloggers.[4] However, facts alone are not enough to sustain an audience's interest. Press releases, product flyers, and corporate brochures—however useful to customers—often do not excite customers either, yet those communications materials are the mainstay of many corporate websites. Those same facts can be incorporated within a blog so that they connect the writer—and by extension, the company—with the reader and the customer.

Bloggers use many of the techniques of new journalism, except that within the context of blogs, the new journalism format changes from one article, or a book, to a series of posts that detail the blogger's life. Corporate bloggers effectively produce a new journalism style of writing through the total body of their work on a blog. Each blog post might well be a single piece entirely on its own, but the whole story is all of the content on the blog over time. The character in the story is the blogger, who writes facts that illustrate a company's products and brand from his personal perspective. Blogging can be very effective when this form of writing is used, and its similarity to the format of new journalism is striking. A journalist writing in the new journalism format is an observer. The irony for new journalism is that the effectiveness of this type of blogging arises because the blogger is both the observer and active participant.

Dr. Greiver is a practicing physician in Canada, and her blog is an online journal of her practice's implementation of a new electronic media record system. Dr. Greiver's blog describes her experiences of implementing an electronic media record system within her practice. Her posts take you through the whole process of how her office converted from paper records and a computer accounting system to a place where virtually all data is managed by computers. Dr. Greiver even uses a handheld computer to enter data during consultation with patients. Her blog provides great insight into the challenges of managing the electronic media record software selection process and the issues a small medical practice faces in planning and implementing an electronic media record system.

Dr. Greiver does not just describe how she implemented an electronic media record but also her opinions, feelings, and frustrations with the whole process. The blog is a wonderful record on how to implement a new electronic medical record, and it also reveals that Dr. Greiver is just as human as the rest of us.[5]

The new journalism form of blog writing takes a lot of time and dedication, something few people can do, although the practice produces some of the most compelling content a corporate blogger can write. If your experts do not have time to conduct this type of writing, another option is to really take the role of the journalist and report on your company's activities in the new journalism style of blog writing.

This new journalism style of writing was used when I was writing the Quotium Technologies web-load testing blog. I had no technical expertise in web-load testing other than the years of experience of working with web developers at several companies and agencies. A non-expert in web-load testing, it was not possible to represent myself as an expert on web-load testing. So, I wrote from the perspective of a new employee at a web-load testing company who was exploring the industry, writing a number of detailed interviews with well-known software testing experts in the industry. The emphasis was on facts, but I also gave my personal reflections on the process of learning about the complexities of the web-load testing market. The blog succeeded in boosting the rankings of the main Quotium website in the search engines.

One of the risks of having a non-expert blogger write a blog for a company is that if the company is attempting to demonstrate company expertise in an area of technical competence, a blogger's lack of expertise might harm the perception of the company's brand. Far better to have someone with expertise within the company write a blog, as this will add more credibility to a blog. However, if the new employee interviewed many of the experts within the company who do not have the time to blog, their expertise will be described in the text.

This new journalism approach to blog writing is very similar to how the anthropologist Jean L. Briggs wrote the book, *Never in Anger: Portrait of an Eskimo Family*,[6] in 1970. Jean Briggs was an anthropology student who studied Inuit society during the 1960s, and she wrote a discipline-changing book on anthropology. Jean Briggs included her personal reflections in her book. Up until that point, anthropology books and articles had all been very objective.

Objective Writing

Objectivity is a key style of journalism writing. In this type of writing, the journalist sticks to the facts as closely as the journalist can determine, and no personal reflections or thoughts are described. The goal of this form of writing is to describe reality, not to connect with the reader.

Objective writing can be very effective with certain audiences. For example, in industries where the changes are fast-paced or where products are technically complex, then customers are eager for as much information as possible. The reasons for this are twofold: one, customers want to remain competitive and up-to-date; two, they want to make sure they are maintaining their existing technical knowledge, as it is their job to do so.

Eric Anderson from Adobe has described his writings as being very non-personal;[7] he does not see the need to personalize his writing. Eric is using objective writing because it works best for his audience and even adds to his credibility for his audience. The Adobe product he discusses is complex software, and customers want to know they are receiving information and advice from a technical expert.[8]

Round-ups

Round-up articles are feature articles that contain quotes from famous people in a community on a particular subject. Bloggers often take quotes from other bloggers when they are preparing essays or feature blog posts that cover important or current issues. A blog round-up post is common in many blogging communities. Typically written and posted within a few days or weeks after a major story breaks, a round-up article can be a very helpful review of what the entire community has written on a particular story. Many bloggers become the focus point for an ongoing discussion between other members of a blogging discussion either through an initial opinion piece or this type of round-up posting.

Another type of round up article is when bloggers ask for comments from community members on a topic and write their posting based on the insights from the community. Linking to everyone's blog and asking for quotes and receiving quotes by email prior to posting an article is a virtual guarantee to having the author's blog post receive additional readership, comments, and links from bloggers who were quoted in posting.

Exposé Writing

Exposé writing or investigative reporting involves extensive research to reveal information that some person or organization is attempting to keep secret. The costs of conducting such research are high for newspapers and magazines; bloggers, however, conduct the research on their own time. Many bloggers do conduct investigative reporting; however, where this form of writing is typically published on corporate blogs, consultants and pundits within the blogging community publish it, as they have the most to gain and little to lose from this form of investigative reporting.

Purposely creating bad publicity by writing an exposé about other community members is not really in the interest of most companies. However, sometimes, it is in the interest of a company to discuss the merits of their competitors. One Boeing blog has an example of this form of writing. Randy Baseler runs the blog *Randy's Journal* at Boeing.[9] The blog discusses the strength of Boeing airplanes in comparison to their only major competitor, Airbus. The blog gives Randy and Boeing the opportunity to talk about the differences in product strategy between the two companies. Essentially Randy is turning his discussion about product strategy on his blog into a discussion of thought or product leadership between the two companies. It would be difficult for a company to present such a discussion within a traditional corporate website, but it is possible on a blog. Since he launched his blog in January 2005, Randy has commented on the differences between Boeing and Airbus planes. He regularly provides statistics and side-by-side comparisons of each company's planes and strategies. He also highlights the methods by which Airbus development funding is obtained.

Randy Baseler is not an unbiased observer for the competition between Boeing and Airbus, but Randy's blog provides statistics and an entry point for further discussion about the differences between the two aircraft manufacturers. His posts help to shape the industry conversation and provide references for journalists and customers. Although each post is not in-depth, reviewing all of the blog posts over time, one of the continuing characteristics of Randy's blog is the discussion about the rivalry between Boeing and Airbus. Randy often represents his posts as revealing information where there is industry disinformation. In the process, he risks Boeing's, and his own, credibility, as each of his posts is subjective, giving his and Boeing's position and opinions about the industry.

Filler Articles

Filling space has always been a problem for newspaper and magazine editors. The solution has been to write filler articles, which are short pieces about almost any subject. Many bloggers want to make sure there is always up-to-date relevant content on their site. Several of the very well known corporate bloggers post several times a day. Typically, such filler items are tidbits or links to other blogs. Not only does this actively give a blog's readership access to more interesting data they would not be able to find themselves due to lack of time, but linking to other blogs encourages links and comment from other blogs. Filler articles are a mainstay of blog writing. Although not every blogger is concerned about having fresh content, this style of article can be used to keep a blog fresh and provides a way to include additional keywords for search engine rankings.

FYI Posts

FYI posts are short tips or leads on other articles. This format of article gives an insight into the types of posts a blogger is reading and is a handy resource for readers to keep to other articles on websites or blogs. However, these posts provide no analysis or opinion, and there is no added value for the blog reader or insight into the mind of the blogger other than the link, which means that, more than likely, people will read the information and move onto the webpage from the link.

Puff Piece Articles

A puff piece is a format of writing most editors will not include in their newspapers and magazines. Puff pieces are not objective and do not add credibility to the reputation of a publication. Corporate bloggers write puff pieces on a regular basis. Product and order announcements are the mainstay of such articles. Little more than press releases or product sheets, such content is typically of not much interest to the wider community. However, even a product announcement, when combined with the ability for readers to ask questions in comments, can provide some value to a company corporate blog.

Conference Reports

One type of writing that has developed because of blogging is conference note taking or conference reports where one or many bloggers write notes about presentations and events at a conference. Most technology conferences feature bloggers taking notes to publish the first conference report on a speaker's session, often before the speaker has finished speaking! The combination of a number of bloggers writing notes from presentation sessions means that people almost do not have to attend the conference, although blogging might also highlight the value of a conference. For those people who do not attend a conference, such notes are a great way to learn what happened at the conference, or for conference attendees, a session they did not attend. A blogger who writes good notes and has good opinions on what happens at the conference will receive many links and good standing in the community. If the conference report is tagged and picked up by RSS search engines quickly enough, conference reports become the basis for a community discussion while people are attending a conference.

We have discussed a number of formats of writing used by journalists and how those formats can be used by bloggers. The next step is to consider what content style each audience prefers. Lastly, moving beyond the article format or style, we will discuss how the characteristics of blogs affect the mechanics of writing a blog post.

MECHANICS OF WRITING A BLOG POST

Blogging is really about having a conversation with the reader. Newspaper and magazine journalists write to report news and reflect upon issues, but other than letters to the editor, any feedback on their work was slow and minimal. Blogging is different because it is online, and your reader has the ability to participate in contributing content to a blog. The best blogs are really a conversation with your audience. If a company dares to listen to their audience and understand them on the fly, a real conversation can develop between corporate blogger and reader.

A blogger does have to create value for the reader. The corporate blogger has to find what is unique about his or her company, or if there is nothing unique about the company or its product, the blogger has to have a unique perspective of the world. That is one reason why corporate bloggers who use the New Journalism style of writing in the blogs are so effective. The bloggers write facts, but it is the employee's perspectives on reality that gives color and interest to the reader. Unless your readers seek objectivity, some readers do not want personality, they just want the facts.

If a blogger has a good grasp of how to use the different formats of articles, he or she can pick the best format for the audience. Consider reviewing your audience. What does your audience want to read? Will a particular audience prefer a feature, filler, objective, or new journalism style of article? Fortunately, there is existing work that can help a company decide on the best style of writing for their audience—know what is being written by the journalists who write for an industry already. A company should review the newspapers and magazines that report on their industry and determine which style of writing will work best for their audience based partly on that existing work. Blogging does provide some new perspectives on writing, and audiences also review the work that other bloggers in your community publish; analyze other bloggers' work for the type of articles published and estimate their level of success in the community.

Consider a technology blogging audience that purchases and uses complex products and who needs to gain access to a lot of information quickly to remain current, safe, or competitive. An objective style of writing may be perfectly acceptable to such an audience. On the other hand, a consumer audience that purchases simple products will be looking for a different style of content from a corporate blogger. Objective writing about a simple product will probably not interest that audience, as there will not be very much to discuss. To gain their interest, a company might use a feature style or even a new journalism style of writing. One other crucial factor in choosing a style of writing is the ability of the writer to write within that style.

HOW A BLOG POST IS DIFFERENT FROM OTHER TYPES OF WRITING

The volume and frequency of blog writing will affect the type of articles you can write. Several successful bloggers write lots of articles every day, and many of their articles are reporting pieces. To write such articles requires time. The frequency of posts is an important factor in determining the success of a blog. With so many articles being produced, the bloggers are basically providing headline news for their audience. Yet, that is a characteristic of blogging; you have the possibility of writing and publishing a lot of articles, unlimited, in fact, and it is a simple matter for your audience to keep track of any updates to your blog, if your audience is reading your content through RSS feeds. There definitely is a place within every blogging community for several bloggers who keep abreast of the community to provide many news reports and links to sites and blogs in the community. You may wonder how many times a week does a blogger have to write, and that depends upon a number of factors such as the ability of the blogger to spend time on writing a blog, the volume of content in a blogging community, the style of writing a blogger wishes to use, and the volume of searches within the blogger's industry.

The length of articles in blogs can be very long because the amount of space available to write an article is almost unlimited with many blogging systems. Yet, a blog may not be the best place to write very long articles, as lengthy articles can be difficult to read on the web. Many bloggers have learned to split up their longer articles into different posts. Rather than giving everything away at once, many in-depth features will take place over a series of blog posts.

Choosing the length of an article is dependent upon a few factors, including building the best web pages for search engine optimization, where typically an article should be 400 words long, so that there is enough content for a page to be spidered and indexed fully by a search engine. In addition, a brief article a few paragraphs long might have a bigger chance of being read by a busy audience. That is part of the medium of blogging. Each blog post is an article written in a diary format, and it is possible to write many updates to the initial blog post, and because it is easier to categorize or identify individual articles with tags, categories, or keywords, short articles can actually be easier to find and read quickly.

Hyperlinking to other documents in blogs is important, as hyperlinks are the currency of the web and the reason why the web is so powerful a medium. One link from a site to another gives you access to a volume of content without having to republish that content on the same page. However, that convenience can also be a hindrance to clarity. The more links there are on a page, the harder it is to follow the source material. There is nothing new in the process of writing a document or article that references other material, but it does mean that blog authors have to be careful in describing the relevancy of their cited material. There are differences between articles that features one or two hyperlinks compared with articles that list ten references. A blog post with a lot of links will be tough to read if a reader needs to click through to each link. Therefore, an author should make sure he or she provides a good synopsis of any hyperlinked material; otherwise, the context of the reference will be lost to the reader who does not have time to click through to read all the facts.

However, one advantage in referencing other blogs is that when you send a trackback or pingback to another blog, the trackback may bring more readers to the article. So citing other articles has two benefits:

- The credibility you gain from citing another blogger's ideas and material (as the more credible an article is, the more likely it is that the article will be read, remembered, and cited).
- Trackback links might bring bloggers or blog readers directly to your blog.

Writing a blog post that includes a lot of research and references to other posts adds credibility and authority to your blog posts. Also, credibility is one of the strongest benefits bloggers are looking for from a blog. Blogging is all about conversations and interaction with blog readers and other bloggers; therefore, blog posts that can include references to other blog posts will help foster conversations between bloggers.

How Blogs Are Read by the Audience

There are a number of factors that determine how a blog article is read by an audience, and those factors include where and when the blog is read, namely,

- Article is found through a search on a search engine.
- Blog article is found through a link.
- Blog is subscribed to by the blog reader in a web feed.
- The popularity of the blog article or the measure of the influence of the blog article.
- The time that blog readers have to read an article.
- Timeliness of blogging; blogging is a quick way to get information out to customers.
- Columnist commenting on the news and others' opinions.

If a blog article is found through a search conducted on a search engine such as Google or an RSS feed search engine such as Technorati.com, it is important to consider that the searcher may be new to the blog when writing any blog article. Include keywords your customers would use to search for you, but also do not assume your audience already knows you when writing your post. Give enough review facts so people can pick up the thread.

When a blog reader subscribes to your web feed and if you allow your feed to syndicate all of the text in your blog post, the blog reader may not actually visit your blog to read your article. Writing for an RSS feed is slightly different. This might seem strange, but as you build more relationships and sign up for more RSS feeds, it becomes more difficult to keep in touch with the industry and blogging community as your network expands. So there is something to be said for not writing as many posts so as not to overwhelm your readers, unless there is a very important news event, one or two postings a day should be sufficient and even welcomed by your weary RSS feed blog readers.

Effective writing for blogging requires an understanding of both your audience and the medium of blogging. You have to engage your audience with blog writing as you would with any type of writing. Although there are some characteristics of blogs that will dictate how you choose to develop your writing style. Blogs are an online medium, and how your audience navigates and reads your content will dictate aspects of your writing. A thorough analysis of your audience's community discussion and writing will help you to develop the writing style that works best for the audience of your blog.

CONDUCTING RESEARCH FOR BLOGGING

In the traditional media, journalists conduct research to generate ideas for stories and understand the facts and the perspectives of people who will be featured in their stories. Journalists can increase the credibility of their stories by researching all the facts. Bloggers also conduct research to find ideas for their blog, and just like a journalist, bloggers gain credibility by including more facts and human perspectives in their blog articles. Here are some tips for conducting research for blogging.

Writing a Blog Post

Conducting research is a very important part of the process of preparing to write a blog post. The quality of your written product will depend upon how much research you conduct. The type of article will dictate what type of research a blogger will need to conduct for his or her blog post. A blogger might want to find data and statistics if he or she is writing a feature article or needs a good description of events to provide a news-reporting article.

A lot of corporate blog posts are about other people's thoughts and opinions regarding issues in an industry; these are typically feature articles on industry discussions. That is when your ability to conduct a narrative analysis of many blog posts that discuss a story you are working on will be very important for the success of your finished article. In pulling together a well researched blog article, you really have to have a good memory for all of the facts pertaining to the story already, as understanding what is happening in an industry will give you insights that can have you including information other people would not have known. If you are just coming up to speed on a story and not aware of all the facts, then make sure you research the background of the story. Go deeper, and research every aspect of the story; if there are people involved, read up on their background, and if they have a blog, read it. Provide cross references in your blog post; the more blogs and references that support an idea or position, the more credibility the idea has. Also, consider the credibility of the source. Is the person an expert and objective? Lastly, how recent is the information? Did the blogger give his or her opinion in light of all the known facts?

Construct a narrative around the story, even if it seems as if it is just a series of facts. Include the series of events, and describe people's personalities with quotes and their opinions. Sketch out the basic facts in an industry discussion. List all of the different views from your research; if there are opposing sides, bundle the bloggers with the same views together and pick some good quotes from their post to add to your own article. Check the accuracy of any facts or views expressed, especially if the topic discussed is not an internal company issue.

Interviewing people involved in a story is a great way to find additional information that might not have been previously published. Interviewing might also help a blogger avoid making any mistakes. Double check sources, even sources cited by a traditional news organization, as they get things wrong too; in addition, you might uncover something they missed. Pull everything together and do not forget to send trackbacks to any blog posts you cited, and you should have a great feature blog post.

Capitalizing on Breaking News

If a news story appears that generates a lot of discussion in a short period, or you have a hunch it will, quickly search the community on the topic to discover the different points of view, and put a synopsis of the discussion together for a blog feature article. A detailed synopsis post with many facts will make a good contribution to the community that will produce comment and discussion. If you want to lead the community, it is not just a matter of providing the facts; you also have to give your opinion. One consequence of a synopsis blog post is that you can trackback or pingback to a lot of different bloggers, who then may respond with their own post and trackback, or comment, on your article. Again, blogging is about dialogue and conversation, so you have to have something to say and contribute, but do not get artificially passionate about an industry issue unless you really do have some passion for the story. Through the process of analyzing the community discussion, you might become the center for the community on that topic. Jeff Jarvis from BuzzMachine[10] was the center and catalyst for issues about customer service with Dell. Although a community will usually focus on opinion pieces or news posts for discussion, if you have something to contribute no one else has said, do so.

Attracting a blog audience requires the audience be able to discover your blog through search engines and direct links in blogs. The content and keywords on a blog will influence how an audience finds a blog. Current issues in the community will bring greater traffic and discussion to a blog because your audience is searching on those topics and tags. It is important to understand that, sometimes, content has to be developed for a blog that has to be derived from research conducted on the web, which is done by monitoring current news items or major items of interest for the community over time.

Blogger Outreach

Once you have researched your community and found the most influential and active bloggers who participate in your community, monitor what is said on their blogs and contribute something with a comment or write a post of your own. Monitoring your community will provide insight, which will give you leads for content. Making sure you link to other blog posts and explaining the value of the content within your blog post may in return result in relationships, friendships, and additional links to your blog and produce traffic over time from other blogs.

You must engage your audience by joining in with their conversations where the discussion is happening, even if that means commenting on other blogs in the community. If you do join a conversation on another blog, it is important to read through the blog with the aim of discovering where you have either a connection to the blogger or can make a useful contribution to the conversation via a comment. You will be more likely to make a connection and actually have a good dialogue with someone if you know more about their background and what interests them.

Keeping the Facts Straight

It is important to monitor web and industry publications for ideas, but it is not the only reason a blogger should conduct research on an ongoing basis.

You should also monitor the web for any online discussion to discover what customers and stakeholders are saying about your company online. If there is a misrepresentation of facts about your company online, those facts need to be corrected, either on the website where posted or you can use your blog to set the record straight. Jonathan Schwartz, the CEO of SUN Microsystems, has done this several times with professional journalists on his blog. A journalist will interview him, and before the journalist has even published his article, to make sure the entire interview was published, Jonathan Schwartz will publish his version of the interview.[11]

Competitive Research

You should also monitor the web to learn more about your competitors, either by monitoring the competitor's website and blogs, if they have one, or by monitoring the blogs of customers who use the competitor's products. The competitive information you discover online could greatly influence the direction of your company on many levels. Even if the consequences of some new initiatives by competitors will take some time to react to, that does not mean you should let them take all the limelight. Certainly, do not be spoilers to your competitors' success; if your competitor comes out with an idea or product that is good, especially if they are also conducting effective blogging, congratulate your competitors on their success.

Market Research

Content and social networking are enticing people away from the mass media toward online tools for self-publishing. It is the customer's ability to discuss or create unique content within a social context that is driving the growth of consumer-generated media. It is much simpler today for a company to research customer conversation's online and conduct the type of market research about their industry that until very recently was not possible. Many companies are now using consumer-generated media for market research, discovering what people think about their products and the industry. This is one very important reason why a company should monitor the online discussions about their brand and industry.

Michael Cornfield, PhD, adjunct professor at the Graduate School of Political Management, George Washington University, and Vice President of Public Affairs, ElectionMall.com, believes online research of consumer-generated media can be tremendously valuable for companies, as "before the Internet came along, community conversations were far less legible than they are today. Although we can't analyze those conversations with probabilistic precision, as with survey research, we can learn a great deal from a combination of statistical and narrative analysis. PR and marketing strategists gain from this pioneering research—and, in a way, so do consumers and citizens, because they are being heard more in their natural (as in unprompted by a researcher) state."[12]

SOME FINAL WORDS ABOUT WRITING A BLOG

Blogs give the blog writer a great deal of flexibility in how you can write content. The facts of what you write are important, but equally, how you conduct outreach to other bloggers and react to blog reader's comments and questions on your blog may have just as much importance as what you write. It may be that the impression you give in how you conduct a dialogue with your audience is just as important as the content for running a successful corporate blog.

Endnotes

1. The Writers Market Encyclopedia. Found formerly on the web at http://www.writersmarket .com/WritersResource/Encyclopedia_Display.aspx

2. http://www.blogsouthwest.com

3. http://stonyfield.typepad.com/bovine

4. Backbone Media Corporate Blogging Survey (2005). Available at http://www.backbonemedia .com/blogsurvey/index.html

5. http://drgreiver.blogspot.com/

6. Jean L. Briggs (1970), *Never in Anger: Portrait of an Eskimo Family.* Harvard University Press, Cambridge, MA.

7. Backbone Media Corporate Blogging Survey, John Cass, Stephen Turcotte, Kristine Munroe (2005). Available at http://www.backbonemedia.com/blogsurvey/index.html

8. Scout Blog (2006), *Northeastern University and Backbone Media Blogging Success Study.* Available at http://www.scoutblogging.com/success_study/blogger_interviews/adobe_eric_anderson .html

9. http://www.boeing.com/randy

10. http://www.buzzmachine.com

11. http://blogs.sun.com/jonathan

12. Intelligence Briefing, John Cass, Vol. 3 No. 3 April/May (2006), *Discovering your customer's opinion about your company with consumer generated media measurement.* Edited by Edward A. Crowley, published by Photizo Group.

CHAPTER 7

Dialogue and the Art of Conversation for Effective Blogger Relations

Blogging gives companies the ability to conduct an online dialogue with their audience in a way that is significantly different from most current written corporate communications methods. Rather than sales sheets or corporate brochures, blogs present the opportunity to capture once private conversations in the offline world and place them on the web for the world to see. In the offline world, private conversations were not open to the public. Customer service calls, sales calls, product discussions, or company interactions about industry issues were once very private. Communication on a blog between a customer and an employee is public and open to all. This openness produces a dynamic that enables customers and industry peers to assess the overall strength of a company's brand by observing how the process of dialogue is conducted on a blog with your company.

Blogs give companies the ability to write unlimited content, which creates the freedom to write more, and in the process removes some of the cultural barriers to writing content that is informal and less promotional, while the ability of an audience to comment on a blog breaks down the distance between employees and customers. Instead of one-way corporate communications, blogging is two-way communication.

Corporate blogging can give the reader either a positive or negative impression of the company and will influence the impression a reader will have of a company's brand. If you do not monitor the discussion online or participate in online discussions about your company or the industry, your company may face potentially harmful consequences. An example of this happened with Dell. Jeff Jarvis from BuzzMachine[1] was the center of a storm about customer service issues with Dell. Although there were problems with the machines, the real issue was how Dell handled the customer service problems online, and Dell was scrambling to catch up with how customers wanted to conduct a dialogue through the web. Creating an open channel for dialogue through blogging and its ability to build more realistic impressions about a company help people to connect with a company, and these are just a few of the important benefits of corporate blogging.

Conducting a two-way dialogue with your audience is the strategy your company should adopt to become an effective blogger. If you develop a corporate blog and allow comments on the blog, you are establishing that you are willing to have a dialogue with your audience, which sometimes means you may be criticized. Although no company has to publish any erroneous comments, there is a rule of etiquette in many blogging communities that if you allow comments and someone posts a critical but respectful comment, a blogger will publish the comment. You then have the opportunity to answer any criticism and give your side of the story, as blogging is a two-way communication between the blogger and the reader.

How you respond to your blog readers who comment is just as important as what is written on your blog. Whether it is through answering customer questions, asking questions, expressing empathy with customer problems, or listening, these are all ways to engage and conduct a dialogue with your readers. Blog outreach, the process of commenting on other blogs in your community, will also affect your reputation in your blogging community. Blogging outreach can bring traffic, help build relationships with other bloggers in the community, and maybe even create more customer evangelists for your company's products.

Now that companies have the ability to converse with their customers more easily through blogging, it is important for a company blogger to know what to say and how to conduct a dialogue with their audience. This chapter is all about the art of blogging conversation; it shows how to connect with an audience by establishing a dialogue through blogging and how it is different from existing methods of marketing communication such as advertising.

UNDERSTANDING THE IMPORTANCE OF DIALOGUE FOR EFFECTIVE BLOGGER RELATIONS

Successful blogging occurs when writing is transparent and open and bloggers are willing to listen to opinions and criticism. Blogging should never be a cynical attempt at dialogue but a real conversation between individuals. Open dialogue, which is the medium of blogging, is the key to effective blogger relations.

Blogs allow corporate bloggers to converse with their audience directly. Such online conversation can demonstrate a company's ideas, abilities, and, in the final analysis, brand to customers and the world. Although dialogue is the medium of blogging, it is also the method by which a blogger grows his or her reputation, and he or she becomes better known in the community by appearing on other blogs through comments, links, and trackbacks. Dialogue then is both how a company should develop content and how eventually a company will achieve its communications goals.

Dialogue is not just about conversation on your own blog, it is also the process of seeking out the places on the web where there is conversation about your industry and interests. Bloggers should search their blogging community for places where conversation and dialogue about their industry occurs. Knowing when and where to conduct a dialogue with other bloggers are important in developing goals for a blog, whereas understanding what should be discussed and who is the best person to communicate with online will help in achieving your blogging goals.

Corporate bloggers may have goals in mind when launching a new blog, such as obtaining more leads through blogging. The way to achieve such goals is not necessarily by writing promotional copy about your product on a blog. Success may only come when a company discusses an issue that is totally unrelated to the product but relates to the company's audience. This occasional disconnect between selling products and the content that needs to be produced drives the need for careful planning about the nature of the type of content and dialogue that should be developed on a corporate blog and the blogging outreach that is conducted by a company.

Content generation is really more about creating a dialogue with your audience, and this dialogue might be very direct in terms of reacting to another community member's blog post with a post of your own or a comment on the other blog. As community dialogue might be unrelated to product discussion, it is sometimes difficult for most marketers to understand how a particular blogging strategy can bring benefits to a company. An analogy would be when marketing people jumped on the search engine marketing bandwagon and paid for pay-per-click search engine ads because it was easy to do. A marketer merely had to pay for an ad and receive a result, a click-through, and, potentially, a customer. The costs for pay-per-click ads for each keyword are rising, and so more marketing people are implementing organic search engine optimization on their websites. Marketers discovered that organic search engine optimization is not a quick fix; you have to write useful content to succeed in attaining high rankings and develop an effective linking campaign. A marketer has to think carefully of a strategy to develop the content that is going to achieve their organic search engine optimization goals. Similarly, blogging requires careful planning and a solid strategy if a company is going to be successful in developing content that will encourage dialogue and conversation.

To achieve a company's goals with a corporate blog, a company might sometimes have to follow a strategy that seems unrelated to their product. For example, Stonyfield Farm sells yogurt but does not write about yogurt. The Stonyfield Farm's content strategy is based upon the psychographics of the audience—they are attempting to create a dialogue with their audience about organic farming and healthy kids. The content of Stonyfield Farm's blogs is only related to yogurt. The blog content draws in an audience who can then conduct a dialogue with the bloggers.[2]

The inspiration for the Stonyfield Farm blogs was the Howard Dean campaign in the 2004 presidential election; the campaign had a big effect on the CEO of Stonyfield Farm, Gary Hirshberg. After watching the benefits of blogging to the Dean campaign in the election, Stonyfield Farm launched five blogs. Over time, Stonyfield Farm reduced its original number of blogs from five to two; to focus on the blogs that had content that was of most interest to their audience. In the Northeastern University and Backbone Media Blogging Success Study 2006, the research interviewers asked Christine Halvorson, the company's blogger, why the company cut down on the number of blogs. Christine said, "We had five different topic areas and all along we considered it one big experiment. So, we put the five out there to see what works. We got rid of one because it never seemed to find an audience. It was sort of an insider's view to the company, you know, I wrote about quirky little things we did as employees. We had a potluck today, in honor of St. Patrick's Day, or whatever it was and it didn't really seem to find an audience which is in retrospect, understandable."

When the Stonyfield Farm blogs first started in April 2004, Christine Halvorson wrote about politics, religion, and other non-business issues. Those posts received a lot of comments. The company started a blog about strong women because most yogurt eaters are women. Christine Halvorson told the interviewer that the other blogs were successful, although Christine did not write about yogurt more than three or four times in two years. She spends a lot of time reading the news about parenting because that is the content strategy of this blog. She was able to connect the content of the blog with Stonyfield Farm yogurt through the example of Stonyfield Farm being one of the first companies to put DHA into their yogurt. DHA is good for developing babies' brains. Christine would not try to pitch the product but asks questions around the subject, whether people know about the importance of their babies eating food enriched with DHA or if they or their babies eat food with DHA in it. Christine said she tries to "raise questions in people's minds" or be provocative by asking question such as, "What do you think of this issue or that?" to generate comments. Dialogue is important for the success of a blog, but only when that discussion is linked to issues your audience is interested in reading and discussing.

For many bloggers, engaging in dialogue is a good measure of success on a blog. A note of caution exists for some corporate bloggers in that they may not actually have a high level of interaction with their readers although there is a large audience. Customers prefer to keep to the sidelines and read blog content because they may be uncomfortable about revealing too much about themselves, privacy concerns, or fear of revealing competitive details to the rest of the industry on the blog. A blogger should realize that confidentiality is important to blog readers and have their contact information available to blog readers when blog readers wish to correspond privately.

HOW BLOGGING DIALOGUE IS DIFFERENT FROM EXISTING MARKETING COMMUNICATIONS TECHNIQUES

Holding a conversation is not something new to the world, but in some ways, it is new to corporate marketing. Most marketing dollars are dedicated toward advertising and direct sales related tasks. Advertising is the process of sending a message to an audience through a medium to generate a response, typically a sale. There is not a lot of room for conversation within this sales model. A generation of marketing people uses the sales model as the center of their marketing efforts. The sales model has often driven marketing efforts at companies because the available media that was available to communicate with customers did not provide an easy or effective method for conducting a dialogue with a company's audience.

Even in media that have examples of two-way conversation, such as TV, radio, and others, with call-in shows, these types of media have advertising, which is a one-way communication using the sale model to encourage people to buy.

The sales model has often consumed the lion's share of a marketing department's budget through the technique of advertising. However, advertising used extensively within corporate marketing departments really features a lack of two-way conversation other than the customer making a purchase. Many companies conduct market research and have product marketing, but the dollars spent on those disciplines are much smaller than the volume of dollars spent on advertising.

Corporate blogging, in contrast, is a method of marketing your company without advertising. With a blog, there is no need to buy an ad, and if a company so chooses, blogging allows a company to talk about their company, products, and method of doing business without the need for promotional sales language.

In fact, attempting to sell your products too much on a blog will probably turn off more customers than attract them to your blog. The sales model does not leave a lot of room for dialogue. Blogging by its two-way communication nature encourages blogger and customer engagement, both as a medium and as a way to achieve success with a blog.

Advertising seeks to persuade customers to buy, but if a customer has questions, the advertising department does not really provide a mechanism for customer interaction. Many companies have market research, customer service, or product marketing where customer feedback is part of the process of answering a company's questions about the effectiveness of its products and services. It is just that with a blogging campaign, a company can easily create content that is accessible through a mainstream medium, the web, and the power of search engines, and in turn, customers can publicly respond to a company on a blog.

There is an art to advertising, and so there is an art to conversation; everyone has the skills from their own personal experiences to conduct a conversation with their customers. Marketing people have to avoid falling into the trap of trying to sell by pitching a product in their blogging community, as they did with advertising. To become an effective blogger, a company has to develop a dialogue with its audience, and because dialogue is a two-way communications process, companies that wish to blog effectively should use the marketing model, not the sale model, to achieve their business goals.

Blogging is a method for gaining sales, traffic, and higher search engine rankings, which uses the marketing model in the same way advertising uses the sales model to achieve goals. Blogging presents the opportunity to achieve a higher return on investment of marketing dollars than advertising in terms of building sales, traffic, customers' feedback, and building better products and stronger brands, as blogs provide a mechanism for dialogue with an audience and the opportunity to use the marketing model much more effectively and easily at a tactical level.

Public relations can be defined as the process of delivering a company's message to its audience, and media relations is where corporate communicators use journalists to connect with their audience through the media. There are limits to the process of effective media relations, in that journalists are effective gatekeepers to an audience. A company did not own this channel of communication or have much of an effective mechanism for response or criticism when a reporter gets their message wrong. Blogging gives public relations the ability to have a direct conversation with customers, bypassing the journalist as go-betweens to a company's audience.

Dialogue is the medium of blogging and as such represents a greater opportunity for you to connect with your audience through two-way communication. Blogging effectively requires a new set of techniques and tactics that are really based on engagement and blogger outreach.

THE MECHANICS OF BLOGGING DIALOGUE

Blogger Engagement on Other Blogs

To conduct a dialogue with your audience, you have to engage the audience on your blog and in your blogging community. Engagement with other bloggers means conducting a conversation with readers and other bloggers. Conversations take part on blogs, in blog articles published by a blogger, and in comments by blog readers, or a post might be written in reaction to another post by another blogger, which, in turn, can be commented upon to continue a discussion between people. Blog conversations can occur between two or more bloggers writing articles that reference other blog posts.

To demonstrate how a conversation happens in the world of blogs, we will look at the example of Lauren Vargas of the blog Communicators Anonymous. She wrote a post called, "The Confusion Rainbow," which explained she had signed up for the anti-astroturfing campaign developed by a number of public relations bloggers, where public relations practitioners would pledge not to engage in astroturfing with their companies or clients. Astroturfing is the process of representing yourself as a customer or fan in the media to make it appear that your product, entertainer, or political candidate has more support than they really do. In the post, Lauren is joining an existing dialogue on Trevor Cook's website, another public relations blogger. Lauren had asked Trevor a question in the comment section of his blog, but Trevor had not answered the question at the time she had published her article. Lauren's article received several comments from a number of bloggers including Trevor Cook and myself. Lauren's blog post is an excellent example of how a blogger can use available tools to ask questions and highlight issues through dialogue. Here is the text of the post and comments from Lauren's blog:

> AUGUST 31, 2006[3]
> The Confusion Rainbow
> Sometimes the line is clearly drawn between right and wrong. Sometimes not. After giving the anti-astroturfing issue quite some thought, I added my name to the anti-astroturfing movement list[4] [link to petition on the New PR Wiki about Astroturfing], but I am still confused. What is Black, White and Grey PR? D-Ring PR[5] and Kami Huyse of Communication Overtones[6] take the reigns of drafting a quasi-creed. Seems like I was not the only one left wondering.
>
> I asked Trevor Cook[7] about "Grey PR" in response to his post,[8] but no answer:
>   Code of Conduct does not mean enforcement, which, unfortunately seems to be the solution.

I am confused about 'grey PR' ... many of us also wear marketing and advertising hats ... where do we draw the line? This is not only difficult at the practitioner level, but with senior management without professional communication experience.

How does peer pressure and corporate direction play a part in the (case-by-case) responsibility of recent scandals?

I suppose the easy answer is, you don't want to work for these individuals or organizations. Things appear to be so clear in the conduct outlines proposed, but real-life issues are hard to define. At times, the rose-colored glasses come off in hindsight based upon customer response. Does this mean I am ignorant? No, I do not believe so, but I do think this is a complex issue that cannot be solved by a creed/code. The solution is practiced steps of defined behavior and consistency—a case-by-case basis does not cut it.

09:24 AM | Permalink

TrackBack URL for this entry: http://www.typepad.com/t/trackback /5851058

Listed below are links to weblogs that reference The Confusion Rainbow:

COMMENTS

I'm sorry Lauren, I didn't mean to ignore you!

I agree that grey PR is complex and I don't think it is open to general rules. It is an area where we have to make judgments on a case by case basis. Is this a harmless, fun way of highlighting a product, service, or cause? Or does it actually mislead people in a potentially harmful way? These are not merely extraneous ethical issues. If it does risk misleading people then it risks damaging the client's reputation.

Posted by: Trevor Cook | August 31, 2006 at 12:05 PM

One thing I don't like about creeds or codes or whatever you want to call them is that they tend to tell you what NOT to do, rather than what to do. And even when they tell you what not to do, people can always find loopholes or define their case as an exception.

I agree with you that case-by-case doesn't cut it, either.

Posted by: Karen Russell | August 31, 2006 at 01:37 PM

Aren't the grey areas those that don't overtly violate the code of ethics, but which each person must make a personal values decision? I think it is a good question Lauren, and I am not sure there are any good answers.

Posted by: Kami Huyse | August 31, 2006 at 01:53 PM

Not any good answers? There are never any simple answers.

Karen, I agree with you about codes being a list of things not to do. So, it would be impossible to write a "code" with all possible scenarios of issue.

Trevor, it's ok ... I know you are a busy guy, it's just the post bothered me from the moment read.

My concern is, personal choice may not be so personal.

Posted by: Lauren Vargas | August 31, 2006 at 06:03 PM

I think the code is useful and relevant. However, like anything else the code will have more effect if more people think you are being watched.

Wearing seat belts did not really happen for most people until a law was passed requiring seat belts to be worn. Even then there were a lot of people who did not wear them. The next step was to allow police officers to make that a reason to stop people. That caught a few more people.

I think that peer pressure, corporate direction, and senior management all have a role to play in astroturfing and grey PR. When you are a single practitioner in a company and you're the sole voice in the dark, it's difficult to make the right choice, but when you are a keystroke away from a whole community who support you in keeping to a code, then that code not only seems the right thing to do, but also something you have to do.

When no one can hide and you know you will be stopped, it makes it a lot easier to make a code work.

Law in a law-abiding society exists because the members agree and maintain those laws. I think this discussion helps to establish what is agreed upon by the community, and if so those rules or practices are more likely to be observed than not.

Posted by: John Cass | August 31, 2006 at 08:21 PM

I like "no one can hide" ... agreed if there were to be a code it would need to be enforced.

Posted by: Lauren Vargas | September 01, 2006 at 05:54 AM

That is the critical point, if you cannot hide behind the corporate firewall anymore, it makes it more difficult not to adhere.

Posted by: John Cass | September 02, 2006 at 08:08 PM

As you can see from the above example, getting involved in an existing blogging conversation is very easy; all you have to do is write an article that references another blog post already engaged in a discussion. However, when you write an article, you have to add something to the conversation. Maybe a synopsis of the existing conversation, if no one in the community has already published a synopsis, or an article that develops some original idea or perspective that adds to the existing conversation.

The process of conversation between blogs involves picking another blogger's post you are interested in discussing and then writing a blog article that references the original article. Make sure you link to the other article, especially if you quote the blogger. Reference the name of the blogger, the name of the blog, and perhaps the title of the article. You will not always have to include all of this information; however, thoroughness in citing other people's work will demonstrate that you are respectful of the other people's published work.

Concentrate on the dialogue in the community when you are engaged in a discussion with your colleagues in your blogging community. Do not be tempted to introduce your own sales agenda, just because you have sales goals to meet. Writing a blog is not the same as writing an advertisement. Although the payoff with advertising copy can be immediate—someone reads an ad, is motivated to respond, and buys your product—the payoff in blogging is having the dialogue with your audience and blogging community. The dialogue demonstrates your expertise, involvement in the community, and what it is like to work with your company. People get to experience you, the company, and the value of your brand through how you write and converse with the community on a blog.

If you are successful in engaging bloggers in your community, you will gain respect and readers, and over time, you can write about the subjects that most interest you, if you have not been able to do that within the context of other bloggers' conversations. Those other bloggers who now subscribe to your blog will start to write their own blog articles in response to your articles or comment on your blog. Real success with blogging only happens once you have established a certain reputation or relationships within the community.

Within the context of optimization for higher search engine rankings, the value of blogging comes from the fact that blogging dialogue is between different blog websites. Many search engines give a higher ranking to webpages that have more links from other websites, which also have related content and keywords. Blogs provide a perfect medium for helping a company to get higher search engine rankings because employees have the ability to write unlimited content and engage other bloggers in a dialogue that might also produce links back to your blog.

Blogging conversations are between different websites, and this is the reason why blogs can be so helpful with the optimization for higher search engine rankings, but it can also bring technical difficulties because blogs are separate websites, owned by different people and organizations. As each blog has a different publishing system, when a discussion occurs between blogs, the mechanisms for tracking conversations can be rather clumsy and not very effective. As we have discussed in previous chapters, there are mechanisms for tracking conversations between blogs: trackbacks and pingbacks. Although not all blogs provide such technical services, and in the case of trackbacks, the mechanism for notifying other bloggers that an article has been cited requires a blogger to remember to copy and paste the trackback URL into his or her publishing system backend.

One important consideration about conducting blogger dialogue and fostering engagement through blogging is to make sure that you are tracking any conversations you conduct with other bloggers. It is easy to monitor the conversation when a blogger sends a trackback to your blog, but more difficult when there is no citation. That is why it is important to use other tools for tracking the conversation about community issues when a discussion occurs without any blogger notifying you. Searches on general search engines and RSS feed search engines such as Technorati.com, using the keywords that will pinpoint a conversation, will enable you to keep up with the thread of a discussion with other bloggers who contribute to a community discussion. Such discussions around individual conversations will also help you to identify new bloggers who write on the same topic.

Commenting

Commenting is an important part of engaging other bloggers, either by joining in an existing conversation or initiating a new conversation. If you have just started your blog and the number of readers is low, one way to increase your exposure in the community is by commenting on other blogs. People may not know you exist or have any sense that it is worth subscribing to your RSS feed. Commenting on other blogs gives you the opportunity to demonstrate your relevance by entering the dialogue where it is happening in the comment sections of other bloggers within your blogging community.

When commenting on a blog, it is important to remember that you are writing on someone else's website and that your comments will be screened either before or after publishing. If you are not respectful to another blogger or their ideas, do not be surprised if your comment does not appear or, even worse, if the blogger writes another blog article critiquing your comments. Do not write a comment for the sake of commenting; write a comment because there is something to discuss. Engage people in conversation; if you are interested and have something to say about your subject, it will not be difficult for you to get into a discussion with other bloggers. Build relationships with important influential bloggers in your community; to do this, you must subscribe to their RSS feeds and read their blogs on a regular basis. Even the most popular bloggers usually do not get a lot of comments on every post. Think of something useful or unique to contribute to a post by writing a comment. Over time, as you comment on a regular basis, a blogger may return the favor, subscribe to your RSS feed, and pay attention to your writing on your blog.

As you comment on other blogs in your community, you will begin to see the same names appearing on the blogs you comment on from other bloggers in your community. You will begin to understand the interrelationships between bloggers in the community. Those interrelationships are important, as each blogging community is different and its members determine the rules of the community. Reading the blogs of the bloggers who participate will give you a good sense of the expectations of how a blogger should act in your community.

Building relationships with bloggers who share your industry will help you to promote ideas within the community. If you are blogger and have developed an idea, but no one reads your blog, no one will read your great idea. However, a blogger who knows a lot of people and can carry on a discussion with a number of other bloggers at the same time will be able to have at least a part of their community pay attention to their ideas.

A big part of blogging is to get people interested in your content, and you do that by engaging in a dialogue with your community. Your comment content must also provide a valuable contribution to other bloggers and the whole blogging community.

There may be occasions when you want to talk with another reader in the comment section of a blog, who is not the owner of the blog. Typically, dialogue in comment sections is between blog owners and their readers, but there is no rule against readers having a parallel discussion within someone else's blog, especially if the discussion is related to the topic at hand. However, the acceptability of such a practice depends on whose blog you are commenting upon. If you want to write a comment that addresses another blog reader's comment, you might be able to send them an email directly by looking for the reader's email address in the signature link. If there is a lot of reader discussion on a blog, then it is probably safe to carry on a third-person discussion with another reader. If not, direct your comments to the blog author. If another reader directly addresses you or makes critical remarks about you or your company, it is perfectly acceptable to post an answer. It may be best to respond to the critic in the comment section of the blog, where the criticism takes place, rather than on your own corporate blog because it demonstrates you have an answer for the reader and responding on your own blog might highlight some comments needlessly.

There is some etiquette to responding to critical comments. A big part of responding to a critical comment is thinking about when to respond and when not to respond. You do not necessarily have anything to gain from responding to a critic, but on the other hand, if you do not respond, the assumption that maybe your critic was correct may arise in the blogging community. Challenging critics can be very dangerous, especially if you do not respond quickly, you are not sincere, or you do not follow-up on the discussion. Most bloggers discover that when a critic is answered, the response deflates a lot of the criticism, as you took the time to respond. If you just joined the discussion, a critic may tone down their criticism once it is realized the critic is not just complaining about someone in the abstract but a real person who is prepared to answer back.

As blogs are separate websites, the mechanisms for tracking conversations are still rudimentary, and coComment and other comment monitoring services have been developed to help bloggers track their conversations on other blogs. The service allows you to track your own comment on another blog and other comments written by other readers on a blog. Once registered, a blog reader can log back into the coComment website and determine if anyone has responded to one of their comments; you have to click through to the original website to follow-up with comment if necessary, but such comment tracking services have proven invaluable in solving the problem of remembering where you wrote a comment and if someone has responded.

Blogger Views on Comments from the Blogging Success Study

In the Northeastern University and Backbone Media Blogging Success Study 2006,[9] twenty corporate bloggers were asked what they thought makes a blog a success, and the participants suggested commenting between bloggers in a public blog was seen as a way to engage other bloggers and readers. Many of the bloggers interviewed in the study thought that the interaction that occurs through commenting back and forth on a blog was very important to the success of a blog.

One blogger in the study, Tim Jackson from Masi Bikes, thought that comments from fellow bloggers on his blog were important, and he believes that it is "a key ingredient to being successful with a blog personally is to network with other bloggers and to do the right thing and post comments and add links and do things like that because you build your strength and credibility within the community and you're not just another, you know, soulless marketer with a blog site." He thought it was especially important to receive comments from influential bloggers within his industry. Tim thought it was important to seek out important blogs in his industry to be able to connect with influential bloggers. Tim said he would "leave comments there to invite that back and forth dialogue." Posts about the latest products, even competitors, generate the most comments from readers on the Masi Bikes blog.

Another blogger in the blogging success study, Jim Cahill from the Emerson Process Management blog, said that commenting on other people's blogs helps with the success of his blog because, "we are trying to build a conversation about the topic at hand and the more you add to the conversation, then over time others will begin in the conversation on your blog. As more people become more blog and RSS aware, we want them to participate."

Blogger outreach was an important issue for the Emerson blog. According to another participant in the blogging success study, Deborah Franke of Emerson Process Management, "you are participating because conversations are going on, the conversations just haven't been as visible. I think people are adopting blogs to be heard and people can jump in and be part of the conversations. Word of mouth has always been around; it just hasn't been on the web. It's also about community. It's about the place. It's about the exchange that is happening. You're not pushing a message at them whether you are commenting or posting. You are simply engaging with the community."

Cathy Taylor, a journalist and blogger at Adweek, described how one of the magazine's competitors, the person who runs the blog Adrants, comments on many blogs. Cathy thought that the Adfreak team would probably comment more if her team of bloggers had the time. Cathy said that the extra comments by the person who runs the Adrants blog gives a greater boost to the Adrants blog compared with the Adfreak blog at Adweek.

Comment Moderation

Allowing comments to appear from blog readers has important implications for engagement with an audience and the perception that your blog is open for discussion. Sometimes, moderating comments on a blog before the comments appear is necessary because of comment spam. If the medium of blogging is all about dialogue, turning on comment moderation, however efficient a blogger might be as a moderator, restricts conversation and dialogue.

Many bloggers do not moderate comments. In the Northeastern University and Backbone Media Blogging Success Study, Rick Short from Indium Corporation described how he leaves commenting open, even to the extent of allowing spam comments to remain on his blog. Rick explained his reasons for being so open with comments, "You need to be believable and credible. Well, you know this is, we already are, but when you start acting in another way you sort of degrade your existing image. We're very well known as a technology company, and as a very high integrity, sophisticated market resource. If I go to market with some filtered, manipulated set of information, that takes us backwards. Our customers are smart enough to go through our comments, and see an ad for offshore gambling and realize that it's just spam, and then overlook it. Or, if some guy starts ranting and raving about how he's my competitor, he's the man, my customers are smart enough to realize."

In the blogging success study, Christine Halvorson from Stonyfield Farm explained that Stonyfield Farm does not review or fact check content before publishing. Christine thought that lack of oversight led to a very human voice for the blog. Christine writes all the content, except for the *Bovine Bugle*, which is written by one of Stonyfield Farm's organic farmers.

Christine Halvorson does moderate comments to make sure the tone of the comment never gets very "nasty," which is something she has seen on many mommy blogs (blogs run by mothers about the topic of motherhood and children), where people will criticize other people for making different choices. Also, Christine would not allow comments that are factually wrong, such as a comment stating that, "babies need to watch television in the first month of life." Christine would do some of her own fact checking or post the comment with her own comment stating that the issues raised have not been proven.

Originally, the Stonyfield Farm blog did not have a comment policy, and Christine decided to create one after receiving a lot of repetitive comments on a post. If all points of view have been stated in comments, Christine decided not to allow any additional comments. Christine moderated any comments that described repetitive viewpoints.

Nokia: Blending Traditional Media Relations with Blogger Relations

There are times when it is okay to contact bloggers outside of the context of an ongoing conversation through email or mail. Companies that believe they have a story that would be of interest to a blogger may send that story to a blogger in the hope that the blogger will respond and write about it on their blog. If the story is not relevant, the blogger may just ignore the email. There is a chance, however, that the blogger may criticize you in the blog post. If, however, you read the blog to understand the blogger and you discover you do have some things in common and relevant to the blog, you may have a good response to your pitch.

One example where pitching bloggers worked well is the Nokia Blogger Relations Outreach campaign. Nokia ran the campaign for three different cell phones. As part of the campaign, Nokia sent 50 N90 cell phones to bloggers for review. The reason for the outreach program was that rather than pass on someone else's review of the telephone through a link, Nokia wanted the bloggers to use and experience the cell phone. Nokia also provides a free return address shipping pack to the bloggers when they have finished reviewing the product. In addition, the campaign ran a companion blog.

Andy Abramson, Nokia's blogging consultant, managed the campaign for Nokia. He has a very strong technology background and runs a well-known VoIP blog.[10]

Once Nokia had sent out the telephones and people had the chance to use them, the bloggers started posting articles about the Nokia phones. Every time a blogger reviewed the N90 product, Andy thanked the blogger for the comments in a reader comment post on the reviewer's blog, answered any questions they might have, and typically linked back to them on the N90 blog, whether the review was positive or negative. He successfully combated any criticism on a blog by responding with a comment and linking back to all posts from the N90 blog. He was completely transparent; whether a blogger has a good or bad perspective on the phone or the campaign, he listened to them, considered, and responded on the N90 blog with links, even to his toughest critics.

Nokia and Andy Abramson combined traditional media relations with blogger relations to build an effective product review program for Nokia cell phones. The Nokia Blogger Relations Outreach program illustrates how a company can use a blog as a way to promote its products and engage in dialogue within blogging communities. Nokia skillfully combined both disciplines to produce successes with the product review program in terms of blogger reviews. They also effectively countered any criticism of the program by responding to any positive or negative references on the Nokia blog with links and in the comment section of any blog critiquing the Nokia blogger relations program.[11]

Living in an Information Age

Marshall McLuhan, who coined the phrase, "the medium is the message," also commented more than 30 years ago on what was happening with the growing importance of culture. He said, "Why should art and culture suddenly become very big business like big science. The reasons are tied up with the fact we are living in an information age, when you live in an information age, culture becomes big business, and the cultural explosion becomes itself culture. It knocks down all of the walls between culture and business."

The medium of blogging is all about dialogue with readers, which means to be successful in conducting a dialogue with an audience, you have to take part of the culture and use the language of your community. If you succeed in learning the art of conversation with your audience, you will build an effective blogging practice.

Endnotes

1. http://www.buzzmachine.com

2. Scout Blog, John Cass, Dr. Walter Carl (2006), *Northeastern University and Backbone Media Blogging Success Study*. Available at http://www.scoutblogging.com/success_study

3. Communicators Anonymous, Lauren Vargas (2006), *The Confusion Rainbow*. Available at http://12commanonymous.typepad.com/my_weblog/2006/08/the_confusion_r.html

4. New PR Wiki. Available at http://www.thenewpr.com/wiki/pmwiki.php?pagename=AntiAstroturfing.HomePage

5. D-Ring PR Blog, Steve Field (2006), *Astroturfing Revisited*. Available at http://field.prblogs.org/2006/08/20/astroturfing-revisited/

6. Communications Overtones Blog, Kami Huyse (2006), *Grassroots Mobilization vs. Astroturfing*. Available at http://overtonecomm.blogspot.com/2006/08/grassroots-mobilization-vs.html

7. http://trevorcook.typepad.com/weblog/2006/07/black_pr_white_.html#comment-19981229

8. Corporate Engagement Blog, Trevor Cook (2006), *Black PR, White PR*. Available at http://trevorcook.typepad.com/weblog/2006/07/black_pr_white_.html

9. Scout Blog (2006), *Northeastern University and Backbone Media Blogging Success Study*. Available at http://www.scoutblogging.com/success_study/

10. http://andyabramson.blogs.com/voipwatch/

11. Blogsurvey Blog, John Cass (2005), *Reviewing the Nokia N90 Blog V*. Available at http://blogsurvey.backbonemedia.com/archives/2005/12/reviewing_the_nokia_n90_blog_v.html

Brand Strategies for Effective Blogging

This chapter describes why it is important to use certain strategies for effective blogging, first by suggesting that building a trusted brand is the best way to build a successful company and then by describing how blogging can help a company to build more trust than traditional forms of marketing communications. An ancient Greek wrote a framework for persuasion thousands of years ago, which illustrates how a blogger can establish credibility through blogging today. Three case studies describe the strategies IBM, Microsoft, and Macromedia used for their blogging efforts and provide you with some ideas through the narrative about how a company can develop a blogging strategy that will build brand trust.

BRAND STRATEGY AIMS TO CREATE TRUST

Brand is a difficult word to define. Some people think the word can be defined by the images associated with a product or company, maybe its name or logo. Others consider that brand describes the value a company provides to its customers. Brand is at the heart of any company's operations, whether thinking about brand

137

strategy is something a company does on a regular basis or not. Marketing is not just about promoting a product; it is also about creating a product that customers will want to buy. That is where brand strategy can help a company to create a product or provide services that people will want. Brand strategy is about creating the idea that your company is to be trusted when it comes to buying a particular product or service.

Public relations strategy aims to identify the unique characteristics of a company or its products and use those unique characteristics to craft a compelling message. A message aimed at persuading an audience to listen and eventually buy products. Public relations professionals do not just look for key benefits; they look for the most unique and defining elements of a company's product and focus on that unique characteristic in all communications. This idea ties well into brand strategy, where companies attempt to define themselves as the best in a particular category of product. Volvo is the classic example. Volvo has a mission to build great cars, and to achieve that goal the company strives to make the safest automobiles possible. The brand strategy of building safe cars infuses everything the company does, from product development strategy to manufacturing. Volvo has worked to push the boundaries of safety in automobiles since the 1940s and was an early innovator in the development of seat belts. Customers trust Volvo to focus on building great cars that are safe and repay the company by buying them.[1]

Any brand strategist would want to achieve what Volvo has succeeded in doing with its brand by dedicating more than 50 years to developing great cars that are safe. Strategists want their customers to think of their company as being a reliable provider of a promised value for a particular need. They wish customers to think of their company whenever they think of that need, just as many customers think of Volvo when they think of the automobile manufacturer with safe cars.

Essentially, Volvo is thought of as the leader, or a leader, in the category of safe cars. The company's position in the industry is almost insurmountable. As long as Volvo does not detour from its brand strategy of safety, the company is safe. Although other smaller rivals might come along and establish beachheads in Volvo's markets, customers will typically give a market leader, in this case Volvo, time to catch up with smaller rivals rather than disrupt their established perception and investment in believing that a particular company is the right choice for a type of product. Once trust is established, it is hard to lose that trust if a company remains dedicated to its brand strategy.[2]

A company seeks to establish brand trust with its audience and customers, as there is a very large payoff in terms of loyalty and market share. This is why a company will seek to establish itself as the market leader in a particular product category. Leadership in building the best products if it also translates into brand trust is an excellent goal for any company to pursue. Establishing brand trust is not merely a matter of repeatedly telling your audience that you are the best at what you do, you have to prove what you say to them and establish your credibility with your audience so that the trust exists that you can perform

Blogging Dialogue: The Medium for Creating Brand Trust

Blogging can be used to conduct a dialogue between an audience and a company. Instead of the sales model, conducting a dialogue through blogging uses the marketing model to transfer information and create knowledge. Creating an open dialogue with your audience through blogging is the perfect tool for building or reinforcing a company's brand in the minds of your audience.

Influential blogs can have as large an audience as some mainstream media outlets. Blogs in some instances have as much if not more power to communicate with targeted groups of people on the web than traditional media publications. Now that Internet search engines are so widely used to find information on the web, the marketplace for information and ideas is in some respects driven by what is a top ranking on Google, MSN, or Yahoo! for a particular keyword. Blogs are perfect tools for getting higher rankings because of their design, as the number of individual blogs makes it possible to obtain links to help with higher search engine rankings when a blogger conducts an effective blogging campaign in a community. Blogs might not have the same prestige as a 100-year-old newspaper, but if you target your audience a blog may be a better way to reach them if it is important to get your message to the right people.

Dialogue can be said to be the medium of blogging in the same way that creating a powerful selling point in advertising is important for effective advertising or, for that matter, in publishing your ads in the media that your audience reads, listens, or watches. However, advertising today lacks credibility with many audiences because people are cynical about the self-promotional nature of advertising.

Most people are overwhelmed with the volume of advertising and there is little opportunity for dialogue in an ad. Advertising uses the sales model to achieve results tactically; in contrast, a company can use a blog to develop a dialogue with its audience if used correctly. Promotional public relations efforts through the media means a company had to rely upon journalists as a go-between to get out their message. A company can use the marketing model to conduct a dialogue with its audience through a blog and in their blogging community.

The marketing model more closely describes what happens on a blog than the sale model used in advertising. Customers can comment and bloggers can respond. A company can make the most impact with blogging if a company conducts a dialogue to establish credibility with an audience, which leads to people listening more and gives a company the opportunity to demonstrate credibility for their products, which in turn can create brand trust for a company.

Although it is possible to conduct a dialogue between a company and their audience, how the dialogue on a blog is developed is critical to the effectiveness of a business blogging effort. That is why the strategies a company employs to engage an audience reading a blog are important. Just as a particular advertising campaign strategy has to work with an audience to be successful, a company has to develop a blog strategy that will be successful for its audience. To succeed with blogging, a company must take steps to establish its credibility.

To establish credibility in your community, you have to be a contributor to the industry dialogue related to your products, perhaps, by discussing new ideas, having a dialogue with customers, and building a connection with customers.

THE GREEKS ESTABLISH CREDIBILITY WITH RHETORIC

Establishing a speaker's credibility is something that has been happening for thousands of years. There are existing ideas in how to persuade an audience and how to establish credibility. Not many bloggers follow ancient classical Greek philosophers in writing their blog posts or comment on other blogs. However, a review of some of the writings of Aristotle about rhetoric provides a framework that will be very familiar to today's contemporary blogger when conducting blogging.

Aristotle (384–322 BC) wrote about rhetoric in his work, *The Art of Rhetoric*. Rhetoric is the art of persuasion using language. He sought to describe how a person would conduct rhetoric. The study of rhetoric was one of the three most important areas of study in ancient Greece and deals with the art of persuasion in public spaces such as public meetings or government. He described three factors that influence the persuasive power of a speaker. They include ethos, pathos, and logos, which can be described as follows:

- *Ethos* is how the character and credibility of a speaker influence an audience to consider him to be believable.
- *Pathos* is the use of emotional appeals to alter the audience's judgment.
- *Logos* is the use of reasoning to construct an argument, either inductive, which uses examples to draw conclusions, or deductive, which uses accepted propositions or facts to come to specific conclusions.

Ancient Greek philosophy might not at first glance appear very relevant to today's marketing world. However, surprisingly, Aristotle's framework for effective persuasion works well for the world of blogging. Within the context of blogging, Aristotle's three factors of influence can be correlated to blogging. Aristotle described how speakers created credibility with their audiences through their speeches. Bloggers hope to create credibility with their audiences by demonstrating expertise, force of argument, and ideas. Aristotle's three factors can be related to blogging in the following way.

Ethos in blogging would be a blogger's level of openness, transparency, and expertise; these are all factors that help to establish the credibility of the blogger by making a blogger believable. Ethos is probably the most important factor, as it relates to how to use blogging as a marketing channel with customers. Customers are cynical about marketing messages through sales and advertising. If you are able to establish credibility as an expert through dialogue that is open and transparent, a blogger and the company he or she represents have the opportunity to present the message to their audience, who will then be much more likely to listen to the blogger and company. Most advertising is an interruption, and customers try to ignore advertising messages, rating such messages with a certain amount of disbelief. Blogging if presented by a blogger with ethos provides two benefits: first, a company's message is heard, and second, the message is seen as much more credible.

Pathos is included in many blog posts by bloggers making emotional appeals to their audience. However, within the context of blogging, we can probably stretch the meaning of pathos to include the personalization of content by bloggers. Most content on corporate websites lacks emotional appeal and connection with audiences. Bloggers will give their personal perspective, even when writing about products and company. Within blogging communities, it is culturally acceptable to include content about a blogger's life, experiences, and personal opinions. Such writing reveals the writer's human side and in the process establishes credibility because of the personal connection with the reader.

Studies conducted on the level of influence on a customer's purchasing behavior by sales people, friends, and family indicate that the closer the person is to the customer, the more influence and more likely a customer is going to listen to them. Blogs can help an audience to get to know a blogger, and by extension a company, as the blogger represents the company, which in turn, will give a blogger more influence with a customer.[3]

Logos is used by many bloggers to support reasoned arguments within a blog post. Many bloggers may not strive to be as rigorous writing a post as academics or journalists are with their work. Some bloggers do work hard to present reasoned arguments on a blog, and there has been more than one case of political leaders and media leaders falling from favor because of the rigor of bloggers uncovering and reporting all the facts in the United States. Making references to other blog posts and websites is also part of the culture of blogging. Citing another blogger adds a lot to the credibility of the blogger when linking to other people's work. Links also extend the value of blogging content because the reader clicks through and reads the original content on the other website. A reasoned argument when accompanied by citation is a big part of blogging culture.

ESTABLISHING CREDIBILITY AND BUILDING BRAND TRUST

One goal of many bloggers is to establish themselves as leaders in their blogging community. Thought leadership means to be known as a leader in your field of expertise, either through developing ideas that are unique or innovative in an industry or by being a very credible person in your industry because of your expertise. Thought leadership effectively means establishing credibility with an audience to produce extra brand equity for a blogger and by extension the blogger's company.

Thought leadership was found to be an important goal by many bloggers in the Backbone Media Corporate Blogging Survey 2005. Respondents to the survey stated that the top three priorities for bloggers starting a blog were[4] "another way to publish content and ideas," "thought leadership," and "build a community." The same respondents were asked what issues continued to be important in their current blogging strategy. Thought leadership and idea sharing were the most important factors.[5] When asked about the impact of their blog on their company, the following factors were identified as bearing the most impact from their blog: "another way to publish content and ideas," "thought leadership," and "RSS syndication."[6]

There are reputation benefits from establishing yourself as a leader in your community, but there are also some practical benefits for search engine rankings. If a blogger establishes himself or herself as a leader in the blogging community with a good following of readers, there is a good chance other bloggers will cite and link to the blogger's posts and comment on those posts. Those links may help with boosting the ranking of a blog in a search engine for any keywords listed on the blog post. Those higher rankings may translate into more traffic to the blog. A blogger, and by implication, the company that employs him or her, will gain credibility and influence in their community by writing blog posts that establish the blogger as a leader in ideas in their blogging community.

TRANSPARENCY IS IMPORTANT FOR BLOGGING CREDIBILITY

We can go back in time to borrow some ideas from ancient Greece for a framework for establishing credibility. Openness and transparency in writing and behavior are a large part of the framework for establishing credibility in blogging. Citing other ideas, bloggers and posts helps to establish the credibility of the blogger, because it demonstrates that the blogger is not only concerned with their own agenda. If an audience believes you are only promoting your own agenda, the rest of your work is seen as less credible. If your goal is to establish yourself as a leader in an industry, one of the steps to establishing leadership is through establishing credibility. Most people do not see advertising as being entirely credible. When it comes to corporate blogging, there could be the temptation to follow the same strategy of constant self-promotion and only discuss your own company in a positive light. A discussion of all the facts, including a critique of your own company, occasionally establishes credibility because an audience can trust you to tell the truth about the industry and your own products.

Transparency and your level of openness will help you to establish trust and credibility with an audience. Transparency is basically the process of disclosing all the facts that your reader would want to know when reading a blog article, for example, a blogger needs to disclose any financial connections with any people or organizations they write about. It is important to reveal those connections, because without full disclosure, readers cannot make up their own minds about the validity of a piece. For example, if it is revealed that a blogger was compensated by an individual or a company who was written about favorably in the blogger's article, the reader asks the question, "Was the piece favorable because that is what the blogger thinks or because that is what the blogger is paid to say?" Disclosure and transparency gives the reader the information they need to make up their own mind about a post and the blogger who wrote it. If you do not reveal an existing connection when writing a blog article, you risk criticism from the community if all is revealed.

According to many bloggers, openness and transparency are the reasons why blogging is by its nature more believable and credible than a traditional website.[7] An audience will appreciate a blogger who is open about themselves and their company because the blogger is not trying to hide behind the veneer of a marketing message. Many bloggers believe being free to express positive or negative ideas about their own company also adds tremendous credibility to any organization.

There are several ways for a blogger to be transparent. Many bloggers prefer a blogger leave comments open for anyone to write a comment without moderation, whereas other bloggers consider comment moderation not only acceptable but required management of a company's brand online. Transparency is not just about commenting; it is also about the content of a blog, how open a blogger is about their reasons for writing content, and his or her willingness to discuss criticism of their company. Jeremy Pepper, a public relations blogger in the Northeastern University and Backbone Media Blogging Success study, described how Robert Scoble, formerly of Microsoft, was one of the best-known examples of a corporate blogger. Robert Scoble was a Microsoft employee who runs his own blog called the Scobleizer. He left the company for personal reasons in 2006. Robert Scoble became the most famous Microsoft blogger because of how he wrote his blog. In part, the success of the Scobleizer was because Robert Scoble regularly criticized his own employer, yet still retained his job at Microsoft. Many Microsoft customers were impressed by Robert Scoble's openness and willingness to discuss delicate company issues openly. Scoble's blog and others at Microsoft helped to change negative perceptions about Microsoft left over from the court case against Microsoft in the late 1990s. Robert Scoble's example has taught a generation of corporate bloggers how to be transparent about their own company.

Taking risks by giving your opinion of a company's position may raise a few concerns with management, but the effort can establish the legitimacy of a blogger with an audience. Transparency builds trust, trust builds interest, and interest builds an audience. The audience that reads the transparent blogger may be like Robert Scoble's audience with Microsoft; their perception of the company was changed from negative to neutral.

Rather than losing control, or losing customers, just the opposite happens when transparency is used as a strategy because your audience is more likely to believe what you tell them when your blog is more transparent. That credibility presents the opportunity to present a company's message and have that message read by an audience.

A company thinking about setting up a blog needs the right person who will be credible when writing for an audience if they are ever going to have a hope of establishing themselves as a leader in the community. Credibility comes from the expertise of the person and their believability in what they state to an audience; in the case of blogging, this means a blogger has to be transparent, as transparency builds trust and credibility.

Brand strategy for effective blogging definitely includes thought leadership, but to really succeed in blogging, sometimes it takes the realization that a blogger has to cite other bloggers and include other people's ideas on their own website. In fact, this is an element of transparency for companies that is important and will help to establish the credibility of a blogger and their company.

CUSTOMER FEEDBACK BUILDS THE MOST BRAND EQUITY

A company should develop a strategy to become effective at conducting blogging. It will probably take some time for you to realize what is possible with blogging. That is all right, as the medium is so different from advertising or public relations that it just makes sense that each company will have to figure out a strategy that works for them and their audience.

Although no comprehensive studies have been conducted to compare the benefits gained from corporate blogging in each company and most evidence is anecdotal on the part of the bloggers themselves or their rankings on search engines, when you read the stories of how customers react to a company based on its actions in a blog it just makes sense that the best strategy to follow for a company is one of leadership through dialogue. Leadership establishes a blogger and company with credibility, which in turn builds trust and brand equity for a company. As the following examples will demonstrate, what is even more important than company ideas is the willingness of a company to listen to their customers by taking customer feedback on existing products or in developing new products.

This customer feedback model was discovered through two surveys conducted in 2004 and 2005, the first Corporate Blogging Survey 2004 conducted on the PR Communications blog and the second Corporate Blogging Survey run by Backbone Media in 2005. Three companies who were corporate blogging stood out from these surveys: IBM, Microsoft, and Macromedia (Adobe has since merged with Macromedia). The three examples demonstrate that the most benefits come to those who concentrate on their customer's ideas. During that 2004 survey, the idea was developed that blogger's could use their blogs to conduct product development. The second survey in 2005 had a "hypothesis that blogs bring most value to companies in the form of product development." The study used case studies from IBM, Microsoft, and Macromedia to describe the strategy each company uses in creating content and interacting with customers. The 2005 study report described the benefits gained from each strategy. The study concluded that listening to your customer and encouraging customer feedback provides a company with the most opportunity for benefits from blogging.

RESULTS FROM THE BACKBONE MEDIA CORPORATE BLOGGING SURVEY 2005

The survey determined that there were a number of benefits to be derived from starting a corporate blog, including quick publishing, thought leadership, building community, sales, and online public relations. The way to build a successful blog was to develop a blogging content strategy, as a company's blog strategy will determine the level of overall success for a blog.

Although the survey results were helpful, the case study interviews with IBM, Microsoft, and Macromedia gave the most insight into what results a company might expect from the content strategy they follow with their blog.

IBM Case Study

Product development and customer service—The study's authors worked with Bill Higgins, a Systems Engineer and blogger at IBM, to develop the case study.

The goal was to understand if his blog had helped with any product development, customer service issues, and brand issues.[8]

At the time of the survey in 2005, IBM had not experienced very much feedback on their public blogs. In fact, there were no examples of an IBM blog post where the company had communicated with a customer to improve a product or solve a customer service issue. None of IBM's key company executives or product managers wrote a blog at the time of the study. Bill Higgins explained that, "at IBM the people who ultimately make product decisions are:

1. Group and brand executives and staff (e.g., Software Group SVP, Software Group Strategy)
2. Product management (a.k.a. marketing)
3. Development leaders
4. Customer service organizations

Most of the existing IBM bloggers on developerWorks are people who use IBM products; they are in services, rather than people who define product scope."

IBM was not getting very much feedback on product development and customer services issues from its public blogging efforts. This contrasts with Microsoft and Macromedia's blogs, where customer feedback was received on company blogs. At that time, one reason might be that the people who build the products did not blog at IBM. There may have been other factors in action; for example, IBM's existing channels of communication with its existing customers may have been preferable to a blog for instance.

However, Bill Higgins thought that, overall, his blog has been successful in terms of thought leadership, building a community, and getting information out to his audience quickly.

Conclusions—IBM has sales of more than $90 billion a year; Microsoft has sales of more than $50 billion a year; Macromedia, now part of Adobe, is considerably smaller. IBM just does not have the same visibility with its blogs that other companies such as Microsoft, SUN Microsystems, and Macromedia had in 2005 in terms of one-on-one communications and feedback from customers. It may be that IBM's markets did not include as many people blogging online as other companies do or that its markets are more heavily business-to-business centered such as Rational Software's testing software.

Bill Higgins at IBM suggested the relative size of IBM's markets and audience meant that the size of the audiences in the markets IBM concentrates on where blogging was taking place was smaller than the markets targeted by the blogs at companies such as Microsoft and Macromedia (Adobe). If a person from IBM is blogging, he or she is not revealing too much information and not asking for feedback. Rather, it is the type of content and who is writing on IBM blogs in 2005 that reduced the opportunities for potential benefits from IBM's blogging efforts.

Microsoft Case Study

George Pulikkathara, Marketing Manager and founder of MSDN Webcasts at Microsoft, is the blogger for MSDN webcasts and described how Microsoft's blogging efforts helped product development and service issues. He provided some examples of how a post or communication on a Microsoft blog has helped Microsoft improve their product and deal with a customer service issue.

The spelling mistake incident—Ken Dyck, a customer of Microsoft, while working in the Microsoft Windows operating system noticed a spelling mistake in the Windows update function. He tried to inform Microsoft of the spelling mistake. He used the Microsoft support site to report the error.[9] To report the spelling error, he would have had to call product support services and register an incident, at a cost of $250. Instead, Ken decided to blog about the bug on his blog[10] in the hope that a Microsoft[11,12] employee would read his blog entry.[13]

George explained that even if someone did register an incident with Microsoft, the staff in the support department does not have responsibility for enacting a change, meaning that when an incident is passed on through existing channels, because of the different levels of people it takes to have an incident reported, any error reported may not make the list of priorities for the development team. Blogging provided a better mechanism for customers to contact Microsoft who build the product to make a change to their software.

If Microsoft does not monitor such issues on blogs and forums, they lose both the customer and maybe leave some negative public relations on the web. Several bloggers at Microsoft are monitoring the web for such customer posts. There was discussion at Microsoft at the time of the survey to automate the process for monitoring customer frustrations and issues expressed on the web by customers outside the Microsoft customer support system. Ideas included appointing a person who would be responsible for monitoring within each product group.

For Microsoft, the issues around customer service and how blogging is helping the company to respond to customers quickly have a lot to do with Microsoft's approach to business in the last few years. George explained that Microsoft was very "goal focused" to get products out by certain dates. Sometimes, responding to an immediate customer issue takes product teams away from those goals. However, people at Microsoft recognized that they are in business to serve their customers, and they saw that blogs would help to connect their product teams to customers directly. George described that blogs have helped Microsoft focus on the customer.

Downloading MSDN webcasts for offline viewing—At one time, users could only stream webcasts when using the Microsoft software LiveMeeting 2003; they could not download the file for later use. One customer, Ronny Ong, wanted to download webcasts[14] provided by MSDN so that he could review the webcasts on his desktop or laptop at a more convenient time. There was no technical way to download the webcasts, so Ronny wrote a VBscript to allow the download. He posted how to download the webcasts on the web where lots of customers downloaded the program. Stuart Gunter and Janco Wolmarans, two other programmers, had a similar issue to Ronny Ong with downloading webcasts. Stuart and Janco were based in South Africa, where it was costly to stream a video over the Internet. The two programmers created a simpler script and set up a website at http://www.webcasty.com/. George Pulikkathara watched the work the three programmers produced by reading their blogs. He decided to meet with the LiveMeeting product team in Washington State to tell them about the situation. The LiveMeeting team had not been aware that anyone would want to download the webcasts and had previously decided not to address the issue of downloading, as the file size of the product was so large. The LiveMeeting team researched a better downloading solution for the next release of LiveMeeting after they heard about the work conducted by Ronny, Stuart, and Janco.

Do not forget about VB5—S. "Soma" Somasegar, the corporate vice president for the Microsoft Developer Division, travels around the country meeting customers and has promoted the use of blogs within his division. Through blog posts and meetings with user groups called PASS (Professional Association of SQL users), Somasegar learned that many customers wanted to continue to get support for the VB5 through customer blogs. Microsoft was going to discontinue its support of Visual Basic 5, as the company wanted to focus on VB6 support. Microsoft determined that support for VB5 would cost more than the support for VB6. When told about the difference in cost for VB5 support on Microsoft blogs, the customers were happy to pay, as they then had the option to ask for VB5 support.

Transparency in Microsoft—All three Microsoft cases are examples of how blogging helped Microsoft communicate with their customers through blogs. With a company as large as Microsoft with more than 50,000 employees, customers do not know whom to contact. Employees at Microsoft are not bad people; they just do not always understand customer needs. Blogs are helping Microsoft to listen and become more customer focused.

Under the direction of Microsoft bloggers like Soma Somasegar, there is a new drive to have more transparency in the company. Microsoft is realizing that to remain competitive, the company has to rely on the expertise and skills of its employees; by empowering each Microsoft employee, each employee effectively becomes a real functioning brand manager for Microsoft whose role is to help the customer no matter what role they play in the company. Sometimes, that transparency means that customers and even employees will criticize Microsoft, but the new management thinking is that such criticism is good, as Microsoft then has the opportunity to react and respond. With blogs, communicating that response quickly and effectively has become a lot easier in the last few years. The payoff for Microsoft's blogging efforts is that customers are changing their perceptions of the company and trusting the company more.

Macromedia Case Study

Macromedia was a successful software technology company with many well-known products; Flash and ColdFusion are examples. Mike Chambers,[15] the product manager for Flash and a blogger, described Macromedia's experiences with blogging. The company has since merged with Adobe.

Product development—Initially, blogs were started at Macromedia to build a better community and get information out to customers more quickly than existing channels. Over time, Macromedia discovered that blogs could be used for the development of their products. This shift in thinking about how blogs could be used for product development was gradual and required a substantial change in thinking about the Macromedia product development process. Formerly, a product would not be announced until 2 to 3 weeks before a release. The company did not want to leak information about a new product to competitors.

Customer community has always been a strong element with the Macromedia brand. The merger between Macromedia and Allaire Corporation in 2001 brought the strong ColdFusion customer and reseller community of Allaire to Macromedia. The company then maintained its customer communities through forums and local user groups. Product feedback was received by talking with customers directly, at user groups, and by visiting specific customers. Blogs were launched in 2002.

Macromedia initially used blogs to get information out to customers quickly. The company wanted to be more open and transparent with their developers. Customers started to give software feature suggestions on blogs spontaneously, and as time passed, Macromedia began to use blogs to discover what new features customers wanted in new versions of products. The Macromedia employees would discuss on their blogs what needed to be done to implement any customer suggestions and report back to customers if they were able to implement any customer suggestions. Macromedia eventually began to understand that the tool of blogging would help their company to get more information from their customers on product development through an open dialogue.

Mike Chambers explained that before blogs, the software development process "was a very closed process, the blogs made it a more open and transparent process." Chambers said, "customers use [our products] more than we do, they know them better than we do, we wanted to tap into that."

Example of "why a simple fix is not always so simple"—Macromedia was working on an update to its Flash product code-named Ellipsis and had asked for feedback from their customers. One customer asked if a fix could be implemented in the next release. When searching for script in the application's scripting editor, a panel window is opened, the "find panel." However, if the panel window remains open, it is not possible to change or edit any text in the scripting editor.

In the development process of Ellipsis, the team determined they would focus on those issues that affected a lot of users and would not risk or touch a lot of the code in the software. Reviewing the "find panel" issue, the Macromedia team had thought that the issue would be easy to fix; however, they realized the following:

1. The problem was not easy to fix.
2. The fix would have been risky, and it would have affected other parts of the application.
3. The fix would cause new usability issues.

Mike Chambers made the following post on his blog about the issue:[16]

> The head of engineering asked an engineer to look into the issue. It looked like it would be an easy fix, and an easy win for users (which is a win for us).
>
> So, the first item that came up was actually usability related. There were concerns that it would be confusing to users if the Find Panel was open but the ActionScript editor had been closed. What should the panel do if the user clicks find then? What if they keep the panel open, but open a new frame of ActionScript? We looked at how other programs handled this (Visual Studio, EditPlus and Notepad), and determined that this would not affect many users, and that the other programs have similar issues.
>
> So, the engineer then looked into how easy and risky it would be from a code standpoint to make the change. It turned out, that in order to make it non-modal, we couldn't just flip a Flag, but rather had to call a new method. Okay, a little more risky, but not that big of a deal.
>
> After further investigation, we discovered that we would actually have to change the window type, which in essence would mean we would have to reprogram the Window. Again, not yet that risky, but now we are getting into more significant changes.
>
> Finally, and the straw that broke the camel's back, we found out that we would have to completely rewrite how the Find panel actually finds data. This is because currently, when you open the Find Panel, it takes a snapshot of the text in ActionScript editor (since the user won't be able to change it). I am not sure why it is done like this, but do know that it is faster than dynamically loading the text each time and keeping the cursor position each time.
>
> Changing how the Find Panel searches text is a big code change and risky. Furthermore, making the change could now lead to significant performance decreases when searching large amounts of text. These factors combined to make the change too risky for Ellipsis, and we deferred it to the next version of Flash (at which time we are basically re-writing all panel and window code).

> Anyways, I just wanted to share this with the list to give some context to why something that may seem simple, doesn't get fixed for Ellipsis. This was an issue that I thought would be very simple for us to fix, but it turned out to be a lot more complicated and risky than I expected.

Here was an example of how Mike Chambers' blog was used to answer a customer's specific request for a fix to the Macromedia application, but because of the work that would be required to fix the issue, the whole project would have taken longer to complete and costs would have risen for customers. With this post, Mike Chambers demonstrated that Macromedia listened to its customers and his team involves the customer in the process of fixing problems. Customers commented on the blog post, stating that they appreciated the understanding they had gained from Macromedia development process and now understood the decision Macromedia made for the development of the product.

When customers were involved in the development of software at Macromedia, it changed their perception of the customer, from "them and us" to "customers and Macromedia employees being part of a team."

Conclusions—Over time, working with blogs, Macromedia slowly realized there were big benefits and manageable risks to opening up the process of product development to their customer community. Internal blogs helped to evangelize the idea of using blogs to encourage feedback and suggestions from customers in an open way. Slowly, through trial and error, Macromedia determined how best to make the process work. The whole process of using blogs to communicate with customers for the development of new products has been a huge success. That success has come in terms of better products, more committed customers, more sales, and positive public relations results.

One of the biggest benefits to Macromedia has come from the increased number of search engine higher rankings. The blog posts of 50 to 60 Macromedia blogs has meant the company has more content on the web, and because the posts are valuable to Macromedia customers, the company's blogs are receiving links from customers. Chambers explained, "weblogs will appear first [on search engines], even before our site, because of conversations, we were getting linked."

One of the factors determining the ranking of a webpage in a search engine is the number of sites linking to a webpage. Through online conversations and discussion, Macromedia's blogs received a lot of links, which in turn gave Macromedia higher rankings and produced more traffic from search engines.

Macromedia's blog strategy was not to develop a lot of blogs, rather, the thinking was that it was more worthwhile to develop a few blogs with quality content rather than develop a lot of blogs with hardly any content. Macromedia had about 50 to 60 blogs. More people could have written a blog at the company; however, Macromedia's blog strategy was only to add content that will bring value to their customers. Macromedia encouraged bloggers to give enough personal information so that customers have a sense of the Macromedia employee and to focus content on product. The blogging strategy was a great success for Macromedia, helping to build a stronger brand with customers by using the techniques of openness and transparency with blogs.

CHOOSING A BLOGGING BRAND STRATEGY

Thought leadership and customer feedback are the best brand strategies to follow for the most benefits from corporate blogging. Evidence for this idea comes from contrasting the three technology company case studies from the 2005 study: IBM, Microsoft, and Macromedia. All three companies were early corporate blog adopters, with blogs dating back to the beginning of the twenty-first century. These companies had some of the most experience with blogging in the industry. Yet there were differences in how each company approached blogging and their content strategies, and those differences produced different benefits and results for each of the companies.

IBM focused public blog content on industry discussion leadership. No product builders or executives wrote a public blog at the time of the survey. IBM did not have a product development blogging content strategy or ask for feedback from customers through blogs.

Microsoft is using blogs in particular departments to combat bureaucracy within the company's existing channels of customer service. Blogs are helping Microsoft to redefine its approach to dealing with customers. Blogs have helped product builders at Microsoft become closer to the customer and listen to feedback.

Macromedia has since merged with Adobe Corporation; however, by 2005, blogs had already initiated a major change in culture at Macromedia. The company's software development processes had been changed since the company started blogging in 2002. When blogging first started at Macromedia, the goal was to send out information quickly to customers. As time progressed, and Macromedia blogger became more comfortable with the medium, the bloggers asked for product ideas from their customers earlier in the software development process. The software development process at Macromedia had once been very closed; because of the introduction of blogs, the software development process at Macromedia became more open and transparent.

The developers and management at Macromedia realized that by letting their customers get involved in the development of their products at an early stage, customers would be more committed to purchasing a product and referring products on their own blogs. Macromedia risked revealing too much information to competitors, but the rewards have proven to be too great to worry about such issues on a public blog. Results were more links to Macromedia websites from customer blogs, higher search engine rankings, and a committed group of customers willing to buy and evangelize Macromedia products.

Microsoft and Macromedia were crossing a cultural divide, from a closed system in product development to one of openness and transparency. Macromedia has already crossed that cultural chasm. Both Microsoft and Macromedia were receiving tremendous benefits from customer feedback for product development and direct traffic and web links for marketing promotion. Using blogs to take customer feedback means that Microsoft and Macromedia customers believed the companies built or changed products based on customer suggestion. If you helped build a product as a customer, you are much more likely to buy the product and tell your peers about the product. Here lies the online public relations opportunity for corporate bloggers. The best ways to market a product are through customer referrals and good public relations. Building a dialogue with a community of online customer bloggers and readers will increase the likelihood of customer comments being generated on your audience's blogs about your company, as customers will be discussing their ideas about your products. That conversation produces direct traffic and links back to a company blog and site, resulting in higher search engine rankings, more traffic, greater brand equity, and customer evangelists.

Endnotes

1. F. Joseph LePla, Susan Davis, and Lynn M. Parker (2002), *Integrated Branding*. Kogan Page Limited, London, p. 70.

2. Geoffrey A. Moore (1995), *Inside the Tornado*. HarperBusiness, New York.

3. PR Communications Blog, John Cass (2003), *Advocacy, Can Fuel Your Demand*. Available at http://pr.typepad.com/pr_communications/2003/12/advocacy_can_fu.html

4. Backbone Media Corporate Blogging Survey (2005), *Question Three*. Available at http://www.backbonemedia.com/blogsurvey/12-priorities-corporate-blog.htm

5. Backbone Media Corporate Blogging Survey (2005), *Question Six*. Available at http://www.backbonemedia.com/blogsurvey/16-factors-blogging-strategy.htm

6. Backbone Media Corporate Blogging Survey (2005), *Question Eight*. Available at http://www.backbonemedia.com/blogsurvey/22-impactcorporateblog.htm

7. Scout Blog (2006), *Northeastern University and Backbone Media Blogging Success Study*. Available at http://www.scoutblogging.com/success_study

8. http://www-03.ibm.com/developerworks/blogs/page/BillHiggins/

9. http://support.microsoft.com/

10. Ken's Meme Deflector, Ken Dyck (2005), *Ken's Bug Reporting System*. http://www.kendyck.com/2005/05/kens-bug-reporting-system.php

11. http://bobwyman.pubsub.com/main/2005/05/getting_attenti.html

12. http://blogs.msdn.com/msdnwebcasts/default.aspx

13. http://bobwyman.pubsub.com/main/2005/05/getting_attenti.html

14. http://msdn.microsoft.com/events

15. http://weblogs.macromedia.com/mesh

16. http://weblogs.macromedia.com/flashteam/archives/2004/09/why_a_simple_fi.cfm

CHAPTER 9

Blogosphere Communities: Lessons from the Automobile Blogging Community

The term *blogosphere* does not only describe one large community of tens of millions of blogs but rather a number of smaller communities each with their own bloggers, social norms, and readership. What works for one community in terms of how you conduct blogging may not necessarily work for another community. To understand a community, a corporate blogger should assess its scope. This chapter provides an assessment of one blogging community, the automobile blogging community; to understand the process of how to assess a blogging community and how a company might use the assessment of the automobile blogging community to develop a corporate blogging strategy for their own company.

This chapter will focus on the lessons companies can learn from one blogging community and how those lessons translate to other industries. The list of automobile blogs was developed in October and November of 2006 to provide enough information for the development of an assessment and strategy recommendations. The assessment of the automobile blogging community is not meant to be comprehensive or up-to-date but rather a demonstration of the steps a company has to complete to develop their own corporate blogging strategy by assessing their own industry's community

The list of automobile blogs will change, as will their characteristics over time. The list is published as a demonstration of the type of research that has to be conducted by a company to make an assessment of their industry's blogging community.

RESEARCH PROCESS FOR THE AUTOMOBILE BLOG ASSESSMENT

The automobile blogging community was researched using the assessment process found in Chapter 2. When conducting an assessment of your community, it is important for each blog's content strategy, blogger background, and the style of writing to be understood and documented. The assessment of individual blogs in a community will help with developing a corporate blogging strategy, from the basic question "Should my company blog?" to "How should my company interact with a community?" There are a series of factors you should record for your assessment of each blog. As part of the automobile blog assessment the following information was researched for each automobile blog in the community:

Name of the blog
URL of the blog
Name of the blogger
Blog started
System used by the blogger
Interaction elements allowed
Commenting turned on
Trackbacks allowed
Social networking tools enabled
Comment tracking tools used by the blogger
Blogger background
    Does the blogger answer comments?
    Does the blogger interact with other bloggers in the community?
Writing style
Volume of comments received by the blogger
Technorati.com ranking

A description of each factor can be found in Chapter 2 of this book.

OVERVIEW OF THE AUTOMOBILE BLOGGING ASSESSMENT

The list of automobile blogs gives us an opportunity to build an overall understanding of the automobile blogging community. That is what you should do in assessing a blogging community—build a good understanding of your industry's blogging community by reviewing as many of the blogs in the community as possible. Conducting an assessment will help a company to understand who is active in the industry, some of the social mores within the industry, and the leading bloggers.

In this chapter, you will find a list of 42 automobile blogs, with a brief assessment of each blog. The blog assessment is not meant to be a comprehensive review of each blog; rather, the assessment aims to provide an example of how you would conduct a community review for a company to be able to develop a corporate blogging strategy.

We also provide a timeline of when each automobile blog was launched and, lastly, a list of blogs in the order of each blog's Technorati ranking. The blogs reviewed range from one blog in the top 100 blogs as considered by Technorati's list of top blogs to blogs that are not very highly ranked. There are many measures of blogging, not just a blog's Technorati ranking; some important blogs may not even be ranked by Technorati. Therefore, it is important to review and assess all of the blogs in your community, whatever the popular industry ranking's state.

Understanding the Types of Blogs in the Industry

The automobile blogging community dates back to 2001, with the blogs The Truth about Cars, Minifile, Ride, and Autoguy. Automobile blogs are divided between blogging publishing companies, such as Gawker Media and Weblogs Inc, and car enthusiasts. Blog publishing companies are conglomerates of a number of different types of blogs, run by professional bloggers. The business model for these sites is to attract a large audience and sell advertising on the basis of the audience. Not quite journalists, these types of bloggers are definitely no longer consumers. Autoblog[1] from the Weblogs, Inc. media group is a great example of this type of blog. What is interesting about this type of professional blogger is that public relations can probably be a very effective way to approach such bloggers. The constant need for stories to maintain the volume and quality of posts means that traditional public relations approaches work well with these professional bloggers.

Car enthusiasts are people who love cars or a particular brand of car and write a blog about the subject. Car enthusiasts have a day job besides his or her blog. Typically, the auto enthusiasts favor one model or manufacturer. The blog Cars! Cars! Cars![2,3] is definitely a consumer blogger, although the blog is running a few Google Adwords ads on the site.

The blog Jalopnik is notable for the number of humorous and entertaining posts related to the automobile industry.

Automobile Manufacturer Blogs

There are not very many automobile vendor blogs, which makes sense, as there are only a small number of companies in the industry. The General Motors FastLane blog has succeeded in generating a lot of publicity and links on the web for the company. But it is too early to tell if the blog has played a significant role in helping the company to get out of its sales doldrums. The insight provided by customers might actually help future General Motor car designs and upgrades, especially as poor sales at General Motors has been a structural issue in that the company was selling the wrong type of cars and trucks during a period of high gas prices.[4] Ford is trying a new tactic based on complete openness with its boldnewmoves.com website.

Both the General Motors FastLane blog and Ford's efforts are an attempt to engage customers through the use of blogs. General Motors has not succeeded in engaging every single customer that asks a question on the blog. Although the reason for the lack of engagement on the General Motors blog may be because of a lack of resources, the response demonstrates General Motors has further to go in understanding the brand perception benefits of communicating directly with customers through a blog.

Overview of Topics in Industry

In the automobile blogging community, the range of topics varied. However, certain patterns of stories were recognized—three themes rise to the top as the biggest discussion topics in the industry.

- A review of a car from the perspective of its drivability, style, power, and value.
- The current state of the green car industry, what companies are doing or not doing to help reduce energy consumption and pollution emissions.
- How badly General Motors and Ford are running their affairs in terms of product development, marketing, and each company's falling market share and profitability.

The constant drone of criticism in blogs aimed at the big American automobile manufacturers has some basis because the sales figures for Ford and General Motors have not been very good in recent years. In fact, both large American manufacturers have lost market share. General Motors launched the General Motors FastLane blog in an effort to engage car customers directly.

Assessment of Automobile Blogging Community Interaction

Critical to the success of any blog is how the authors interact with the rest of the community. Commenting, trackbacks, and linking to other blogs were all actions that were regularly conducted by members of the automobile blogging community. Some of the most highly ranked Technorati auto blogs conducted all of these activities.

Professional bloggers and non-professional bloggers were the bloggers who were most willing to engage in conversation through comments on a blog and link to other blog posts within a blog in the community. Many of the articles in these blogs cited traditional media articles as sources for stories, whereas the blogs run by traditional media companies tended not to cite other blogs or link to other bloggers. Those companies generated their own stories and reviews.

Probably, the blog with most comments was the General Motors FastLane blog, run by the automobile manufacturer General Motors; early in the launch of the General Motors FastLane blog, General Motors received more than 150 comments on a post.

Technorati Rankings

The blogs in the automobile blogging community with the highest Technorati ranking are run by professional bloggers or bloggers whose full-time job is writing a blog. Autoblog and Jalopik have the top Technorati rankings. Most of the highest Technorati-ranked automobile blogs are multiple-author blogs.

The top Technorati-ranked media blogs included the Detroit Press and Edmunds.com. Media-related blogs make up about one fourth of the automobile blogs that are highly ranked in Technorati. Traditional media blogs do appear in the top 30 blogs; typically, those blogs are multiple-author blogs, although the blogs at Edmunds.com authored by some of the company's auto writers do appear in the top 30 blogs by Technorati rankings.

Non-professional writer blogs or ordinary people do not appear very much in the top 30 Technorati-ranked automobile blogs. The Auto Prophet, Cars! Cars! Cars!, MyFordDreams, Carpundit, and Autoguy are all under this type of blog.

ASSESSMENT AND STRATEGY RECOMMENDATIONS

Compared with some blogging communities, it does not appear that the automobile blogging community is all that large. For example, the public relations blogging community had more than 500 members in 2006; although the volume of comments in community blogs is certainly very active. I suspect that many existing automobile forums developed in the 1990s capture a lot of the discussion in the community, as the industry is so small, with so few blogs dedicated to automobiles. The community does have some significant highly ranked Technorati blogs; therefore, this is a large audience for this type of blog. There is definitely an opportunity for any company to create a successful automobile blog and become an important leader in the industry.

If you were to start blogging in the automobile blogging community, you would need multiple authors with some expertise in the automobile industry to keep up with the frequency of posts. As a lot of news happens in the automobile industry, any blogger who wants to be successful, unless they focus on a particular aspect of the automobile industry, will need to write frequently to cover all that happens in the industry. Many of the automobile blogs have multiple authors. To keep up with the pace of the industry, building a multiple-author blog is one strategy that would enable a blog to keep up with the volume of writing necessary to build a significant blog in the community.

Articles on car reviews, energy-efficient cars and trucks, and issues related to Ford and General Motors are subjects regularly discussed in the automobile blogging community. Discussing the state of the industry in the United States with the larger manufacturers is a current top-of-mind topic for many automobile bloggers. Any blog that can bring perspective, opinion, and some different points of view will definitely be cited by other blogs in the industry. More analysis of European and Asian automobile manufacturers might be one way to provide some unique insight into how European and Asian manufacturers are affecting the U.S. automobile market. Building relationships with people or bloggers with expertise in European and Asian car manufacturers to gain further insight would be one way to develop some interesting scoops.

If you conduct your own reviews by driving the cars, this would add tremendous credibility to a new blog for the automobile community. There is a definite opportunity in the automobile industry for more blogs run by someone who is an expert on how to handle cars and give opinions on the drivability of automobiles. In fact, many of the blog posts in the automobile blogging community that review cars appear to be just links to original traditional media publication reviews. A real opportunity in the automobile blogging community exists for good independent reviews of cars. You would have to have contacts with automobile manufacturers to be able to drive their automobiles early; or conduct more comprehensive reviews once the automobiles have arrived in the dealer's lot.

Communicating with blog readers is definitely a feature of the automobile blogging community. Any blogger should be prepared to engage the readership on their blog by answering comments. Citing and referencing other automobile blogs in your blog would also help to connect with other bloggers in the automobile community. As so many traditional media companies are cited by blogs in the industry, anything you can do to build relationships with traditional media journalists would help a new blog.

LESSONS LEARNED FROM THE AUTOMOBILE BLOGGING COMMUNITY

Building a justification for starting a corporate blog in the automobile industry would be very easy—there is a large audience with just a small community of blogs as of the end of 2006. Traffic, links, and success would only be a matter of time and effort on the part of company. However, one writer would probably not be enough; having a group of writers makes a lot of sense for this industry. Critical in building a successful blog will be having bloggers who also conduct blogger outreach; such outreach will take more time but will help a blog to get more traffic and links. If a company was in the automobile industry, it would also have to build a writing strategy that included the three foremost topics in the industry: reviews of cars, fuel efficiency, and the debate about American car manufacturers. A company would have to consider how its products fit into these three topics. While you could just state your opinion on the issues. But if a company's products related directly to one of the topics, it would provide more opportunities to put a company's products in the context of the overall industry discussion.

When conducting your own audit of your industry, reading the blogs in the industry is a big task, but one that is very worthwhile. You will learn what the most important topics in your blogging community are, how other blogs handle the resources needed to blog in your community, and if there is a sufficient audience for another blog. Use the audit model to build a justification and help you develop a strategy if you decide to move forward with a blog.

In addition to using currently available tools to measure the standing of different blogs in your community, it is important to keep abreast of the development of blogging measuring services when you conduct an assessment of your community.

Lastly, here is the overview of the automobile blogging community. First, the list of automobile industry blogs, then the timeline of the blogs, and lastly, the automobile blogs listed in order of highest ranking on Technorati.

Automobile Industry Blogs

Name of the blog: Autos Blog for the *Detroit News*
URL of the blog: http://info.detnews.com/autosblog/index.cfm
Name of the blogger: Daniel Howes, Scott Burgess, Mark Truby, David Shepardson, Christine Tierney, David Phillips, Brett Clanton, Bryce Hoffman, and Josee Valcourt
System used by the blogger: Custom?
Interaction elements allowed: Limited to comments
Commenting turned on: Yes
Trackbacks allowed: No
Social networking tools enabled: None
Comment tracking tools used by the blogger? Uses the *Detroit News* forum software
Blogger background: All of the bloggers are journalists on the staff of the *Detroit News*.
Does the blogger answer comments? A quick scan through several posts reveals that each journalist blogger does not appear to answer comments on the blog.
Does the blogger interact with other bloggers in the community? No, the bloggers do not interact with the rest of the community in their blog posts. From this review, it appears the blog is more of an editorial writing post than a blog.
Writing style: Thoughtful articles on the state of the industry
Volume of comments received by the blogger: Quite high, probably due to the forum
Technorati.com ranking: 8,532 (however, these links represent links to the whole paper)

Name of the blog: The Truth about Cars
URL of the blog: http://www.thetruthaboutcars.com/
Name of the blogger: Robert Farago, Jonny Lieberman, Sajeev Mehta, Frank Williams, and Jay Shoemaker
Blog started: November 2001
System used by the blogger: WordPress 2.0.4
Interaction elements allowed: Yes. Also, a reader can sign up for comment email notification and register for the blog's commenting system.
Commenting turned on: Yes
Trackbacks allowed: No
Social networking tools enabled: No
Comment tracking tools used by the blogger? Yes
Blogger background: Multiple-author blog, a combination of freelance journalists and enthusiasts

Does the blogger answer comments? Yes
Does the blogger interact with other bloggers in the community? Not that I can judge from looking back over a month of posts.
Writing style:
Volume of comments received by the blogger. High, the blog is very active
Technorati.com ranking: 9,906

Name of the blog: MotoringFile
URL of the blog: http://motoringfile.com/
Name of the blogger: Gabriel Bridger is the managing editor, and the blog is also written by a staff of writers.
Blog started: October 2002
System used by the blogger: WordPress
Interaction elements allowed:
Commenting turned on: Yes
Trackbacks allowed: No
Social networking tools enabled: No
Comment tracking tools used by the blogger? D/N
Blogger background. MotoringFile is a blog dedicated to the MINI. Started by Gabriel Bridger, the site has grown to support advertising and a number of contributors.
Does the blogger answer comments? Yes
Does the blogger interact with other bloggers in the community? Yes
Writing style: News articles, filler pieces, and scopes on MINIs
Volume of comments received by the blogger: Medium to high
Technorati.com ranking: Not ranked

Name of the blog: Ride
URL of the blog: http://www.angelfire.com/retro/browsers/
Name of the blogger: James G. Halmayer
Blog started: September 2002
System used by the blogger: Blogger
Interaction elements allowed:
Commenting turned on: Yes
Trackbacks allowed: No
Social networking tools enabled: No
Comment tracking tools used by the blogger? D/N
Blogger background: Personal blogger
Does the blogger answer comments? Yes
Does the blogger interact with other bloggers in the community? Yes
Writing style: Filler pieces, video
Volume of comments received by the blogger: Low
Technorati.com ranking: 130,332

Name of the blog: Just-Auto.com
URL of the blog: http://www.just-auto.com/blogs.aspx?
Name of the blogger: David Leggett
Focus of the blog: Articles about the automobile industry, in depth
Blog started: March 2003
System used by the blogger: D/N
Interaction elements allowed:
Commenting turned on: Yes
Trackbacks allowed: No
Social networking tools enabled: Yes, del.icio.us and dig.com
Comment tracking tools used by the blogger? No
Blogger background: Former Director of Forecasting for the Economist's
Intelligence Unit's automobile sector.
Does the blogger answer comments? Not that I can see
Does the blogger interact with other bloggers in the community? Did not
see any links to other blogs
Writing style: Opinion pieces and investigative articles about the car industry
Volume of comments received by the blogger: Low
Technorati.com ranking: 8,759

Name of the blog: UKPylot's MINI Blog
URL of the blog: http://miniblog.guapacha.com/
Name of the blogger: D/N
Blog started: July 2003
System used by the blogger: WordPress
Interaction elements allowed:
Commenting turned on: Yes
Trackbacks allowed: Yes
Social networking tools enabled: No
Comment tracking tools used by the blogger? D/N
Blogger background: A MINI owner
Does the blogger answer comments? Yes
Does the blogger interact with other bloggers in the community? Yes
Writing style: Journal style of writing and filler pieces
Volume of comments received by the blogger: Low to medium
Technorati.com ranking: 994,759

Name of the blog: Autoguy
URL of the blog: http://autoguy.blogspot.com/
Name of the blogger: Rick Todd
Blog started: December 2003
System used by the blogger: Blogger

Interaction elements allowed:
Commenting turned on: Yes
Trackbacks allowed: No
Social networking tools enabled: No
Comment tracking tools used by the blogger? D/N
Blogger background: An American law graduate living in Dubai writes about cars.
Does the blogger answer comments? Yes
Does the blogger interact with other bloggers in the community?
Writing style: Thoughtful articles and commentary about the current state of the automobile industry, along with journal articles about his car experiences
Volume of comments received by the blogger: Low
Technorati.com ranking: 143,068

Name of the blog: Cars! Cars! Cars!
URL of the blog: http://carscarscars.blogs.com/index/
Name of the blogger: Robert Schulties
Blog started: December 2003
System used by the blogger: Typepad
Interaction elements allowed:
Commenting turned on: Yes
Trackbacks allowed: No, were once turned on
Social networking tools enabled: No
Comment tracking tools used by the blogger? D/N
Blogger background: No details
Does the blogger answer comments? Did not see any answers
Does the blogger interact with other bloggers in the community? With links to a lot of blogs
Writing style: Review of the latest news from the industry
Volume of comments received by the blogger: Low to medium
Technorati.com ranking: 57,350

Name of the blog: Carpundit
URL of the blog: http://carpundit.typepad.com/carpundit/
Name of the blogger: Anonymous blogger
Blog started: March 2004
System used by the blogger: Typepad
Interaction elements allowed:
Commenting turned on: Yes
Trackbacks allowed: Yes
Social networking tools enabled: No
Comment tracking tools used by the blogger? D/N
Blogger background: Boston-based lawyer

Does the blogger answer comments? Yes
Does the blogger interact with other bloggers in the community? Yes
Writing style: Carpundit writes about cars, politics, and the news. Short opinion pieces about cars
Volume of comments received by the blogger: Low
Technorati.com ranking: 88,496

Name of the blog: Grant's Auto Rants
URL of the blog: http://grantsautorants.blogs.com/blog/
Name of the blogger: Grant W. Repsher
Blog started: April 2004
System used by the blogger: Typepad
Interaction elements allowed:
Commenting turned on: Yes
Trackbacks allowed: No
Social networking tools enabled: No
Comment tracking tools used by the blogger? D/N
Blogger background: An automotive marketing and customer relationship management specialist living in Detroit, MI. Grant writes for automotive news and is founder of a car-related website, www.servassistonline.com.
Does the blogger answer comments? Did not appear to answer comments
Does the blogger interact with other bloggers in the community?
Writing style: Thoughtful opinion pieces on using cars and the state of the car industry
Volume of comments received by the blogger: Low
Technorati.com ranking: Not ranked

Name of the blog: Future Cars, Hybrid Cars
URL of the blog: http://futurecars.blogspot.com/
Name of the blogger: Amit
Blog started: May 2004
System used by the blogger: Blogger
Interaction elements allowed:
Commenting turned on: Yes
Trackbacks allowed: No
Social networking tools enabled: No
Comment tracking tools used by the blogger? D/N
Blogger background: Engineering and SEO expert
Does the blogger answer comments? Does not appear to answer comments
Does the blogger interact with other bloggers in the community?
Writing style: Short articles about hybrid card
Volume of comments received by the blogger: High
Technorati.com ranking: 200,241

Name of the blog: Sir Warrior–S13 Blacktop SR20DET Project
URL of the blog: http://sirwarrior.blogspot.com/
Name of the blogger: Kane
Blog started: May 2004
System used by the blogger: Blogger
Interaction elements allowed:
Commenting turned on: Yes
Trackbacks allowed: No
Social networking tools enabled: No
Comment tracking tools used by the blogger? D/N
Blogger background: The blogger is writing about their car project
Does the blogger answer comments? Yes
Does the blogger interact with other bloggers in the community?
Writing style: Post-by-post description of this bloggers work on building a car
Volume of comments received by the blogger: Low
Technorati.com ranking: 1,364,559

Name of the blog: Autoblog
URL of the blog: http://www.autoblog.com/
Name of the blogger: Large group of blog authors
Blog started: June 2004, article about the launch http://bigblogcompany.net/
archives/000273.html
System used by the blogger: Blog Smith
Interaction elements allowed:
Commenting turned on: Yes
Trackbacks allowed: No
Social networking tools enabled: Yes, Technorati.com linking blogs
Comment tracking tools used by the blogger? D/N
Blogger background: Multiple authors
Does the blogger answer comments? Yes
Does the blogger interact with other bloggers in the community? Yes
Writing style: Auto articles about cars and the industry, typically based on
other media articles
Volume of comments received by the blogger: High
Technorati.com ranking: 29

Name of the blog: AutoMuse
URL of the blog: http://www.vehicleinfo.com/AutoMuse/
Name of the blogger: E. L. Eversman
Blog started: July 2004
System used by the blogger: Moveable Type 3.11
Interaction elements allowed:
Commenting turned on: Yes

Trackbacks allowed: Yes
Social networking tools enabled: No
Comment tracking tools used by the blogger? D/N
Blogger background: Chief counsel for vehicle information services and a writer for AutoGuide.net.
Does the blogger answer comments? Yes
Does the blogger interact with other bloggers in the community? D/N
Writing style: Articles on the law about the autos and also opinion pieces on cars in general
Volume of comments received by the blogger: Low
Technorati.com ranking: 35,598

Name of the blog: Alternative Energy Blog
URL of the blog: http://alt-e.blogspot.com/
Name of the blogger: James
Blog started: August 2004
System used by the blogger: Blogger
Interaction elements allowed:
Commenting turned on: Yes
Trackbacks allowed: No
Social networking tools enabled: No
Comment tracking tools used by the blogger? D/N
Blogger background: D/N
Does the blogger answer comments? D/N
Does the blogger interact with other bloggers in the community? D/N
Writing style: Writes about energy-related issues, touches on use of energy by cars
Volume of comments received by the blogger: High
Technorati.com ranking: 16,063

Name of the blog: Jalopnik
URL of the blog: http://www.jalopnik.com/
Name of the blogger: Mike Spinelli, Davey Johnson, Ray West, Mike Austin, and Robert Farago
Blog started: October 2004
System used by the blogger: D/N
Interaction elements allowed:
Commenting turned on: Yes
Trackbacks allowed: Yes
Social networking tools enabled: Yes, del.icio.us, digg
Comment tracking tools used by the blogger? Yes
Blogger background: Multiple-author blog

Does the blogger answer comments? Yes
Does the blogger interact with other bloggers in the community? Yes
Writing style: Scoops, videos, comments on the industry, cars, and other publication articles
Volume of comments received by the blogger: High
Technorati.com ranking: 379

Name of the blog: Chrysler Weblog
URL of the blog: http://www.chryslerweblog.com/
Name of the blogger: D/N
Blog started: October 2004
System used by the blogger: WordPress
Interaction elements allowed:
Commenting turned on: Yes
Trackbacks allowed: No
Social networking tools enabled: No
Comment tracking tools used by the blogger? D/N
Blogger background: D/N
Does the blogger answer comments?
Does the blogger interact with other bloggers in the community? D/N
Writing style: Comments on the cars and the people who make the cars
Volume of comments received by the blogger: Medium
Technorati.com ranking: 151,556

Name of the blog: If It's Got an Engine…
URL of the blog: http://dorri732.blogspot.com/
Name of the blogger: Dorrington Williams
Blog started: November 2004
System used by the blogger: Blogger
Interaction elements allowed:
Commenting turned on: Yes
Trackbacks allowed: Linking
Social networking tools enabled: No
Comment tracking tools used by the blogger? D/N
Blogger background: Interested in cars since early childhood, a car enthusiast who is also a nuclear engineer
Does the blogger answer comments? Yes
Does the blogger interact with other bloggers in the community? Yes
Writing style: Opinion articles, short fillers about his own cars, automobiles in general, and the industry
Volume of comments received by the blogger: Low
Technorati.com ranking: 288,082

Name of the blog: Views on Car News
URL of the blog: http://carpoint.blogspot.com/
Name of the blogger: Rashmi
Blog started: December 2004
System used by the blogger: Blogger
Interaction elements allowed:
Commenting turned on: Yes
Trackbacks allowed: No
Social networking tools enabled: No
Comment tracking tools used by the blogger? D/N
Blogger background:
Does the blogger answer comments? D/N
Does the blogger interact with other bloggers in the community? D/N
Writing style: Short articles on cars, some coverage of the industry, and hybrid cars
Volume of comments received by the blogger: Medium
Technorati.com ranking: 228,488

Name of the blog: General Motors FastLane Blog
URL of the blog: http://fastlane.gmblogs.com/
Name of the blogger: Multiple-author blog; principal author is Bob Lutz, a leading General Motors executive
Blog started: January 2005
System used by the blogger: D/N
Interaction elements allowed:
Commenting turned on: Yes
Trackbacks allowed: Yes
Social networking tools enabled: No
Comment tracking tools used by the blogger? D/N
Blogger background: Executives at General Motors
Does the blogger answer comments? Yes, but in posts, occasionally
Does the blogger interact with other bloggers in the community?
Writing style: Articles on General Motors cars and events, product feedback is solicited
Volume of comments received by the blogger: Very high
Technorati.com ranking: 3,061

Name of the blog: Tapscotts Behind the Wheel
URL of the blog: http://tapscottbehindthewheel.blogspot.com/
Name of the blogger: Mark Tapscott with Marcus MacFarland
Blog started: February 2005
System used by the blogger: Blogger

Interaction elements allowed:
Commenting turned on: Yes
Trackbacks allowed: Yes
Social networking tools enabled: No
Comment tracking tools used by the blogger? No
Blogger background: Traditional print media journalist turned blogger
Does the blogger answer comments? Do not know
Does the blogger interact with other bloggers in the community? D/N
Writing style: Car reviews, opinion, and review of the auto blogs
Volume of comments received by the blogger: Low
Technorati.com ranking: 17,011

Name of the blog: The German Car Blog
URL of the blog: http://www.germancarblog.com/
Name of the blogger: Christian
Blog started: March 2005
System used by the blogger: Blogger
Interaction elements allowed:
Commenting turned on: Yes/no linked to a forum site for commenting
Trackbacks allowed: No
Social networking tools enabled: Yes, del.icio.us, Technorati linking
Comment tracking tools used by the blogger? D/N
Blogger background: Blogger works for Audi
Does the blogger answer comments? D/N
Does the blogger interact with other bloggers in the community? D/N
Writing style: Filler articles based on articles published in other media, comments on cars
Volume of comments received by the blogger: High in the forum
Technorati.com ranking: 7,950

Name of the blog: The Auto Prophet
URL of the blog: http://theautoprophet.blogspot.com/
Name of the blogger: D/N
Blog started: March 2005
System used by the blogger: Blogger
Interaction elements allowed:
Commenting turned on: Yes
Trackbacks allowed: No
Social networking tools enabled: No
Comment tracking tools used by the blogger? D/N
Blogger background: Engineer working for an American auto company
Does the blogger answer comments? Yes

Does the blogger interact with other bloggers in the community? Yes
Writing style: Talks about cars and politics, commentary on industry and cars, filler pieces including videos
Volume of comments received by the blogger: Medium
Technorati.com ranking: 35,203

Name of the blog: RaceDriven.com: The Blog
URL of the blog: http://racedriven.blogspot.com/
Name of the blogger: Brian Vermette
Blog started: March 2005
System used by the blogger: Blogger
Interaction elements allowed:
Commenting turned on: Yes
Trackbacks allowed: No
Social networking tools enabled: No
Comment tracking tools used by the blogger? D/N
Blogger background: Motor sports and car enthusiast
Does the blogger answer comments? Could not see any
Does the blogger interact with other bloggers in the community? Yes
Writing style: Articles about the car industry, and car racing
Volume of comments received by the blogger: Low
Technorati.com ranking: 168,181

Name of the blog: MyFordDreams2 and MyFordDreams
URL of the blog: http://myforddreams2.blogspot.com/ and http://myforddreams.blogspot.com/, respectively
Name of the blogger: D/N
Blog started: April 2005
System used by the blogger: Blogger
Interaction elements allowed:
Commenting turned on: Yes
Trackbacks allowed: Yes
Social networking tools enabled:
Comment tracking tools used by the blogger? D/N
Blogger background: A man who wanted to comment on the Ford Motor company
Does the blogger answer comments? D/N
Does the blogger interact with other bloggers in the community? D/N
Writing style: Articles about Ford and the car industry
Volume of comments received by the blogger: Low
Technorati.com ranking: 60,205

Name of the blog: TCC Confidential
URL of the blog: http://www.thecarconnection.com/blog/
Name of the blogger: Marty Padgett
Blog started: May 2005
System used by the blogger: WordPress 1.5.1.1
Interaction elements allowed:
Commenting turned on: Yes
Trackbacks allowed: No
Social networking tools enabled: No
Comment tracking tools used by the blogger? D/N
Blogger background: D/N
Does the blogger answer comments? D/N
Does the blogger interact with other bloggers in the community? D/N
Writing style: Opinion pieces on cars, the industry, and life
Volume of comments received by the blogger: Low
Technorati.com ranking: 83,736

Name of the blog: Auto IT
URL of the blog: http://auto-it.blogspot.com/
Name of the blogger: D/N
Blog started: July 2005
System used by the blogger: Blogger
Interaction elements allowed:
Commenting turned on: Yes
Trackbacks allowed: No
Social networking tools enabled: No
Comment tracking tools used by the blogger? No
Blogger background: D/N
Does the blogger answer comments? D/N
Does the blogger interact with other bloggers in the community? D/N
Writing style: Articles about auto technology and future cars
Volume of comments received by the blogger: Low
Technorati.com ranking: 264,898

Name of the blog: The BMW Blog
URL of the blog: http://bmwblog.net/
Name of the blogger: Daniel Feies
Blog started: August 2005
System used by the blogger: WordPress 2.0.2
Interaction elements allowed:
Commenting turned on: Yes
Trackbacks allowed: Yes

Social networking tools enabled: No
Comment tracking tools used by the blogger? D/N
Blogger background: A software designer at Microsoft writes about cars and BMWs
Does the blogger answer comments? D/N
Does the blogger interact with other bloggers in the community? D/N
Writing style: News and commentaries on BMW and MINI's links to conference speeches
Volume of comments received by the blogger: Low
Technorati.com ranking: 287,192

Name of the blog: Left Lane News
URL of the blog: http://www.leftlanenews.com/
Name of the blogger: Nick Aziz
Blog started: September 2005
System used by the blogger: WordPress
Interaction elements allowed:
Commenting turned on: Yes
Trackbacks allowed: No
Social networking tools enabled: No
Comment tracking tools used by the blogger? D/N
Blogger background: Professional blogger
Does the blogger answer comments? D/N
Does the blogger interact with other bloggers in the community? Yes
Writing style: Reviews of cars and scope on the car world
Volume of comments received by the blogger: high
Technorati.com ranking: 1,210

Name of the blog: Autopia
URL of the blog: http://blog.wired.com/cars/
Name of the blogger: John Gartner, Mark Durham
Blog started: September 2005
System used by the blogger:
Interaction elements allowed:
Commenting turned on: Yes
Trackbacks allowed: No
Social networking tools enabled: No
Comment tracking tools used by the blogger? D/N
Blogger background: Multiple authors
Does the blogger answer comments? D/N
Does the blogger interact with other bloggers in the community? D/N

Writing style: Short articles about issues related to the car industry, not very much on the cars themselves
Volume of comments received by the blogger: Low to medium
Technorati.com ranking: 6,192

Name of the blog: Straightline
URL of the blog: http://blogs.edmunds.com/Straightline/
Name of the blogger: Richard Homan, Michelle Krebs, Steven Cole Smith, and Ken Gross
Blog started: October 2005
System used by the blogger: D/N
Interaction elements allowed:
Commenting turned on: Yes
Trackbacks allowed: No
Social networking tools enabled: No
Comment tracking tools used by the blogger? D/N
Blogger background: Journalists write auto-related posts
Does the blogger answer comments? D/N
Does the blogger interact with other bloggers in the community? Mainly mainstream references
Writing style: Short articles on industry news
Volume of comments received by the blogger: Low to medium
Technorati.com ranking: 13,838

Name of the blog: Karl on Cars
URL of the blog: http://blogs.edmunds.com/karl/
Name of the blogger: Karl Brauer
Blog started: October 2005
System used by the blogger: D/N
Interaction elements allowed:
Commenting turned on: Yes
Trackbacks allowed: No
Social networking tools enabled: No
Comment tracking tools used by the blogger? D/N
Blogger background: Karl Brauer, is editor-in-chief of edmunds.com
Does the blogger answer comments? Yes
Does the blogger interact with other bloggers in the community? Yes
Writing style: Commentary on the car industry and reviews of cars
Volume of comments received by the blogger:
Technorati.com ranking: 36,017

Name of the blog: The Driving Woman
URL of the blog: http://blogs.edmunds.com/women/
Name of the blogger:
Blog started: October 2005
System used by the blogger: D/N
Interaction elements allowed:
Commenting turned on: Yes
Trackbacks allowed: No
Social networking tools enabled: No
Comment tracking tools used by the blogger? D/N
Blogger background: Multiple-author blog
Does the blogger answer comments? D/N
Does the blogger interact with other bloggers in the community? D/N
Writing style: Articles on cars and the car industry
Volume of comments received by the blogger: Low
Technorati.com ranking: 71,768

Name of the blog: The Car Curmudgeon
URL of the blog: http://www.stabile.org/autos/
Name of the blogger: Chris Casarez, Donald Lee, Gregg Hall, Gregory Ashton, James Hunt, Matt Keegan, and Rick Stabile
Blog started: December 2005
System used by the blogger: WordPress 1.5.2
Interaction elements allowed:
Commenting turned on: Yes
Trackbacks allowed: Yes
Social networking tools enabled: Yes, del.icio.us
Comment tracking tools used by the blogger? D/N
Blogger background: Multiple-author blog
Does the blogger answer comments? D/N
Does the blogger interact with other bloggers in the community? D/N
Writing style: Rants and thoughts related to cars and car driving
Volume of comments received by the blogger: Low
Technorati.com ranking: 1,364,559

Name of the blog: MotorAlley
URL of the blog: http://motoralley.blogspot.com/
Name of the blogger: David Wassmann
Blog started: December 2005
System used by the blogger: Blogger
Interaction elements allowed:
Commenting turned on: Yes

Trackbacks allowed: No
Social networking tools enabled: No
Comment tracking tools used by the blogger? D/N
Blogger background: Worked in product development and marketing in the car industry
Does the blogger answer comments? Yes
Does the blogger interact with other bloggers in the community? Yes
Writing style: Articles on the car industry
Volume of comments received by the blogger: Low
Technorati.com ranking: 144,278

Name of the blog: The Blog for Auto Bloggers
URL of the blog: http://autobloggers.blogspot.com/
Name of the blogger: Multiple-author blog
Blog started: December 2005
System used by the blogger:
Interaction elements allowed:
Commenting turned on: Yes
Trackbacks allowed: No
Social networking tools enabled: No
Comment tracking tools used by the blogger? D/N
Blogger background: Multiple-author blog
Does the blogger answer comments? Yes
Does the blogger interact with other bloggers in the community? Yes
Writing style: Bloggers discuss what happens on their Auto blogs
Volume of comments received by the blogger:
Technorati.com ranking: 2,060,324

Name of the blog: KickingTires
URL of the blog: http://blogs.cars.com/
Name of the blogger: David Thomas, Patrick Olsen, Mike Hanley, Kelsey Mays, Beth Palmer, Eric Rossi, Amanda Wegrzyn, and Joe Wiesenfelder
Blog started: 2006 cars.com
System used by the blogger: Moveable Type
Interaction elements allowed:
Commenting turned on: Yes
Trackbacks allowed: No
Social networking tools enabled: No
Comment tracking tools used by the blogger? D/N
Blogger background: Journalists writing for the blog
Does the blogger answer comments? Yes
Does the blogger interact with other bloggers in the community? Yes

Writing style: Reviews on cars and the industry
Volume of comments received by the blogger: Medium
Technorati.com ranking: 9,000

Name of the blog: Automotive News from Popular Mechanics
URL of the blog: http://www.popularmechanics.com/blog/automotive
Name of the blogger: Ben Stewart
Blog started: January 2006
System used by the blogger:
Interaction elements allowed:
Commenting turned on: Yes
Trackbacks allowed: No
Social networking tools enabled: No
Comment tracking tools used by the blogger? D/N
Blogger background: D/N
Does the blogger answer comments? D/N
Does the blogger interact with other bloggers in the community? D/N
Writing style: Articles on cars, reviews, and the industry
Volume of comments received by the blogger: Medium
Technorati.com ranking: 36,924

Name of the blog: The Auto Blog
URL of the blog: http://www.partstrain.com/blog/
Name of the blogger: Rowen Pierce
Blog started: January 2006
System used by the blogger: WordPress 1.5.2
Interaction elements allowed:
Commenting turned on: Yes
Trackbacks allowed: Yes
Social networking tools enabled: No
Comment tracking tools used by the blogger? D/N
Blogger background: D/N
Does the blogger answer comments? D/N
Does the blogger interact with other bloggers in the community? D/N
Writing style: Reviews of cars and the industry
Volume of comments received by the blogger: Low
Technorati.com ranking: 86,153

Name of the blog: Automotoportal
URL of the blog: http://www.automotoportal.com/
Name of the blogger: blogger names not listed
Blog started: February 2006

System used by the blogger:
Interaction elements allowed:
Commenting turned on: Yes
Trackbacks allowed: No
Social networking tools enabled: No
Comment tracking tools used by the blogger? D/N
Blogger background: D/N
Does the blogger answer comments? D/N
Does the blogger interact with other bloggers in the community? Could not see any references
Writing style: Articles about cars and the industry
Volume of comments received by the blogger: Low
Technorati.com ranking: 4,553

Name of the blog: AutoblogGreen
URL of the blog: http://www.autobloggreen.com/
Name of the blogger: Sebastian Blanco, Sam Abuelsamid, Mike Magda, Derrick Y. Noh, and Bruno Vanzieleghem
Blog started: April 2006
System used by the blogger: D/N
Interaction elements allowed:
Commenting turned on: Yes
Trackbacks allowed: No
Social networking tools enabled: No
Comment tracking tools used by the blogger? D/N
Blogger background: Multiple-author blog
Does the blogger answer comments? D/N
Does the blogger interact with other bloggers in the community? D/N
Writing style: News articles about the green auto industry
Volume of comments received by the blogger: Low
Technorati.com ranking: 30,214

Name of the blog: The Car Blog
URL of the blog: http://thecarblog.com/
Name of the blogger: Mike Rundle, Matthew Oliphant, Paul Scrivens, Jason Fried, Didier Hilhorst, Eric Lorraine, Sage Olson, and Eric Etten
Blog started: April 2006
System used by the blogger: Custom
Interaction elements allowed:
Commenting turned on: Yes
Trackbacks allowed: No
Social networking tools enabled: No

Comment tracking tools used by the blogger?
Blogger background: Multiple-author blog
Does the blogger answer comments? D/N
Does the blogger interact with other bloggers in the community? D/N
Writing style: Articles on cars and industry issues and opinion pieces
Volume of comments received by the blogger: Medium
Technorati.com ranking: 34,705

Automobile Blog Timeline

November 2001	The Truth about Cars	http://www.thetruthaboutcars.com/
October 2002	MINI Weblog	http://motoringfile.com/
September 2002	Ride	http://www.angelfire.com/retro/ browsers/
March 2003	Just-Auto.com	http://www.just-auto.com/blogs.aspx?
July 2003	UKPylot's MINI Blog	http://miniblog.guapacha.com/
December 2003	Autoguy	http://autoguy.blogspot.com/
December 2003	Cars! Cars! Cars!	http://carscarscars.blogs.com/index/
February 2004	Autoworld	http://autoworld.tblog.com/however, not active
March 2004	Carpundit	http://carpundit.typepad.com/ carpundit/
April 2004	Grant's Auto Rants	http://grantsautorants.blogs.com/blog/
May 2004	Future Cars, Hybrid Cars	http://futurecars.blogspot.com/
May 2004	Sir Warroior–S13 Blacktop SR20DET Project	http://sirwarrior.blogspot.com/
June 2004	Autoblog	http://www.autoblog.com/ (article about the launch: http:// bigblogcompany.net/archives/000273 .html)
2004	The Truth about Cars	http://www.thetruthaboutcars.com/ index.php/
July 2004	AutoMuse	http://www.vehicleinfo.com/AutoMuse/
August 2004	Alternative Energy Blog	http://alt-e.blogspot.com/
October 2004	Jalopnik	http://www.jalopnik.com/
October 2004	Chrysler Weblog	http://www.chryslerweblog.com/
November 2004	If It's Got an Engine…	http://dorri732.blogspot.com/
December 2004	Views on Car News	http://carpoint.blogspot.com/
January 2005	General Motors FastLane Blog	http://fastlane.gmblogs.com/
February 2005	Tapscotts Behind The Wheel	http://tapscottbehindthewheel .blogspot.com/

March 2005	The German Car Blog	http://www.germancarblog.com/
March 2005	The Auto Prophet	http://theautoprophet.blogspot.com/
March 2005	RaceDriven.com: The blog	http://racedriven.blogspot.com/
April 2005	MyFordDreams2	http://myforddreams2.blogspot.com/
	MyFordDreams	http://myforddreams.blogspot.com/
May 2005	TCC Confidential	http://www.thecarconnection.com/ blog/
June 2005	At Home Mechanic	http://www.athomemechanic.com/
July 2005	Auto IT	http://auto-it.blogspot.com/
July 2005	MPHBlog	http://www.mph-online.com/blogs
August 2005	The BMW Blog	http://bmwblog.net/
September 2005	Left Lane News	http://www.leftlanenews.com/
September 2005	Autopia	http://blog.wired.com/cars/
October 2005	Straightline	http://blogs.edmunds.com/ Straightline/
October 2005	Karl on Cars	http://blogs.edmunds.com/karl/
October 2005	The Driving Woman	http://blogs.edmunds.com/women/
December 2005	The Car Curmudgeon	http://www.stabile.org/autos/
December 2005	MotorAlley	http://motoralley.blogspot.com/
December 2005	The Blog for Auto Bloggers	http://autobloggers.blogspot.com/
2006	KickingTires	http://blogs.cars.com/
January 2006	Automotive News from Popular Mechanics	http://www.popularmechanics.com/ blog/automotive
January 2006	The Auto Blog	http://www.partstrain.com/blog/
February 2006	Automotoportal	http://www.automotoportal.com/
April 2006	AutoblogGreen	http://www.autobloggreen.com/
April 2006	The Car Blog	http://thecarblog.com/
	Detroit News	http://info.detnews.com/autosblog/ index.cfm
	Brakebias—Tiempo Borré	http://hondakid86.blogspot.com/

Automobile Industry Blogs by Technorati Ranking

Name of the Blog	URL of the Blog	Technorati Ranking
Autoblog	http://www.autoblog.com/	29
Jalopnik	http://www.jalopnik.com/	379
Left Lane News	http://www.leftlanenews.com/	1,210
General Motors FastLane Blog	http://fastlane.gmblogs.com/	3,061

Name of the Blog	URL of the Blog	Technorati Ranking
Automotoportal	http://www.automotoportal.com/	4,553
Autopia	http://blog.wired.com/cars/	6,192
The German Car Blog	http://www.germancarblog.com/	7,950
Autos Blog for the *Detroit News*	http://info.detnews.com/autosblog/ index.cfm	8,532*
Just-Auto.com	http://www.just-auto.com/blogs.aspx?	8,759
KickingTires	http://blogs.cars.com/	9,000
The Truth about Cars	http://www.thetruthaboutcars.com/	9,906
Straightline	http://blogs.edmunds.com/Straightline/	13,838
Alternative Energy Blog	http://alt-e.blogspot.com/	16,063
Tapscotts Behind The Wheel	http://tapscottbehindthewheel.blogspot.com/	17,011
AutoblogGreen	http://www.autobloggreen.com/	30,214
The Car Blog	http://thecarblog.com/	34,705
The Auto Prophet	http://theautoprophet.blogspot.com/	35,203
AutoMuse	http://www.vehicleinfo.com/AutoMuse/	35,598
Karl on Cars	http://blogs.edmunds.com/karl/	36,017
Automotive News from Popular Mechanics	http://www.popularmechanics.com /blog/automotive	36,924
Cars! Cars! Cars!	http://carscarscars.blogs.com/index/	57,350
MyFordDreams2	http://myforddreams2.blogspot.com/	60,205
MyFordDreams	http://myforddreams.blogspot.com/	
The Driving Woman	http://blogs.edmunds.com/women/	71,768
TCC Confidential	http://www.thecarconnection.com/blog/	83,736
The Auto Blog	http://www.partstrain.com/blog/	86,153
Carpundit	http://carpundit.typepad.com/carpundit/	88,496
Ride	http://www.angelfire.com/retro/browsers/	130,332
Autoguy	http://autoguy.blogspot.com/	143,068
MotorAlley	http://motoralley.blogspot.com/	144,278
Chrysler Weblog	http://www.chryslerweblog.com/	151,556
RaceDriven.com: The blog	http://racedriven.blogspot.com/	168,181
Future Cars, Hybrid Cars	http://futurecars.blogspot.com/	200,241
Views on Car News	http://carpoint.blogspot.com/	228,488
Auto IT	http://auto-it.blogspot.com/	264,898
If It's Got an Engine…	http://dorri732.blogspot.com/	288,082
The BMW Blog	http://bmwblog.net/	287,192
UKPylot's MINI Blog	http://miniblog.guapacha.com/	994,759
Sir Warroior–S13 Blacktop SR20DET Project	http://sirwarrior.blogspot.com/	1,364,559

The Car Curmudgeon	http://www.stabile.org/autos/	1,361,559
The Blog for Auto Bloggers	http://autobloggers.blogspot.com/	2,060,324
Grant's Auto Rants	http://grantsautorants.blogs.com/blog/	Not ranked
MotoringFile	http://motoringfile.com/	Not ranked

*However, these links represent links to the whole paper.

Endnotes

1. http://www.autoblog.com/
2. http://carscarscars.blogs.com/index/
3. http://www.forbes.com/bow/b2c/review.jhtml?id=7883
4. New York Times, Micheline Maynard (August 6, 2006), *Toyota Drove to the Bank in a Ford.* Available at http://www.nytimes.com /2006/08/06/weekinreview/06maynard.html?ex=1312516800 &en=8c866413678ec951&ei=5090&partner=rssuserland&emc=rss

CHAPTER 10

Blogs from the Customer's Perspective

The design and visual impact of a blog can be less important to a blog reader than what a blogger writes if a real connection with readers is made through a blogger's writing. Making a good impression that connects with an audience involves many factors including writing style, openness, and transparency. Although content is what brings a blog reader to a blog, the one factor that keeps readers returning is a blogger's ability to reveal himself or herself and connect in an authentic way with readers through writing.

Many blog readers want to read the blog of someone who is personable, humorous, and likeable. That is not always the case for some blog readers; how you come across is not as relevant as the content. Going against the grain, some bloggers espouse technical expertise rather than personal content to capture the reader's attention. Those bloggers may be right, for some customers want content more than anything else.

Blog readers are even beginning to expect that a company will respond to their requests and questions on the customers' blogs even when a question was not originally posted on the company's blog. Because of the changing nature of media, customers have the ability to publish writing that can be found globally and easily. In a world where the content from consumer-generated media can appear in the top 10 rankings of a Google, MSN, and Yahoo!, such instant and global access to the web means companies can no longer hide from customer criticism. Companies have to respond quickly or face critical publicity about a lack of response.

A series of online survey interviews were conducted with several blog readers of various corporate blogs for this chapter, including Microsoft, Masi Bikes, and Indium Corporation. In this chapter, you read the blog readers' perspective on why they read blogs. The chapter describes a series of factors that reveal why people read blogs and some tips on what readers want from a blogger. Quotes from the blog readers' interview transcriptions demonstrate the value that blogging provides to a company and describe how credibility is important to how a blog reader judges a blogger.

BUILDING TRUST THROUGH BLOGGING

It is possible to build trust in a company's brand through blogging. All that is required is that the person doing the blogging connects with blog readers. Once trust is developed between the audience and the person who writes the blog for a company, people who have a connection with a blogger may be more willing to consider a company's products and brand. A company can use blogging as a way to break through the barriers people throw up against advertising messages. People believe that the individuals writing a blog have more freedom to give their honest opinion about products. Blog writing is not considered advertising if a corporate blogger can build a relationship with an audience. Blogging, therefore, essentially helps a company to reach an audience through the content on a blog, through the writer's opinions, and by how the blog is run. A blog can really demonstrate the passion an employee has for a product or a company, and once trust is developed between a customer and a blogger, passion, when revealed in a blog, will be read and considered much more carefully by blog readers than if read in a company advertisement.

An example of a blog where the blogger has really established trust with his audience is Tim Jackson of the MASI Guy blog for Masi Bikes. Tim Jackson works for Haro Bicycle Corporation. He is the sole member of the marketing team for the Masi cycles division of Haro Bicycle Corporation. Several readers of the blog agreed to give their opinions about the MASI Guy blog.

James Thomas is a MASI Guy bike blog reader who believes that openness, transparency, and writing style are the factors that add the most credibility to Tim Jackson's blog. James said that Tim's blog gives readers a true sense of his approach to his job as brand manager at Masi. He said,

Though Tim obviously wants to promote Masi Bikes, the blog does not read at all like marketing material. I think the genuine, sometimes offbeat content allows readers to put a personal face with the company and the products. If potential customers want to read technical specs on the bikes, they can check out the Masi website. If they want a casual peek into life at Masi and the thoughts behind the products, they can check out the blog.

Building a connection with blog readers by providing a lot of content that reveals the personal side of an employee on a blog lies at the core of what corporate blogging should be all about.

James Thomas had always had a favorable impression of Masi Bikes because he had friends in college that rode Masi bikes. However, he did not know very much about the latest bikes from Masi until he ran across Tim's blog. James explained that he has built a connection with the Masi brand through reading the blog. He said,

I can see the passion for cycling that goes into the bikes makes me, maybe subconsciously, like the brand a bit more. I have never met Tim personally, but through his blog and the comments that he makes on my blog, I feel like I know him a bit. That personal connection that the blog creates certainly influences my perception of the company. I would probably not buy a new Masi just because I read the MASI Guy blog, but if all other factors were equal, the personal connection created by the blog would influence me to choose a Masi over another functionally equivalent, similarly priced bike. I guess a better way to express that is that people are more comfortable buying from someone they know. Tim's blog makes readers feel like they know someone in the bike business.

Jeff Mosser, another Masi blog reader, said that it is Tim Jackson's role at the company and his authority as a blogger that gives the blog credibility. He said, "If I met Tim in the street, I feel like I could instantly strike up conversation with him." Jeff has a new impression of Masi Bikes because he read the blog, and now he is considering purchasing a Masi bike.

He also thought that Tim's interaction with his readers and the speed at which he responds to blog reader comments really "breaks down the corporate wall and makes the company seem more personable ... like they are still small enough to care about individual customer concerns ... not just selling X number of units for the most profit." James also said there are a lot of factors that help to make Tim Jackson's blog interesting, including the following:

- openness and transparency of the blogger,
- writing style of the blogger,

- content of the blog,
- interaction with blogger,
- interaction with other blog readers,
- frequency of posts,
- how quickly the blogger responds to comments,
- the blogger's role at their company,
- the authority of the blogger.

Another MASI Guy blog reader, Annie Bakken, reads Tim Jackson's blog because,

> Tim blogs less as a Masi representative and more just as Tim, and I am way more likely to trust someone who comes across as a regular ol' dude who likes to ride his bike, as opposed to someone who has a blog just as a promotional device. If the only thing he blogged about was Masi, I wouldn't still be reading.

She went onto say, "it comes down to Tim being a nice guy with a family who likes to ride his bike, not an industry shill. If I thought his blog was only a marketing ploy I wouldn't bother with it."

Big companies can appear impersonal to customers. Blogging can be a way for a larger company to build trust with customers through individual employee blogs. "One Louder" is a blog run by Heather Hamilton, an employee at Microsoft. Heather Hamilton is the staffing manager for Microsoft's marketing central sourcing team. Most of the blogs at Microsoft are developer blogs used to conduct outreach to customers; only a small number of blogs at Microsoft are involved with marketing or staffing.

As a reader of Heather's blog, Viki Lutz has changed her impression of Microsoft since she started reading the blog. Viki said, "I only thought of MS as a large corporation, but now, Heather has added a human aspect to the company's brand. That's a big change!" Viki initially started to read Heather's blog because she was interested in learning more about Microsoft's recruiting style. Viki said Microsoft's recruiting style "seems more personal—especially when mega-corporations like MS are automated and impersonal."

Another One Louder blog reader, Brett Norquist, said,

> I worked for Microsoft for nearly 10 years as a contractor, vendor, and full time employee. In my current job, Microsoft is our largest client so I know the company quite well. I do believe that Microsoft has changed as proven by allowing Heather, Scoble, and others to maintain blogs and discuss topics that are not always favorable. But they are authentic and, in Heather's case, a better-informed candidate is probably the type she's after.

As the blog readers demonstrate, if a corporate blogger can build a connection with readers, the trust developed with the blogger can (if there is authenticity) extend to the blogger's company as well.

WRITING PERSONAL AND ENTERTAINING CONTENT

Blog readers want to read good content, and good blog content means that the writing is from a blogger's personal perspective. A favorite blogger almost becomes a friend to the reader, and readers know their favorite bloggers quite well if the blogger does a good job of personalizing their posts. To build a relationship between a blogger and readers takes time, and a company should carefully assess who should blog when developing a blogging content strategy. The person's expertise and the potential blogger's ability to write engaging stories and introduce a personal touch into blog posts should be considered in the choice of blogger candidate.

The only way a blogger has to connect with a reader is through the content on a blog; therefore, it is important to try to develop content that is personal and engaging rather than content that is dry or unresponsive. The important priority in blogging is to personalize your writing and reveal more of yourself because that is what will really engage readers. The dilemma for any blogger is to know what to reveal and what not to reveal, what is entertaining, and what is irrelevant to an audience. With blogging, there is plenty of space to explore, make mistakes, and be human. The best advice that anyone can follow in writing a blog is don't try and fake being real for your customers, but just be yourself, and people will see the humanity in you, and make a connection if there is one to make.

According to the Northeastern University and Backbone Media Blogging Success study on blogging success,[1] one technique that a blogger can use to build a successful blog is by personalizing blog posts and creating entertaining content. Success in part then can be said to come from the personality of the blogger, whose personal writing style will influence the interaction and reading habits of the audience. A blog reader can learn a lot about a blogger's "personality" from the humor they use, the personal experiences they describe from their role in their company, and the passion expressed by a blogger for their topic. The more entertaining a blogger is, the more captivating and riveting the content, the higher the chance for blogging success. Good blog writing has to contain content about the topic of the blog that interests an audience, but it is the inclusion of personal perspectives on issues in an industry that keep readers coming back for more.

Several readers had opinions about the writing style and personalization presented by Tim Jackson's blog. One reader, James Thomas, believes he really knows Tim Jackson. He believes Tim's writing to be informal, even conversational. He said,

> If I met Tim I would know that we are both bike geeks and that we would have no shortage of things to talk about. Tim enthusiastically shares his passion for cycling and I think that enthusiasm is infectious. I think he is a bike geek, maybe even an extreme bike geek. Beyond that, of course, I think Tim is someone who is optimistic, outgoing, and chooses to live his life to the fullest. People like to be around someone like that, in real life and in the blogosphere.

Annie Bakken said that the Masi blog has raised Annie's awareness of the Masi brand. Now that she knows someone at the company, she notices the company more when she does walk into a bike shop. Annie thought that the ability to interact with Tim through his blog meant that it had given her the ability to understand that he is a "good guy" and "Internet friend" rather than "some dude who works for Masi." She was much more inclined to take his opinion about bikes into account based on her reading of Tim's blog.

Sometimes, a picture is worth a thousand words. Jeff Moser, another MASI Guy blog reader, thinks the blog has a good blogging style. He thought the blog contained, "Lots of pictures, smaller paragraphs with good content and lots of information. Sometimes bloggers lose me if they ramble on too long. A good picture adds reality to the post too. I'd like to see more pictures of day to day operations at work though...."

Heather Hamilton's recruiting blog from Microsoft also has some blog readers who think her blog is personal. Viki Lutz believes Heather's content was very personal. She said, "I continue to read because Heather is professional AND personal—her content varies between cutting edge information and occasional rants (which makes her more of a person than anything else)." Viki was able to describe Heather from the content on Heather's blog and said,

> I feel as though I would know exactly where her knives are kept in her kitchen! LOL! (Based on her pictures posted on her blog and loooong post about her updates and remodeling projects.) Overall, I think Heather and I share a lot of the same values and have a lot in common—just based on how she writes and interacts with others on her blog. I would describe her as an independent woman who takes on home improvement projects from Hell and really tells you "like it is"—as she has proclaimed that she is "a Staffing Manager, Microsoft Employee Evangelist, Quasi-Marketer, and Truth-Teller."

Brett Norquist described how he first started reading Heather's blog, and why he continues to read the blog,

I started reading Heather's blog when Scoble linked to it back a couple of years ago. I continue to read her blog because I enjoy the style of her writing and she writes about topics that interest me. I hire people for our small company and I like many of her suggestions on how to keep your best employees happy. A while back, she also wrote up some very humorous summaries of The Apprentice, which I enjoyed. She also updates her blog regularly. I also like how she mixes work-related posts with personal experience posts that range from cooking to TV shows to whatever is on her mind. I never know what to expect but the surprise factor makes it that much more interesting.

The interviews with the blog readers of the MASI Guy blog and Heather Hamilton's blog prove that a company can gain a lot of trust from customers when employees write about their personal perspectives and work on a corporate blog. The blog readers who read the MASI Guy blog think that Tim is not just an expert in their field but also a friend and someone who shares a passion for the sport of cycling. Blog readers believe Tim Jackson has made a connection with them, and the relationship built by writing on a blog gives Tim, and by extension, Masi bikes, authority in the eyes of the blogs readers. The same relationship exists between Heather Hamilton and her readers. Rather than a shared passion for cycling, Heather's blog takes the rather mundane topic of recruiting and adds some zest that have blog readers enjoying Heather's content because she puts a personal face to Microsoft recruiting.

Being successful in blogging is not just about generating content on your own blog; it is also important to carry that same personal touch to other blogs when a blogger conducts outreach. The comments and trackbacks made by a corporate blogger can also be personal and hopefully entertaining. It is even more important for bloggers to write well when conducting blog outreach, because the outreach practiced within a blogging community will draw people back to a blog if the comments posted on other blogs are of interest to blog readers.[2]

INDUSTRY CONTENT PROVIDES GREAT RELEVANCY FOR AUDIENCES

Blog readers will be most interested in industry-related content on a blog. That is certainly what draws a lot of blog readers initially to a blog, although it is the personal spin on content that keeps readers returning for more. Several of the blog readers of the MASI Guy blog started reading Tim Jackson's blog because it was about cycling. Tim's credibility as a cyclist was established because of his writings about the bicycle industry on the blog, whereas Tim Jackson's personal content engaged blog readers and developed trust and greater awareness of the Masi brand. The entertaining content about the bicycle helped to establish further credibility for Tim and, by extension, Masi bikes. It is because Tim cycles and works for a bike company that his authority as a bike blogger was enhanced as someone who had not only passion for the subject but also experiences in the industry.

Heather Hamilton's blog is all about recruiting, and Heather provides insight and tips on recruiting and getting a job at Microsoft. Although the recruiting and job-related content is important, it is Heather's personal spin on the content that really engages blog readers.

Dr. Ron Lasky is a blogger with Indium Corporation, which provides products and services for electronic assembly materials and the companies who use their services, such as electronic assembly manufacturers. Dr. Lasky is a senior scientist with Indium Corporation. Many of the blog readers who responded to the surveys about Dr. Lasky thought that his industry-related content was important in establishing the credibility of his blog. One blog reader, Don Ballard, described Dr. Lasky's blog content. He said, "It is also interesting interspersed with other topics to add some variety. Plus, I value Dr. Ron's advice and opinion." He went on to say that the blog's writing style was "Very easy to read ... for the layman, interesting, talks about current and valid points." The content was credible because of "Dr. Ron's status within the area, his education and his knowledge. He is a subject matter expert and is very helpful with his readers."

In the Northeastern University and Backbone Media Blogging Success Study, an opposing viewpoint comes from Eric Anderson, a blogger from Adobe. He questioned whether personalizing blog writing really is a successful blogging strategy to follow. Although many bloggers in the study suggested that a personal approach would bring more success to a blog, Eric Anderson did not think that content that includes personal information fuels blogging success. Eric concentrates on technical content, avoiding personal details when writing a blog post. In the Backbone Media Corporate Blogging Survey 2005, when interviewing bloggers at Macromedia (which has since merged with Adobe), the Macromedia bloggers suggested that non-personalization of blog posts was a company-wide strategy, and that this non-personalization strategy has been shown to be successful for the Macromedia blogs.

Eric Anderson is a product manager at Adobe, with a very technical audience, whose reason for reading Adobe blogs is probably the knowledge garnered from the blogs. Eric Anderson's blog content might not be entertaining, but it is riveting to such a highly technical audience who are affected by Adobe's product development cycle.

Another possibility is that the amount of acceptable or preferred personalization in a blog post by readers might be different, depending upon the culture of the industry. The way people write technical material may include humor or personal reflection that is only understood by industry participants. To the non-industry observer, such comments would not be perceived as entertaining or personal, yet in the context of the industry, those blog posts may be very entertaining and personal.

A blog has a higher chance for attaining success if the content is industry related and is interesting to its readers. In addition, a blogger in a unique role might develop interesting content because of their unique personal perspectives.[3,4] However, for some audiences, it is just the content that matters rather than the personalization of that content.

BLOG READER COMMENT RESPONSIVENESS

Commenting on a blog or conducting a conversation on the web in public is very new for most corporate websites. The ability to interact with a blogger through comments is not new to the web, as forums have been around since the early days of the web. However, a blog is different from a forum in that a discussion is always initiated by the blogger when a blog post is published and is between the reader and the blogger, rather than in a forum where the discussion can be between forum members.

Managing the blog comment moderation process on blogs is a new and developing cultural phenomenon. Customers do not want their comments edited, and if comments are moderated, it is important to make sure comments are published promptly and answered quickly. When customers ask questions on a blog, they really want answers to their questions. Whether and how a company responds will influence customers' perceptions about the company. It is not just that a single blog reader does not receive a response; it is also that the rest of the customer community can see a company's lack of response on a blog post. If a company does not answer any comments on a blog, most customers and bloggers in the community will come to believe that a company is not interested in joining in on the conversation in the community. Starting a blog with open comments sets the stage for the belief that a company is willing to answer any comments. If you do not respond in some manner, people will be disappointed.

Heather Hamilton's blog readers believe that commenting and interaction are important. Blog reader, Brett Norquist, said that Heather's comments are an important part of her blog. He said,

> Like Scoble, the comment section is as important as the main posts, if not more so. Her style is relaxed but informative. I'd read her if she didn't work at Microsoft. She [Heather] ripped me good once in her comments section, which is cool because it tells me she reads them. I often don't agree with her point of view but she makes me think often and challenges what I experienced at MS when I worked there.

Viki Lutz said that Heather gained a lot of credibility by interacting with her readers. She said, "I especially like it when Heather responds to her readers— I feel like even as an 'outsider' from her corporate world, she's allowing me to partake in conversations and just be a member of her own e-community."

Both of these blog readers find the chance to interact with a corporate blogger an important part of blog reading, an opportunity that adds a dimension that would not be possible on a static webpage. Brett Norquist even makes the point that when Heather Hamilton challenges him, rather than turning him off from reading Heather's blog, Brett believes the interaction makes it worthwhile to return to read more.

At Dr. Lasky's blog at the Indium Corporation, blog reader Don Ballard said that Dr. Lasky's interaction with his readers and how quickly he responds to comments adds a lot of credibility to what Dr. Lasky writes on his blog. He said, "I have also called upon Dr. Ron for advice on several occasions with regards to RoHS/WEEE and he has always helped me out."

BLOGGING TIPS LEARNED FROM THE INTERVIEWS

If you have an open comment section, expect your customers to ask customer service questions, even if you go to great lengths to inform your readers that you do not want to answer customer service questions on your blog. Blogging is all about conversation and discussion. If a customer has a question for your company and there is an open channel through the comment section of a company blog, customers will use that channel. If you do not answer the customer's questions, more than likely, the blog readers will become annoyed and write it on the web in blogs or on other websites. It is far better to have any critical conversation occur on your own blog, where you can give your point of view.

Always remember that running a blog is a little like having a number of customers eavesdropping on your customer support calls. Speed is important in answering any queries. If you do not have an immediate answer, let people know you are working on the answer and will get right back to them. Do not disappoint your readers; try to answer any comments quickly.

A blog is a dialogue between a company and its customers. A company must decide how they will manage customer relations through a blog. If you set the expectation that a customer who writes a comment will receive a response, if you do not reply, you will lose credibility. Not only will you disappoint the customer, but also everyone else who will be able to read that you did not reply.

Any corporate blogger should carefully consider their comment response strategy when developing a blog. The best scenario is to be able to answer any customer queries through your customer service department. If your company is not able to handle the volume of feedback, make a statement on the blog comment form letting people know. Plus, if a customer leaves an email address and comment, send the customer an email with a statement that they may not receive an answer to their question, but you appreciate their input. One tip for your blog designer is to program your blog publishing system so that all blog readers who commented have the option to subscribe by email to any comment thread in a blog post, and also make sure blog readers can unsubscribe easily.

There will be occasions when blog readers make inappropriate comments, so set expectations with your readers that sometimes comments will need to be moderated. Setting expectations goes a long way in avoiding customer frustrations. Otherwise, your company will give the impression that you are not listening to customer feedback, and although this is always bad on an individual call from a customer, when this happens in full public view on a blog website, the negative customer perceptions can be very bad for a company's reputation within its customer community. Customers see your lack of response and act accordingly.

To recap, here are some success strategies for blog responsiveness:

- Answer every customer question; answer them through comment follow-ups or additional blog posts. A company could answer several customer questions if they are all the same sort of question at the same time. Remember to send an email back to the original customer so they know that your company has answered the customer's question.
- Create more blogs for each product, thereby directing customer responses to the appropriate product.
- If you answer any comments in a blog, make sure that your identity is known in the comment post, and especially if the person who makes the comment is the principal blogger on the site, make sure you identify with the company. Lastly, provide your contact information in the comment post so people can ask questions directly.

BLOG READER PRIVACY

Blog readers are very concerned about their privacy; therefore, it is important to give your readers the option of making a comment anonymously in a blog post. If you give the option of anonymity, your corporate blog is likely to receive more comments. Some blog readers may not want their identity revealed because they do not want their competitors to know what they are writing on the web. Giving blog readers the option to post anonymously respects blog readers' privacy and may provide some more interesting feedback and comments for a corporate blog.

Go one step further and give your readers the option of sending you an email. Display your email address on your blog. You might receive questions from blog readers who do not want their identity or the question widely known. If you do receive an email from a blog reader and want to publish the content, you should return to the blog reader and ask their permission to republish the content.

There are some disadvantages in allowing anonymous postings. If someone makes a statement that is unsubstantiated, you, or the person attacked, cannot defend yourself against unknown assailants. The attacker might have more to gain than just a grievance—the anonymous poster might be a competitor. That is why it is important to write a good blogging policy that sets the expectation that you will not allow libelous attacks. Here you will protect the privacy of blog readers who wish to remain anonymous but also will be able to remove libelous posts by setting expectations upfront. You can also ask people who make critical comments to identify themselves in their comment; otherwise, you will not publish a comment.

PRODUCT FEEDBACK

Customers enjoy being able to give feedback to a blogger. Giving feedback encourages customers to feel that they are part of the process of developing a product or company. As we saw in the interviews with the three MASI Guy blog readers, the readers were happy to have the chance to chat directly with Tim Jackson who works at Masi Bikes.

In the Northeastern University and Backbone Media Blogging Success Study, Tim Jackson from Masi said that one of the most important ingredients from the blog has been the ability to ask for feedback from the readers. Tim said that the effort has helped to "shape the products that are coming out." It also gives pride of ownership with customers and retailers who read the blog in a way that is much more of a personal connection with the Masi brand.

POSTING PICTURES

Blogging is all about writing and has become extremely important because the text on blogs allows people to find blog pages through text searches on search engines. Yet blogging is also about connection with people, and for the reading public, posting pictures about a blogger and their company provides an extra layer of connection. As Jeff Moser, a Masi Guy blog reader said, "Lots of pictures, smaller paragraphs with good content. Sometimes bloggers lose me if they ramble on too long. A good picture adds reality to the post too." With picture-sharing websites proliferating,[5] pictures can also be another way for readers to find a corporate blog by searching for pictures with distinct tags.

TENURE COUNTS

Being around for a long time in your blogging community and being the first to market does make a difference for a blog reader. If you are one of the first companies to blog in your community, you will have a longer time to develop relationships with customers.

James Thomas is a blog reader of the Masi blog. Tim Jackson, the blogger, works for Haro Bicycle Corporation. James talked about his reasons for choosing to read Tim's blog,

> I started reading MASI Guy simply because it was one of the first bike blogs that I discovered. Actually, Tim's blog was one of three bike blogs that I read early on and inspired me to start my own blog. I continue to read the MASI Guy because I am interested in hearing an industry insider's perspective on all things bike related.

FOLLOW THE CONVERSATION

The conversation about your company may not be happening just on your blog, it may happen elsewhere on the web, so it is up to each company to monitor what customers are saying about their company and the most important issues in the industry. An important reason for companies to start blogging is that customers are developing content on their own blogs and also using blogs as a space to discuss vendors and products in the marketplace. Sometimes, customers initiate that discussion; sometimes, bloggers or consultants in an industry initiate the discussion. It takes time to blog, and many customers do not always have the time to write about and keep up on the issues of the day. Occasionally, customers who blog will even ask questions about a product or company and publish those questions, hoping the community or the company will engage them with an answer.

A lot of the controversy about Jeff Jarvis in his blog, the BuzzMachine, and his concerns with the customer service issues at Dell were because Dell initially did not engage Jeff through the web and blogs when he posted his complaints about his Dell machines. The world has changed, and customers are coming to the point where they expect a company to monitor what is being said about them.

Make sure you are monitoring the web for conversation about your company and industry issues. Select the tags that you have to follow, and conduct the outreach and comment on the blogs you need to comment on. Your customers are expecting you to conduct this sort of outreach in the new world of blogging.

Ken Dyck was a Microsoft customer who was featured in the Microsoft case study[6] in the Backbone Media Corporate Blogging Survey 2005. He had made a post about a spelling mistake[7] in Microsoft's Windows on his own blog, and employees at Microsoft picked up the post and responded. Ken talked about why he thought it was not necessary to post comments on a company's site if you want to get feedback as a customer; he said, "Depends on the company—for Microsoft, I knew that Scoble has all sorts of feeds set up, I knew it would fly past what he was reading. I would not use that as a strategy for every company, I really tried my post as an experiment, and it worked."[8] Ken Dyck and Jeff Jarvis are good examples of customers who have come to expect that companies will monitor what is being said about them. If you do monitor the web and respond to a query or discussion, not only will you probably be able to dissipate any negative comments about your company but you will also impress customers with your monitoring and response.

Endnotes

1. Scout Blogging Blog (2006), *3.5 Entertaining Writing Style and Personalization: Northeastern University and Backbone Media Blogging Success Study.* Available at http://www.scoutblogging.com/success_study/writing_style/entertaining_writing_style.html

2. Scout Blogging Blog (2006), *3.5 Entertaining Writing Style and Personalization: Northeastern University and Backbone Media Blogging Success Study.* Available at http://www.scoutblogging.com/success_study/writing_style/entertaining_writing_style.html

3. Scout Blogging Blog (2006), *3.5 Entertaining Writing Style and Personalization: Northeastern University and Backbone Media Blogging Success Study.* Available at http://www.scoutblogging.com//success_study/writing_style/entertaining_writing_style.html

4. Blogsurvey Blog, John Cass (2005), *Ken Dyck Interview about the Microsoft Case Study.* Available at http://blogsurvey.backbonemedia.com/archives/2005/07/ken_dyke_interv.html

5. http://www.flickr.com

6. Backbone Media Corporate Blogging Survey (2005), Microsoft Case Study. Available at http://www.backbonemedia.com/blogsurvey/52-Microsoft-case-study.htm

7. Ken's Meme Deflector Blog, Ken Dyck (2005), *Ken's Bug Reporting System.* Available at http://www.kendyck.com/2005/05/kens-bug-reporting-system.php

8. Blogsurvey Blog, John Cass (2005), *Ken Dyck Interview about the Microsoft Case Study.* Available at http://blogsurvey.backbonemedia.com/archives/2005/07/ken_dyke_interv.html

CHAPTER 11

The Future of Blogger Relations: Podcasting, Web 2.0, and Social Media

Web 2.0 and *social media* are terms that describe websites that allow the active participation and sharing of information among a community. Podcasting with audio or video, millions of people who share pictures, 3D environments where people buy and sell services and products, these are all trends that will continue to evolve as the development of Web 2.0 and social media websites continues. In this chapter, we will discuss how podcasters, both audio and video, and Web 2.0 websites can be used by companies to connect with or build a community and how some of the techniques used in blogging can also be used with the emerging technologies to find new ways to connect with audiences through the web.

INTEGRATING SOCIAL MEDIA INTO BLOGS

This book has been about providing companies with strategies and tools for developing an effective corporate blogging campaign. Effective blogging, in part, is the process of interacting with bloggers and blog readers for the purpose of discussing relevant topics rather than attempting to pitch or sell products. To achieve effective blogging, your focus must be to develop and engage in conversations that are relevant to the community, as blogs are written by individuals, who can connect with people in a more personal way than a corporate marketing department. If conducted well, blogging gives companies the opportunity to really connect with their customers. Bloggers give companies a better way to develop trust with an audience. That trust is developed from an employee giving his or her opinions and contributions, whose passion or lack of is open to the world. The personal experiences and perspectives of a blogger are what interests blog readers and keeps them coming back for more. If writing can do all this and more, think what audio, video, or interactive 3D can do for building relationships with your customers.

As more individuals have built and published their own content, blogging has grown in popularity. Bloggers discovered one another through the search engines by searching for content and conversations that interested them. Then as relationships between bloggers were built those individual bloggers became a community.

Blogs are part of the Web 2.0 and social media technology movement where websites are used to facilitate audience participation between community members to build content and value. Search technology has been an important factor in the success of social media websites, both within Web 2.0 websites and as a way of attracting visitors to the website through search engines. Major search engines do not index all information in their databases, and you have to go to websites that specialize in different types of data to find content or people effectively. For example, Flickr[1] provides one of the best image databases on the web that have been described or tagged by its members. Tagging is the process of assigning a keyword to information such as images, videos, or text articles that can then be cross-referenced with similar information. Although search engines do not index all information on the web, search engines are portals for finding websites to find information you seek. Search has expanded to new types of search engines that find content based on RSS feeds such as Technorati. The concept of search is used extensively by social media websites to provide analysis and access lots of data and users. For example, MySpace lets you discover people with similar interests through search within its network of member websites, and YouTube[2] lets you search through videos uploaded by YouTube members. Search is important to social media because it helps you find the content, sites, and people who share your interests.

As blogs are published by many people and organizations on different websites, there is no central website that coordinates which member is a member of a particular blogging community. Usually, on social media websites, there are search tools for finding all relevant content or people within the confines of a social media website. Now, some Web 2.0 websites enable people to use data from different website data sources. Called *mashups*, the combinations of different data sources allow people to search across websites to create something

You also want to make sure that new listeners will find your podcast through the major search engines. Finding content within a podcast can be difficult because podcasts are audio rather than text. It is difficult to search the audio within the podcast, although audio search engines do exist such as Singingfish. One way to make sure your podcast is searchable and easy to navigate is by highlighting each audio section within a podcast with show notes. Show notes can be published in a blog or on a website and make the process of finding spots with a show easier, as notes describe each section of a podcast. Alongside each section of text highlighting a portion of the podcast in the show notes is the time the section of a podcast occurred. Show notes are an easy way for listeners to jump to a section within a podcast program, skipping any part of the show they do not want to listen to. Putting podcast show notes in text means your audio podcast is searchable in the text search engines such as Google, Yahoo!, and MSN.com.

If a company encourages participation and feedback from its listener audience and especially if the audience contributes to a show, a podcast can help a company to build a more interactive community. Probably, the best way to describe how a company can use podcasting is for you, the reader, to listen to several podcasts where the show successfully builds a community.

FOR IMMEDIATE RELEASE PODCAST:
NEVILLE HOBSON'S INTERVIEW

For Immediate Release, or *FIR*, is a podcast hosted by Neville Hobson and Shel Holtz, two communications professionals who reside in Europe and the United States, respectively. http://forimmediaterelease.biz/ is the companion blog for the podcast. The *FIR* podcast has become a mainstay of the public relations blogging community, especially those bloggers who were previously involved in a virtual conference called the New PR Blogging Week organized by the public relations community in 2004 and 2005. The podcast has helped to develop a strong sense of community among communications professionals and those people interested in new social media communications. An interview with Neville Hobson, one of the show's hosts, is reproduced here, as his insights into how to use podcasting for business demonstrate the value of podcasting.

Neville Hobson suggests that podcasts can be used for a variety of business purposes, from podcasts that simply promote an event or product in the same way a traditional press release will promote a new product to building a community with a podcast.

Traditional news releases are carefully scripted and refined, although social media tools such as podcasts are much more informal. Neville Hobson suggests that a company can also develop a podcast that helps to describe a company's story much better than a traditional news release. He said that, "Podcasts can add something that provides a wholly different angle to the communications process. A podcast could include a conversation between the company and a user of one of your products. In a podcast the conversation between a customer and the employee would introduce something very informal, and add something a little more compelling so people will take notice. The customer would talk about how he uses it."

Content is critical in developing a podcast, and he suggested, "You have to have something that people really want to listen to, you have to have the content."

However, personalization of that content is also important. Neville described how he and Shel Holtz would introduce content that is relevant to their audience, but it is how he and Shel discuss the content that puts a personal spin on the show. Their discussions, and sometimes disagreement, about issues in new media communications really connect the show to the audience. He described how personalization works for podcasting: "Personalization is a subset of your content, the topics people really want to hear. What's key is what podcasters do with the content, how they interpret the content; thinking back to the *FIR* listeners survey, what people like about the show is the interaction between Shel and Neville, that is when you get to the nitty-gritty of the content."

Secondarily, Neville suggested that podcasts could be used to develop a community. Neville described that when he and Shel initially launched the podcast, they had not realized the podcast's potential for building community, but that quickly became rather obvious within the first month when their *FIR* podcast was highly successful at soliciting responses from the communications community. Neville said, "We did not set out to build a grand community. The reaction from the community was that people wanted to build the community within the first month of the first episode of the podcast starting."

In the *FIR* podcast, Shel and Neville have a number of topics they decide they are going to discuss in the next issue of the show. Listeners send in comments by email, audio comments, or through the show's blog. Shel and Neville include those comments in their show, either by reading out the comments or replaying the comments in an audio segment. Then the two podcasters discuss the comments. Neville said, "That's the secret to community building, involve your audience. You also have to build your community by including your audiences as contributors directly to the show."

The accompanying blog with show notes also enables people to write comments on what happened in the show. Many people comment on the show, and those comments are used in subsequent shows. Neville said, "We see this on our show notes all the time: someone makes a comment on the blog, someone makes a comment on that comment, and then we have a nice conversation in the episode."

The *FIR* podcast has four additional correspondents, two in the United States, one in the United Kingdom, and one in Australia who provide their own commentary that adds to the content of each episode. Neville explained that each correspondent's content adds to the content of the show, and their contributions have been noted by many listeners in listener surveys as being a highlight of the show.

Frappr is a map location service using Google Maps. The *FIR* podcast uses the service to connect audience members together. The podcast uses the Frappr service to develop a map of its community. Listeners to the show are spread out all over the world, but concentrated in Europe and North America. Show listeners are not just communications professionals but also those people who are interested in communications. Audience listeners include a dentist, a Boeing employee, an investment banker, and engineers. Commenting on the background of his show's listeners, Neville said, "All of these people are interested in communication; they have found our show to be relevant to that interest. We provided a catalyst to build a community, and the community has responded by helping to build up the podcast because of the contributions to the community. In a sense, everyone delivers the podcast, as the community makes up a good proportion of the content."

Neville Hobson believes that content is the most important factor that will add credibility to a podcast. Neville said, "If your content does not resonate with your listeners, the things you talk about, the topics you discuss—not how they are delivered—then you will not build a credible podcast."

The reason why podcasting can be so effective in reaching people is because most marketing efforts are scripted. Podcasts can be very informal. Being open and transparent and informal can be a way to really reach people. Neville said, "It's the informality, the humanness of podcasting which provides some sort of insight into a person at the company. As a customer you know about the company, but with podcasting the medium lets you gain an understanding of the person very quickly. If they are not honest, you will find out that as well."

Podcasters can also be approached in the same way that bloggers can be approached through blogger relations. Neville explained, "Conducting effective podcasting relations can be literally the same as you conduct blogger relations. For a podcast, you would listen to a number of podcasts over time, get a sense of the person and how influential that person is. Then you'd approach them, you'd find some connection with them, and leave a comment. It's important to prep people well before approaching them with a story—not much different than how you would approach people in a traditional media space. Whatever you are doing with your relationships in a social media space, get the podcaster to become interested in a product. A person will write about the product, an opinion, a blogger will write an opinion; the blogger's opinion's will more likely be more open and unedited, journalists posts will be edited, and less open, and the relationship with podcasters will be much different." Basically, over time, from a public relations point of view, one of the objectives in podcasting relations is to build relationships with podcasters.

VIDEO LOGGING

If video killed the radio star, you can expect that video podcasting will become more important in the future. Videos will probably not replace blogs and audio podcasts but video will definitely play an increasing important role for corporate communications. Although many companies have produced product description videos, a regular video or podcast is something new for businesses. Producing a regularly scheduled video log can help a company to build an audience and enhance their industry's community in the same way that audio podcasts have done.

Video takes more attention from viewers than audio podcasting and is also more emotional, as the words and pictures take more senses to watch and listen. Many of the same tips for audio podcasting apply to video logging. Make good show notes, build a community; however, perhaps, what is most interesting is that video logging can be used for conversations between video loggers. A video log shot in response to another video log is something that is happening on video logger blogs and also in video uploading services such as YouTube. Therefore, the possibility exists for companies to issue video logs to address other video logs produced in their industry, in the same way that blogs are used for discussing industry issues.

Video can be an exceptional great way to showcase a company's products, but like blogging, videos can also be used to reveal more of the human side of a company. Microsoft has attempted to use videos to connect with its developer community, through its Channel9.msdn.com website. The site was set up to show customers inside Microsoft through video, blogs, forms, and a wiki. Channel9 is a comprehensive website for Microsoft's customer community, who can register as members, participate, and contribute to the Microsoft developer community. Videos lead on the front page of the website. Microsoft video reporters interview employees within Microsoft. The reporters all have a technical background, and the videos are informal. The videos shown on Channel9 are less about selling product and more about revealing the human side of Microsoft. Typical interviews are with software managers and systems engineers, often highly technical, and the video interviews explore people's experiences working within Microsoft. Although companies do not have to do everything that Channel9 does, the site is an excellent example of how a company can build a community using video. Members comment on each video and exchange opinions.

Video is a great way to build community; some of the most successful video logs are focused on community news. Dan Karleen is one of the founders of Berks.TV, a production of Pipe Up! Media, LLC, an Internet TV channel covering greater Reading, PA, and all of Berks County. Dan was interviewed, and he described how video logging could be used for building community. He said,

With our vlog there is a sort of "Berks.TV culture" emerging, stemming from building upon previous stories and relationships by doing in-depth follow-ups, e.g., with local music bands branching out into new efforts; it is a great way to get to know people over time (and to let the community get to know people over time) with video being the central rallying point for the community feel. With a regional vlog there is very much the opportunity to create a community that spans online and offline boundaries. The ease of publishing video in a blog enables this.

Critical to the success of the Berk.TV video log are contributions from community members; ideas from the community keep the coverage relevant to the community.

Dan gave some tips for developing a video podcasting that really connects with viewers. He said,

Keep at it over time, and focus on what you're passionate about.... Seek contacts and interviews that can help build vlog referrals either online or offline. Expect to be surprised, and be open to heading in new directions. Seek ways to connect with local bloggers—e.g., by interviewing them for your blog. Try to make connections that will resonate outside the community as well. Don't forget to optimize your blog for search engines. If you can share responsibility with a partner or partners, this helps keep things manageable and ideas fresh.

Lastly, Dan describes what makes video logging so different from audio podcasts and blogging. He said, "The excitement of video on the web generates a lot of interest and encourages people to spread the word to their friends and colleagues," and, "People love seeing themselves on video, and they're thrilled to be mentioned on the web. People are excited to Google their name and have their appearance on Berks.TV show up at the top of the list. I can't think of anyone who's turned down an interview request."

SOCIAL MEDIA OVERVIEW

Blogs, podcasts, YouTube, Flickr, and Second Life are all Internet-based websites and communities that use social media culture and Web 2.0 technologies to give people the ability to contribute content, build community, and maintain connections easily. Social media sites make it easy to find people with the same interests by providing links to groups and communities or enable people to catalog content through tagging.

To summarize social media, the web strategy allows people to easily do the following:

Contribute content—Social media participants can contribute content, thus reducing the costs of content development for the founders of social media sites and increasing the number of potential contributors.

Describe content—Members of a social media website are given tools to describe any content they contribute to the website. Keyword, tags, or categorization all help other site members to find content that interests them.

Find content—Search boxes, RSS feeds, and groups are all ways for social media participants to find content easily within a social media website.

Build community—Social media members can easily build communities around content.

Start and continue conversations—Once a community is developed, the social media website encourages more interaction between members for discussion or more content creation.

Here is an overview of some of the problems with social media:

Lack of editorial review—News and information might not be all that relevant to the audience. Sometimes, content may be bogus or attempts at spamming a social media website for search engine juice.

No initial fact checking—Fact checking is often left up to community members; a lot of social media websites use traditional media as sources, and even then no fact checking is conducted.

Quality of the content is dependent upon members—The same issues apply to social media website as traditional media, but maybe there is only so far you can go with volunteers—although Wikipedia, the people-produced encyclopedia, has produced content that is the equal of professionally produced encyclopedias. In contrast, stories in Digg are sometimes promoted by groups of people who have a disproportionate affect on Digg top stories.

Disclosure rules are looser—Unlike traditional journalists, community members are not held to a code of ethics on disclosure, although there are growing social rules within social media sites. Disclosure can be an issue.

Keep up with the latest trends in social media and Web 2.0 technologies. Extend the community on your blog by connecting with communities within social media website communities such as Flickr and YouTube. Join those communities, participate if the community on those sites is active for your industry, or start the community within the website.

Social media websites represent distinct yet not separate communities that can also be connected through blogger outreach. Trackbacks might not be available, but comments certainly are on many of these websites, although it may require somebody to register as a member before they can comment.

Besides commenting within those communities, some social media websites can be integrated into blogs. Flickr images and YouTube videos can be integrated into blogs, either through posting within a blog article or appearing on the side navigation of the blog.

Many bloggers use content found on social media websites in their articles, both because it is an easy way to integrate some great content into a blog and because the content then connects their blog to the community that exists within the social media website. There is a symbiosis between blogs and Web 2.0 websites. Each provides links and content to the other depending upon the needs of the blogger or community member. That content can then be accessed by each website's community, blog readers can see the link and content on a blog, and social media community members can see the content links within a blogger's social media portal within the social media website. Bloglines is a great example of this in action; rather than build a blog roll within a blog, bloglines allow bloggers to post a link to their list of RSS feeds. This makes it easier for a blogger to have only one place where they create a list of blogs they read, and tell the world about—in the blogger's bloglines account. Essentially, if there is information, such as RSS feeds, images, or bookmarked websites that can be managed more efficiently as a service elsewhere, it is a good idea to manage that information within a Web 2.0 website and then integrate the information into your blog. Not only do you then have a better way to manage such information, but you also connect your blog to the community that is using the Web 2.0 website to manage its information.

Flickr

Flickr is one of the most important social media websites on the Internet. It is a social media website that allows you to upload and store photographs. Your photographs can be either public or private; if classified as private, you can make them available to just friends and or family. Flickr gives you access to a wealth of photos, people, and the ability to grow your own community of contacts based on pictures rather than text that is posted on your blog.

Flickr lets you tag each photograph with different keywords, which you can then search in the network of available public photographs. You can search for other users and also create or join groups of people who have formed groups for discussions around photographs. It is possible to discuss photographs with people within Flickr, enabling you to keep in touch with friends, colleagues, and family or find new people based on the types of photographs you search for.

Pictures can also be associated with maps. Flickr is owned by Yahoo!, so the site integrates with Yahoo mail.

A widget is a piece of software that can allow the easy integration of another social media website into a blog, allowing people to quickly integrate content on your blog into any social media website to which they belong or encouraging people to join such communities. A widget or badge can be placed on a blog to display your latest pictures and encourage your blog readers to join you in your conversation within the Flickr website. You can also set up the badge to show different groups of pictures or a random selection of pictures from Flickr.

Digg

Digg is a website that enables registered members to submit links to news from other websites. A Digg member writes a comment about a news story and submits the link and brief overview to Digg. Other registered members vote on the news articles submitted by members, either giving each story a boost or voting down the story by burying it. The collective wisdom of the members will push news stories to the top of the home page. As a story ages, it takes more votes to remain at the top of the page.

People who submit stories to Digg regularly and reach the home page of Digg are called Top Diggers, who attract a following of people or friends. Digg content is entirely developed by registered users. Digg also enables people to connect with people interested in the same types of stories. Digg is both a news site and a community-building website. Stories appear on the upcoming stories page. Many bloggers now provide widgets and links on their blogs and in their articles to encourage Digg members to reference their articles and promote them. A highly promoted article on Digg can generate a lot of traffic for a website owner. Sometimes, groups of friends promote each other's articles in an effort to get a story to the top of the pile on the Digg home page. However, if Digg or the community believes someone is spamming Digg, the site may get banned from Digg.

Digg.com and websites similar to Digg allow blog readers to highlight favorite and interesting articles to a wider group of people. Digg and Slash.org (another well-known social media website) are important for the technology industry. A corporate blogger will want to monitor the web to determine which social media news websites are important for their industry and participate by joining the site or encouraging their readers to promote their stories with a widget in their blog post if the reader believes the story is worth the vote.

MySpace

MySpace allows people to build an online blog for themselves and share the content with other people. Since 2004, the site has become one of the most popular sites on the web.

As part of the process of building a MySpace blog, a member fills out a number of personal details. This allows MySpace to target advertising to each MySpace member using the demographic data provided by the MySpace user. The demographic information also enables other people to find people on MySpace with similar interests. Video sharing, groups for different topics, and more are all features within MySpace that allow users to find other people, network, and become friends.

MySpace, Facebook, and Friendster are all social networking sites that allow people to build their own profiles and share and swap information. The importance for corporate bloggers is the size of the communities within these sites. Even if you have your own blog, if large parts of your audience are members of these social media communities, consider setting up an account to promote your company and products within these communities.

YouTube

You can upload videos to YouTube to be seen by the community. YouTube has fast become a very popular website, both for the community within the website and the ability of people to link to the videos. Members can register to upload videos, and videos can be tagged with keywords and given text descriptions so that content can be easily identifiable. Social media websites such as YouTube are successful because they provide a mechanism for its users to meet and exchange discussion with one another easily. People can upload video files, and people could share them. YouTube succeeds because the company lets its users develop the content for the site and also facilitates the building of a community around any content. YouTube gives users tools to track other users and communities.

Companies can promote their video logs using YouTube. However, YouTube owns any content and videos uploaded to the site, until the content is removed. Many companies have used YouTube to create and promote entertaining and funny videos, hoping that an entertaining video will create buzz and interest from YouTube watchers. However, such efforts are really promotional rather than conversational. The videos aim to attract attention through buzz rather than build audiences through dialogue. Videos can also be used for conversations just like blogs. YouTube represents an opportunity for a company to get more recognition of their content, and also, a company can encourage other video loggers to make videos that comment on the company video or incorporate video content in the YouTube member's video.

Second Life

Second Life is a 3D virtual world that lets you create characters. The world is not really a game; the environment allows people to develop and build houses, clothes, or communities. The creators of Second Life built the world, but the people who participate within the world create all of the experiences in Second Life. There is an economy within Second Life using a currency called Linden dollars, as the company that developed the environment is called Linden Labs.

Second Life is another social media Internet-based service that encourages individuals to come together to form different groups. Unlike blogging and other social media tools, Second Life is not intuitive or easy to use for most people. It takes some time to learn how to build a character and how to interact within the 3D world. However, if you succeed in entering Second Life, you have the opportunity to interact with people on an entirely different level in real time. Using 3D visual and chatting technology, it is possible to connect with people on the web in an entirely different way.

Second Life gives companies a way to connect with a community of people. The environment allows even more interaction with participants, so that videos, text, audio, the chatting in real time is all used to build a connection between a company and its audience. Just as text is used to connect with blog readers in blogs, Second Life and similar environments allow the full range of web-based technologies, including 3D technology, to be used to have a conversation with customers.

We are already seeing a growing number of Second Life blogs and podcasts. These sites intersect with the Real World and search engines. Over time, Second Life will become easier for people to use, and there will be more integration into the Real World and searchable content on search engines for Second Life. If Second Life does not make its environment easier to use, other 3D environments may leapfrog the environment. However, Second Life's leadership position will be tough to assail because the community wants them to succeed.

Philip Rosedale, or Philip Linden, as he is called in Second Life, is the CEO and founder of Linden Lab, the company that built Second Life. Philip answered some questions about the environment and how the Second Life can be used to build community.

An Interview with Philip Rosedale of Second Life

John Cass: "How does Second Life monitor community discussion to build better services for its community?"

Philip Rosedale: "Linden Lab prides itself both in its transparency and the egalitarian ideals on which it was founded. Resident feedback forms a cornerstone of our development strategy, and we do the utmost to listen to what our community is telling us. This includes regular Second Life Views conferences in which we invite a broad spectrum of residents to formally sit down with Linden executives, to virtual town-hall meetings, to ongoing resident dialogue on the Second Life blog (which in fact features one of the highest comment counts of any WordPress blog). This is all to say, we take community discussion very seriously."

John Cass: "This is a general question, but I think it needs answering for most marketing people who are not familiar with 3D interaction environments. How does Second Life enable its members to build their own community?"

Philip Rosedale: "Second Life offers its residents a broad range of tools to help them engage with the community around them, whether that be in a business, social, or creative sense: 3D modeling and scripting capabilities help residents form the "physical" world around them; social networking functionality allows residents to form groups, view each other's profiles, and communicate individually or among the group; commerce tools allow residents to transact and build successful in-world businesses. All of these functions are vital in helping to solidify the sense of community within Second Life."

John Cass: In terms of building community, what does the future hold for social media?

Philip Rosedale: "Social media is and will continue to be a vital part of community building. The fast pace of technological advancement allows for continued improvements upon ways in which individuals can stay connected … in turn, communities will more readily embrace these technologies and they will find more widespread acceptance. Imagine the potential that the web held in 1994—what was once a novel concept is now ubiquitous not only for companies, but for individuals as well. Second Life, and other sophisticated inter-personal technologies are simply advanced ways to network with fellow human beings. Perhaps in a few years time having a virtual presence will be akin to hosting a personal blog, or even as pervasive as individual email addresses."

John Cass: "Does Second Life monitor the web for online discussion about its brand? Do you act on any community feedback and discussion about Second Life, although the discussion is off the Second Life website and interactive environment?"

Philip Rosedale: "We at Linden Lab take into account the whole spectrum of commentary surrounding Second Life, though actual resident feedback remains our highest priority. From a day-to-day standpoint, our focus is on improving the Second Life platform—because of this, we don't always have the capabilities to manage this discussion, which is why our official Second Life Forums were disbanded earlier this year. This in no way means we're not interested in the debate itself, and we very much encourage this to take place in any number of third party websites and message boards. Wherever our residents choose to air their concerns, there will be an attempt on our part to hear them out."

Endnotes

1. http://www.flickr.com
2. http://www.youtube.com
3. http://www.tagbulb.com

INDEX